K. Warren

Report on the Transportation Route along the Wisconsin and Fox Rivers, in the State of Wisconsin

Between the Mississippi River and Lake Michigan

K. Warren

Report on the Transportation Route along the Wisconsin and Fox Rivers, in the State of Wisconsin

Between the Mississippi River and Lake Michigan

ISBN/EAN: 9783337148454

Printed in Europe, USA, Canada, Australia, Japan

Cover: Foto ©ninafisch / pixelio.de

More available books at **www.hansebooks.com**

44TH CONGRESS, } SENATE. { Ex. Doc.
1st Session. No. 28.

REPORT

ON THE

TRANSPORTATION ROUTE

ALONG THE

WISCONSIN AND FOX RIVERS,

IN THE

STATE OF WISCONSIN,

BETWEEN THE

MISSISSIPPI RIVER AND LAKE MICHIGAN.

BY

GOUVERNEUR K. WARREN,
MAJOR OF ENGINEERS AND BREVET MAJOR-GENERAL, U. S. ARMY.

WASHINGTON:
GOVERNMENT PRINTING OFFICE.
1876.

ERRATA.

Page 3, last line but one, 867 of date left out.
Page 3, last line, *ine* left off of *determine*.
Page 6, third line from top, change *work* to *works*.
Page 6, twentieth line from top, after *Fox River* insert *and*.
Page 6, tenth line in contents of Chapter IV, change *maps* to *map*.
Page 6, fifteenth line in contents of Chapter IV, change *terms* to *term*.
Page 6, third line from bottom, change *relation* to *relations*.
Page 7, seventh line from top, change *example* to *examples*.
Page 10, fourteenth line from top, change *hyphen* between *map* and *scale* to a *comma*.
Page 13, nineteenth line from top, change *Dake* to *Dukes*.
Page 15, eleventh line from bottom, change *suggesting* to *suggested*.
Page 17, seventeenth line from bottom, change *Cantley* to *Cautley*.
Page 20, seventeenth line from bottom, for *Maskontens* read *Maskoutens*.
Page 20, ninth line from bottom, for *Meskonsing* read *Meskousing*.
Page 23, twenty-fourth line from top, change *Ouseonsin* to *Wisconsin*.
Page 23, twenty-fourth line from bottom, change *Ouseonsin* to *Wisconsin*.
Page 24, second line of Chapter III, change *improvement* to *improvements*.
Page 24, twentieth line from bottom, change *Jenne* to *Jenné*.
Page 24, fourteenth line from bottom, change *Jenne* to *Jenné*.
Page 24, sixth line from bottom, change *improvement* to *improvements*.
Page 25, third line from top, change *and* to *into*.
Page 30, eleventh line from top, *the lower ferry* should be included in quotation-marks, and *probably Bridgeport* should be included in a parenthesis.
Page 31, fifth line from top, change $1,108.17 to $1,180.17.
Page 31, seventh line from top, change $779.00 to $799.00.
Page 33, twenty-fourth line from top, change $17,022.92 to $17,922.92.
Page 34, twenty-first line from bottom, insert *the* before *two*.
Page 35, eighth line from bottom, insert *comma* after *Wisconsin River*.
Page 37, fourteenth line from top, change *hte* to *the*.
Page 38, nineteenth line from top, change *channel* to *canal*.
Page 39, fifth line from top, change *engines* to *engineers*.
Page 40, seventh line from bottom, change *Packwauka* to *Packwaukee*.
Page 41, first line from top, change *work* to *works*.
Page 41, sixth line from top, change *complete* to *completed*.
Page 42, thirteenth line from bottom, change *this* to *the*.
Page 43, total of column for 1859, change from $36,051.34 to $46,051.34.
Page 46, ninth line from top, strike out *Total* $330,000.
Page 50, twenty-first line from top, change *This* to *The*.
Page 50, twenty-second line from top, change *lower* to *level*.
Page 50, twenty-fourth line from bottom, put *semicolon* after *replacing* and change *and* to *it*.
Page 50, nineteenth line from bottom, change *This* to *The*.
Page 53, twenty-sixth line from bottom, change *Apuckaway* to *Puckaway*.
Page 53, twenty-first line from bottom, change *Apuckaway* to *Puckaway*.
Page 53, tenth line from bottom, change *Apuckaway* to *Puckaway*.
Page 56, eleventh line from top, change *Apuckaway* to *Puckaway*.
Page 56, fourteenth line from top, change *Apuckaway* to *Puckaway*.
Page 57, in first table, change *Apuckaway* to *Puckaway*.
Page 57, in first table, change $75.09 to $735,095.
Page 59, tenth line from top, insert *commas* between the words *her* and *worth*, and *naming* and *that*.
Page 64, ninth line from bottom, change *there* to *then*.
Page 65, third line from top, change *on* to *an*.
Page 65, eleventh line from bottom change *sheets* to *sheet*.
Page 66, twentieth line from top, change *denudations* to *denudation*.
Page 67, in heading to table, change *comma* between 1822 and 1845 to a *dash*.
Page 68, twelfth line from top, in column headed "December," change 1,45 to 16.45.
Page 81, ninth item under first column, headed "Total distance," change 16,000 to 16,500.

Page 82, fifth line for the formula $h = \frac{v^2 \sin 2a}{134}$ read $h_{\prime\prime} = \frac{v^2 \sin^2 d}{134}$; for *a* on same line read *d*.

Page 83, in table, under column headed "Nearest gauge reading," the *minus sign* should be placed after the numbers on the *first, second, third, fourth, twenty-second, twenty-fourth,* and *fortieth* lines.
Page 83, thirteenth line from bottom of table, change *Kraps* to *Knapps*.
Page 90, twenty-fourth line from top, insert *comma* after the word *engineering*.
Page 97, eleventh line from bottom, after the word *could* insert *realize the benefits*.
Page 98, twenty-fourth line from top, change *position* to *portion*.
Page 100, first line of foot-note, change *Cantley* to *Cautley*.
Page 101, fourth line below table, strike out after *river*, *at the same scale*.
Page 105, sixth line from bottom, insert *comma* between the words *these* and *even*.
Page 107, eleventh line from bottom, insert *cases* after *all*.
Page 109, in title of table, change 160 to 165.
Page 110, change 160 to 165 in title of each table.
Page 112, in estimate for Blue River culvert, change 5,983 *cubic yards* to 598.3 *cubic yards*.

LETTER

FROM

THE SECRETARY OF WAR,

TRANSMITTING

The final report of Maj. G. K. Warren, Corps of Engineers, on the improvement of the route of water communication between the Mississippi River and Lake Michigan.

FEBRUARY 15, 1876.—Referred to the Select Committee on Transportation-Routes to the Seaboard and ordered to be printed.

WAR DEPARTMENT, *February* 14, 1875.

The Secretary of War has the honor to transmit to the United States Senate the final report of Maj. G. K. Warren, Corps of Engineers, on the improvement of the route of water-communication between the Mississippi River and Lake Michigan along the valleys of the Fox and Wisconsin rivers, and letter of the Chief of Engineers submitting the same.

The recommendation of the Chief of Engineers that the report and maps and diagrams accompanying the same be printed is respectfully concurred in.

WM. W. BELKNAP,
Secretary of War.

OFFICE OF THE CHIEF OF ENGINEERS,
Washington, D. C., February 11, 1876.

SIR: I transmit herewith the final report of Maj. G. K. Warren, Corps of Engineers, on the improvement of the route of water-transportation between the Mississippi River and Lake Michigan along the valleys of the Fox and Wisconsin rivers, but more especially relating to the part along the Wisconsin.

Examinations were made in 1866 and instrumental surveys during 1867, and some minor ones in 1868 and 1869. The causes of delay in presenting this report will be found stated in it.

The improvement of this route is now in charge of Maj. D. C. Houston, Corps of Engineers. It forms part of the Northern Transportation Route between the interior and the seaboard, which was directed to be reported upon by the act approved June 23, 1874. Major Houston reports:

The survey of the Wisconsin River, under the direction of Major Warren, in 1 contains all the information bearing upon the subject, so far as a survey can determ it.

This is the survey now finally reported upon; it is the only survey of the river between Portage and the mouth that has ever been made, and the maps have not been published.

The publication of these maps and report now will supply information required by the act first authorizing it, as well as the more recent one of 1874. This report closes with the year 1869.

Major Warren has long been connected with western and eastern river improvements, and his presentation of the subject is intended to bring out views regarding the improvement of shallow rivers of considerable slope, small volume, and movable bed.

The conclusions reached by Major Warren are adverse to the permanent improvement of the Wisconsin River by a system of canalization or rectification of its low and high-water channels, and that a canal along its banks is the only method of permanent improvement.

A plan of operations, with detailed estimates of cost, is given for the construction of a canal from Portage to the mouth, of the capacity of the Fox River improvements, for $4,000,000, in the space of two years.

He is of opinion, however, that a larger capacity should be adopted, and recommends location-surveys to be made to determine the best line for the improvement, as soon as the requisite capacity is decided upon. Breadth of canal and locks rather than depth is held to be the ruling idea, in a canal adequate to steam-navigation, because the depth at low water on the Upper Mississippi must always be limited. A transfer at some point in the way to the seaboard will be necessary, and as the lake vessels require depth, this transfer should be made at Green Bay, the canal being adapted to the navigation of the steamboats and barges of the Upper Mississippi.

The maps and diagrams are not numerous, and have been prepared with special view to the inexpensive photolithographic process, so that their publication with the report is recommended.

The present method of improvement of the Wisconsin is on trial on its own merits, and it is too soon for the Department to announce the final result, but the publication of this report with the data it contains, will enable others to form an opinion of the nature of the undertaking, and aid in a more speedy solution.

Very respectfully, your obedient servant,
A. A. HUMPHREYS,
Brig. Gen. and Chief of Engineers.

Hon. W. W. BELKNAP,
Secretary of War.

CONTENTS.

LETTER OF TRANSMITTAL.

CHAPTER I.

AN EXPLANATION OF THE DELAY IN NOT SOONER COMPLETING THIS REPORT, BEING A GENERAL STATEMENT OF OCCUPATION ON PUBLIC DUTIES FROM 1866 TO 1874, INCLUSIVE.

CHAPTER II.

EARLIEST HISTORICAL ACCOUNTS OF THE ROUTE OF THE FOX AND WISCONSIN RIVERS.

INTRODUCTORY REMARKS—HISTORY OF DISCOVERY, ETC., BY JOHN G. SHEA—Events leading to discovery—Adventures of the Sieur Nicolet, A. D. 1639—Discovery delayed by Indian wars—Discoveries by Father Marquette and the Sieur Jolliet—Captivity of, and discoveries by, Father Hennepin, 1680-'81—His rescue by Lieutenant Du Luth—EARLY HISTORY OF MICHIGAN, BY C. LANMAN—Condition of the country at the time of English occupation, in 1760—Condition not changed by the English occupation, which nominally ended in 1783—Wonderful changes wrought by the American Republic—NOTE BY JONATHAN CARVER, 1766—RECOMMENDATION OF LIEUT. Z. M. PIKE, U. S. A., 1805—REPORT OF MAJOR LONG, U. S. A., 1817 AND 1819—MAP OF THE ROUTE, BY CAPT. H. WHITING, FIFTH UNITED STATES INFANTRY, 1819, WITH NOTES.

CHAPTER III.

HISTORY OF THE IMPROVEMENT OF THE ROUTE ALONG THE FOX AND WISCONSIN RIVERS, SINCE SURVEYS AND IMPROVEMENTS WERE BEGUN—PROGRESS OF THE IMPROVEMENTS DOWN TO 1870.

Survey under War Department, in 1836, by Mr. Center, C. E.—Survey under the War Department, in 1837, by Mr. Pettival, C. E.—Bill for the improvement of these rivers, and for a canal to unite them, reported by United States Senate Committee in 1839—Survey of the Fox and Wisconsin rivers, under the War Department, by Captain Cram, in 1839—Report upon survey and estimates of Captain Cram, made by Committee of House of Representatives in 1846—Survey of Green Bay, under War Department, by Mr. Williams, in 1845—Lands granted to the State, on its admission into the Union, for improving the navigation of the Wisconsin and Fox rivers, and for constructing a canal to unite them, act approved August 6, 1846—Operations in 1848; report of Board of Public Works for 1848—List of rapids on Lower Fox River, with the fall at each—Operations in 1849; report of Board of Public Works for 1849—Character of the Wisconsin, and difficulty of improving its channel, stated by Alton—Operations in 1850; report of Board of Public Works for 1850—Operations in 1851; report of Board of Public Works for 1851—Plan of improving the Wisconsin River, by Acting Commissioner Croswell—Operations in 1852; report of Board of Public Works for 1852—Condition of the Wisconsin River improvement and a plan for continuing the same by Acting Commissioner Richardson—Table of expenditures on the Wisconsin River—Table of total expenditures to date—Surrender of the works of improvement, lands, &c., by the State to a company June 1, 1853—Company chartered with conditions July 6, 1853—Condition and character of the works in 1854, by C. D. Westbrook, jr.—Reservoir on the headwaters of the Wisconsin as a means to increase its low-water depth, suggested by Mr. Westbrook—Additional lands granted to the State by Congress—Increased capacity of the improvement required by the State—Condition of the work January, 1859; report of the Chief Engineer of company, Mr. D. C. Jenné—Condition of the improvement in 1860; report of the President of the company to a committee of the State legislature—Navigation of the Wisconsin can be improved by running a steamboat; money expended otherwise would be of no avail; from same report of president of company—Expenditures from October 3, 1856, to December 31, 1859—Expenditures from beginning of improvement in 1848 to 1859—Operations in 1860-'61-'62; report of Superintendent of company—Increased capacity necessary for passage of gun-boats; estimated cost of, by Mr. Jenné, C. E., in 1862—Renewal of interest in the improvement by the United States—Report of committee on naval affairs, Thirty-seventh Congress, upon this improvement, with estimates for an increase of capacity, so as to pass gun-boats, 1863—Company having failed to perform its agreement the works of improvement, land, &c., were sold in 1866—Green Bay and Mississippi Canal Company incorporated by the State August 15, 1866—Examination and estimates of cost of improving this route, required by act of Congress, approved June 23, 1866—Condition of these rivers, improvements, &c., 1866—Condition of the Lower Fox River improvement in 1866—Condition of the Upper Fox River improvement in 1866—Condition of the Wisconsin River in 1866—Works of improvement, &c., in 1867—WORKS OF IMPROVEMENT IN 1868—WORKS OF IMPROVEMENT IN 1869—CONCLUDING REMARKS TO CHAPTER III.

CHAPTER IV.

REPRESENTATION OF SURVEYS MADE IN 1867-'68-'69; THEIR OBJECT AND EXTENT; MAPS AND DIAGRAMS CONSTRUCTED FROM MEASUREMENTS; TABLES OF HYDRAULIC DATA; ANOMALOUS PHYSICAL FEATURES CONSIDERED, AND REFERRED TO A GENERALIZATION OF SIMILAR EXHIBITIONS ELSEWHERE.

Preparations for the survey—Instructions for conducting the surveys—DESCRIPTION OF THE MAPS AND DIAGRAMS MADE FROM THE SURVEYS—Continuous plot-scale 200 feet to an inch—Cross-sections of the valley, scales 400 feet horizontally, and 40 feet vertically, to the inch—Longitudinal profile of the valley—Plots of current measurements for volume—Maps of river on a scale of two inches to the mile—General map of the route from Green Bay to the Mississippi River—Sheets of river-gauge curves—GENERAL DESCRIPTION OF THE BASIN OF THE WISCONSIN RIVER—Form of basin, geographical position, &c.—General elevation above the sea—Geological formations in the basin—Climate—DESCRIPTION OF FEATURES OF THE VALLEY—Definition of terms valley, &c.—Slopes and terraces not overflowed at high water—Marginal lands and islands overflowed at high water—THE RIVER-BED—Sand-bars, &c.—Their formation—Action at low-water—Very bad sand-bars in the Mississippi below the Wisconsin—Very bad sand-bars in the Wisconsin at the junction—Movement of sand-bars down stream—Sources and quality of the sand—Comparison of the Wisconsin sand with other water-moved sands—Gravel and bowlders in river-bed—Falling trees and snags—Bed-rock—BRIDGES—HIGH AND LOW WATER STAGES AND THEIR DURATION—ICE—SLOPE OF WATER SURFACE—Table of measured slopes at low-water—BEND EFFECT—VOLUME OF DISCHARGE—Method of measuring volumes—Table of measured and low-water volumes—Explanation of construction of table—Volumes at a stage one foot above the low water of 1867—Volumes at Skinner's Bluff for all stages—ANOMALOUS PHYSICAL FEATURES OF THE WISCONSIN AND FOX RIVER BASINS—The near approach of the streams without uniting—Peculiarities in the course of the Wisconsin—Peculiarities in the course of the Upper Fox River—Lower Fox River—Analogies between the Lake Winnebago basin and the Lake Winnipeg basin in British America—Probable former extent of Lake Winnebago, with diagram—Hypothesis consistent with above-noted conditions—Previous attempts at generalization in regard to Fox River—PROBABLE CHANGE OF DRAINAGE OF THE FOUR LAKES NEAR MADISON—Explained by the same hypothesis which is applicable to an extensive area.

CHAPTER V.

METHODS OF IMPROVING NAVIGATION.

PRELIMINARY REMARKS—Relation of the United States and corporate companies to the improvement—Difficulties heretofore not appreciated—Influences controlling former plans and operations—Future plans based on the new data—IMPROVEMENT

BY CANALIZATION, regulation, or rectification—Hydraulic formulæ applicable—The Humphreys-Abbot formulæ adopted—Small practical bend effect—Width of rectified river at low water for different depths—Slopes for uniform depths and different widths—Requirements which must be met in works of construction for river rectification, so as to produce a desired navigable depth at low water—Conditions demanded at high water—How to begin the work discussed and illustrated by example—Section of regulated river for both high and low water channels—Further protection against scour—ESTIMATE OF MONEY AND TIME REQUIRED FOR CANALIZING IMPRACTICABLE—Conclusions to be drawn from the success attending similar works on the Garonne—Example in the case of the Ohio River—Conclusion with regard to canalization of the Wisconsin River—IMPROVEMENT BY MEANS OF RESERVOIRS AT THE SOURCES—Doubtful possibility of success.—Immense cost—Great danger attending such works—METHOD OF IMPROVEMENT BY DAMS AND LOCKS—Difficult and expensive, if not impracticable—Never recommended, and special data not obtained for depth to bed-rock—IMPROVEMENT OF NAVIGATION BY MEANS OF CANAL ALONG THE VALLEY—Data for making location—Provisional location—Objectionable features and alternative to avoid them—CHARACTER OF CANAL AND LOCKS—Description of locks, with general directions as to construction—Bills of lock-material—Estimated cost of a lock—Summary of cost of all the lift-locks; of all the guard-locks—Cost of feed-weirs connected with lock; of feed-pipes; of culverts; of waste-weirs; of bridges; of walling; of rip-rap; of grubbing; of clearing land; of engineering the work to be done in two years—Grand total cost—Additional cost for five-feet draft—Annual expense of superintendence and repairs.

ILLUSTRATIONS.

Two wood-cuts and nine photolithographic sketches, to accompany letter-press.

MAPS AND DIAGRAMS.

PLATE 1. General map and profile of the route, showing also the outlines of sheets 1 to 8, inclusive, on a larger scale.
PLATES 2 to 9, inclusive, are reduced from the twenty-four sheets of the original survey of the Wisconsin River, from Portage to its mouth.
PLATE 10. Diagram of observations for stage of water on Lake Winnebago, on the Wisconsin River, and on the Mississippi at Prairie du Chien, during the years 1867, 1868, and 1869.

LETTER OF TRANSMITTAL.

ENGINEER OFFICE, UNITED STATES ARMY,
Newport, R. I., November 26, 1875.

GENERAL: I have the honor to transmit herewith my final report on the transportation-route along the Fox and Wisconsin rivers, but more especially relating to the latter stream.

The text of the report is divided into five chapters, each of which, while forming a component part, is intended to be nearly complete in itself.

Chapter I is a brief account of my different occupations since I took up this subject in 1866 down to the present year. This appears to me called for by the length of time taken. It also furnishes a means of ready reference to any of the reports of the numerous other works on which I have been engaged during this same period.

Chapter II is an account of the early history of the route, which has special interest from its being the pathway to the discovery of the vast Mississippi Valley, and as in a measure certifying to its natural advantages, by showing that it was the first one to open the great Northwest to white men.

Chapter III is a chronological account of all improvements of the route from the first beginnings down to 1870, compiled from all available sources. The cost and condition of the works, as nearly as could be ascertained, is given from year to year; also, extracts from the laws, and estimates of cost of different kinds of improvement as designed by different engineers.

Chapter IV is an account of the surveys made by and under my direction in 1867–'68–'69, and of the maps and diagrams prepared. It contains a description of the river and valley and of all the features that influence one's appreciation of the question of navigation. In this chapter are tables of all the hydraulic data obtained from the measurements of the survey. It concludes with an account of some anomalous physical features along the route, and of the former expanse of Lake Winnebago, suggesting changes similar to what I have shown to have taken place in regard to Lake Winnepeg, in British America.

Chapter V is a presentation of the subject of improving the route for transportation along the valley of the Wisconsin, and no pains or effort has been spared to make this as complete and decisive as possible. It is shown here that any improvement in the natural bed of the river, intended to secure such commodious channel of navigation as the country desires, is impracticable.

The subject of canalization of the river is treated of at length. The extent and uncertainty of the time required, and the great cost and uncertainty at best of final success, condemn it. The plans of having reservoirs at the sources, or of making slack-water navigation by dams and locks, are shown to be impracticable.

A canal along the valley is the only resource, and a provisional location for one is made, with a detailed estimate of the cost of constructing it, if made of the same character and capacity as the present locks along the Lower Fox River. This estimate amounts to $4,000,000, and the time required to complete it is two years, if pushed with all practicable dispatch.

The feasibility of a canal at moderate expense being established, while no other plan seems practicable in my judgment, justifies urging an immediate and thorough survey, for determining the best route for the canal. This survey should have in view the selection of the best route for a canal of the capacity of the existing improvement on the Lower Fox River, and also for such a more capacious channel as may be needed in the proximate future when the through route shall have become established.

The report is so divided into chapters, with tables of contents, that it will be unnecessary to read it all, unless the reader desires information upon all of the general subjects into which the chapters divide it.

To facilitate the presentation of the subjects, a few small plates of octavo size have been prepared for the text, if printed; and in this case the original map-scale of two miles to an inch, the general map and profile of the route from Green Bay to the Mississippi, and a diagram of river-gauge curves should be photolithographed.

I have in this report said nothing of the importance of the route as a line of water-transportation. Its importance is here taken as already well established. This matter was treated of by me in the annual report of the Chief of Engineers for 1868, pp. 357–359.

There are three appendixes to the report, which may be useful for reference to, but which I do not think need to be published. A is a report of Assistant D. W. Wellman, from which I have taken part of the description of the valley in chapter IV; B is the details of the estimates of costs of canal-locks on the provisional canal-location; C is the detailed specifications of the material and manner of constructing composite locks.

Very respectfully,

G. K. WARREN,
Maj. of Engineers and Bvt. Maj. Gen., U. S. Army.

Bvt. Maj. Gen. A. A. HUMPHREYS,
Brigadier-General and Chief of Engineers, U. S. A.

REPORT.

CHAPTER I.

AN EXPLANATION OF THE DELAY IN NOT SOONER COMPLETING THIS REPORT, BEING A GENERAL STATEMENT OF OCCUPATION ON PUBLIC DUTIES FROM 1866 TO 1874, INCLUSIVE.

In giving an account of the time taken by me in completing this final report on the improvement of the route of water-transportation along the Fox and Wisconsin rivers, (more particularly of the latter stream,) it will be necessary to refer to the other work I have had to carry on at the same time, in order that a proper allowance may be made for the slow progress in this one. This duty was begun under the act of Congress making appropriations for certain river and harbor works approved June 23, 1866, and was assigned to me by instructions from the Chief of Engineers, United States Army, dated July 31, and August 2, following.

By these instructions my headquarters were established at Saint Paul, Minn., which place I reached early in August, and at once set to work to organize surveying and reconnoitering parties for the different works intrusted to me, and to gain the preliminary knowledge necessary to make proper organizations, and to properly equip and instruct them. It was a field remarkably free from acquired engineering data, so that while the acquisition of what was known was easy, it left nearly everything yet to be determined.

The duties assigned me, along with that which is the subject of this report, were to make "surveys and examinations," *first*, " of the Mississippi River between Fort Snelling, and the falls of Saint Anthony, and the Upper or Rock Island Rapids of the Mississippi, with a view to ascertain the most feasible means of economizing the water of the stream, of insuring the passage at all navigable seasons of boats drawing 4 feet water;" *second*, " of the Minnesota River from its mouth to the Yellow Medicine River, in order to ascertain the practicability and expense by slack-water navigation, or otherwise, of securing the continued navigability of said stream during the usual season of navigation;" *third*, " of the Zumbro River, Minnesota;" *fourth*, " of the Cannon River, Minnesota;" *fifth*, " of the Fox and Wisconsin rivers, in the State of Wisconsin;" *sixth*, " to examine and report upon the subject of constructing railroad bridges across the Mississippi River between Saint Paul, in Minnesota, and Saint Louis, in the State of Missouri, upon such plans of construction as will offer the least impediment to navigation."

The act of Congress provided for a survey and examination of the Saint Croix River above the ledge, and as it was supposed the stream referred to was the one forming part of the boundary between the States of Wisconsin and Minnesota, this was also intrusted to me. The examination, however, disclosed no such locality on this river as the "ledge," and it was afterward ascertained that the river designated in the act of

Congress was the one forming part of the boundary between the State of Maine and the foreign province of New Brunswick, and' I was relieved of further consideration of it.

My estimate of the cost of making these examinations, surveys, and reports was $70,000, but as they could not be made this season, and as the act of Congress required a report to be submitted at the next session, the work was laid out so as to gain a general knowledge of the whole field, at an estimated cost of $21,000, and thus comply, as far as practicable, with the law. It is unnecessary to state here any of the details of the different examinations, except that of the Fox and Wisconsin rivers. For making this, about $2,000 was allotted, and it was given in charge of Bvt. Major Charles R. Suter, United States Engineers, with instructions as to the character of the examination to be made. I gave my personal attention almost entirely to the Mississippi between the Falls of Saint Anthony and Saint Louis, only examining the Wisconsin River at its junction with the Mississippi.

The results of all our work that season, as well as could then be exhibited, were given in my report dated January 21, 1867, printed as House Ex. Doc. No. 58, Thirty-ninth Congress, second session. In this report, pages 41 and 42, and pages 73 to 103 inclusive, relate entirely to the Fox and Wisconsin rivers. A general map, on a scale of six miles to an inch, accompanying this report, was published at the office of the Chief of Engineers, United States Army, but it is not bound with the regular public documents, as published by Congress. This report was not reprinted in the succeeding annual report as has been customary since; the important parts of it have therefore been incorporated in this report, in chapter III. The examination of the Wisconsin River, in 1866, showed a necessity for a thorough survey of it, a thing which had never yet been done. This was duly reported, and an estimate of $15,000 was submitted for making such survey.

Progress made in 1867.—The act making appropriations for rivers and harbors, &c., was approved March 2, 1867. Before anything could be done on the Wisconsin I was employed, as a member of the Board of Engineers at Keokuk, Iowa, to report upon the plan of improving the navigation at the Des Moines Rapids of the Mississippi by means of a canal. This occupied me exclusively from March 22 to May 15, and on returning to Saint Paul, preparations for making the survey of the Wisconsin were at once commenced, by setting up river surface-gauges and preparing quarter-boat, &c. There was an allotment of $40,000 made this year for conducting surveys on the Wisconsin River and Upper Mississippi River. There were also appropriations of $96,000 for building and operating two dredge and snag boats on the Mississippi; of $40,000 for one such boat on the Wisconsin River; and of $37,500 for removing snags and bowlders from the Minnesota River. The report we had rendered of the result of the examination of the Zumbro and Cannon rivers failed to procure for them any appropriation from Congress.

The amount of work on my hands prevented my giving my personal attention to any one of them continuously, and the survey of the Wisconsin, from Portage City to its mouth, was placed in charge of Major Suter. High water prevented a commencement of the survey until August 26, and it was finished to the Mississippi River, a distance of 119 miles, on the 6th of November. An account of this survey will be given in another place. The dredge and snag boat for the Wisconsin River was not procured this year. The method of dredging proposed, was to scrape the crest of the sand-bar down the stream, and, as the operations were in a measure experimental, it was thought best to limit these to the two boats on the Mississippi River. The smallest of these boats was unable to operate at the mouth of the Wisconsin, where she was tried, because of the very shoal water. Capt. D. W. Wellman, civil engineer, was however employed, out of the fund for this Wisconsin boat, to accompany the surveying party, and while aiding it, gain such knowledge as would enable him to best provide for the wants of navigation on that stream. Notwithstanding every effort that was made to make the survey funds hold out, they became so exhausted that most of the assistants had to be discharged in December, before the notes were all plotted even in pencil. Captain Wellman and two assistants were retained, who continued the labor of plotting and constructing the maps.

There was a brief annual report submitted by me September 14, 1867. (See Annual Report of Chief of Engineers of that year, pp. 259 to 263.) I also made a personal examination of the Wisconsin River, from the upper railroad bridge down to the mouth.

Progress in 1868.—In January, 1868, Major Suter was relieved from duty with me, and I placed the completion of the maps in the hands of Captain Wellman, who continued the work, assisted by Messrs. Dake and Rich. An additional allotment of $14,000 from the appropriation for surveys enabled me to continue the office-work on the Wisconsin maps, and also on those of the Mississippi.

On April 6, at the urgent solicitation of friends of the Wisconsin River improvement, I made a report of progress, which was printed as House Ex. Doc. No. 247, Fortieth Congress, second session. In that report the condition of the maps at that time is stated, and on p. 5 the importance of these river-surveys is treated of. (See also pp. 7 and 8.)

On April 18, 1868, I also made a report on the harbor of Alton, Ill., (See House Executive Document No. 257, Fortieth Congress, second session.)

The propositions which were about this time being urged in Congress to authorize the bridging of the Ohio River, at Bellair and Parkersburgh, caused my being sent for by the chairman of the Senate Committee on Post-Offices and Post-Roads, for consultation. This was owing to my having been engaged on the investigation of the general subject of bridging the Mississippi. I then went to Steubenville and surveyed the bridge across the Ohio at that place. The report of this, dated June 29, is included in the report of the committee dated July 16, printed as Senate Report No. 168, Fortieth Congress, second session. I aided in the preparation of the committee report, and the bill to regulate bridging the Ohio River submitted with it.

This session of Congress made no additional appropriation for surveys or completing maps, and that on hand was used to complete the plotting and construction of the maps in pencil, and to supply any omissions in the former field-work that became apparent when the notes were all worked up. The annual report, dated August 31, 1868, pages 301 to 305, of the printed Annual Report of the Chief of Engineers for 1868, gives the condition of the maps at that date. The field-notes had all been plotted on a scale of 200 feet to an inch, making twenty-four sheets, each 10 feet long. These had been reduced to a scale of two inches to a mile, but nearly everything was still in pencil.

On pages 351 to 356 is a comparison of several plans of improving the Wisconsin River, which indicates that a canal, in part or whole of the distance along the valley, would be the most reliable one. It was seen from this that a special location-survey, to estimate the cost of a canal, was very desirable, but as there were no adequate funds for doing it, I was compelled to limit myself to making additional examinations and measurements, so as to define the outline of the foot of the bluffs and terraces, and obtain the approximate altitude of the terraces, where the survey had failed to do so. Some accurate additional information was obtained from the maps and profiles kindly furnished us by the officers of the Milwaukee and Saint Paul Railway Company. These additional examinations occupied Captain Wellman and one assistant during the autumn. I made a personal examination of the entire line of the Fox and Wisconsin route, and purchased the small steamboat Winneconue, to remove snags from the Wisconsin, but the water was too low to make any use of her that season.

The operations on the Mississippi and Minnesota rivers, &c., gave me a good deal of work. (See Annual Report of Chief of Engineers for 1868, pp. 299 to 385, inclusive.) In addition, a survey of the battle-field of Gettysburgh was begun under my direction, and early in October I was appointed one of a special commission to examine into the condition of the Union Pacific Railroad and the other branch lines east of the Rocky Mountains. Had I known the labor and time this was to take from me, I should have plead inability to perform it while retaining charge of my other works. We did not finish the work of this commission until December 11. I then returned to Saint Paul, where I was unable to attend to anything but the disbursements and similar matters.

Progress in 1869.—On January 15 I was made a member of the joint commission to examine the line of the Union Pacific and the California Central Railroads, to report upon their condition and point out the proper line on which the two roads should unite. The work on this commission occupied all my time in the field till April, and after that until May 15 in Washington, and the labor was very exhausting. The report was published by the Interior Department, but not generally distributed. When this labor ended, I was appointed commissioner to examine and report upon the five last completed sections of the Union Pacific Railroad; after doing which I returned to Saint Paul on July 14. Here I found a large accumulation of work requiring my attention, but had to at once leave it again to take charge of the construction of the bridge across the Mississippi at Rock Island. A curious complication of requirements had arisen here from incompatible conditions in the acts of Congress relating to the kind of bridge and its cost, or, at least, if not incompatible in reality, the authorized interpretation of the laws made them so. The attention of every one under my control was at once given to this matter to the exclusion of everything else, and by the 20th of September (the date of my annual report for 1869) a solution was reached as far as it was possible, and everything put in train for proceeding with the bridge in the way which it has since been completed. My connection with the Pacific Railroad commissions aided me very much at Rock Island, although both greatly interfered with the report on the Wisconsin, which is the occasion of their being mentioned here.

The Wisconsin River is again reported on by me in the printed Annual Report of the Chief of Engineers for 1869, pp. 190 and 191, my whole report occupying pp. 187 to 211, inclusive. I there recommend that $100,000 be appropriated to test the practicability of improving the navigation by wing-dams, before finally resorting to the project for a canal, which my study and experience were leading me to, notwithstanding such plan found little favor with the public.

The office-work on the maps was nearly suspended from June till November. Captain Wellman resurveyed the vicinity of the railroad-bridges to ascertain the changes in the river-bed at these places. He then submitted a general report, which closed his connection with the work.

In September and October, 1869, the "Winneconne" was employed removing snags and impending and fallen trees from the shores between Portage City and Sauk City. The obstructions thus removed are every year recurring, and the remedy is but a temporary one.

In October of this year I engaged Mr. Jacob Blickensderfer, an experienced canal-engineer, and together we examined the whole route along the Fox and Wisconsin rivers, and afterward, with such data as we possessed, made an approximate location for a canal along the Wisconsin River, and prepared detailed estimates of cost of constructing it. A large force was now employed in inking and lettering the maps, but I could not take up the preparation of the final report, because of the necessity I was under of preparing a report, to be submitted to Congress, pointing out required modifications of the laws in regard to the Rock Island bridge before the building of the superstructure could be commenced. The data for this report had been obtained during the summer and autumn by my assistant, Major Benyaurd, United States Engineers, and I completed it on December 4. It is printed as House Executive Document No. 31, Forty-first Congress, second session. The remainder of December was employed in attending to the current office business.

The other works carried on under me in 1869 were the operations of the dredge and snag boats on the Upper Mississippi, the survey and construction of map of the battle-field of Gettysburgh, and the construction of a wagon-road from Du Luth to the Bois-Fort Indian reservation.

Progress in 1870.—The winter at Saint Paul was one of unusual changes of temperature, the thermometer being frequently above the temperature of melting snow, so that affections of the throat and lungs became very prevalent. I was well worn out with the long-continued hard labor, and suffered so much from colds that I could do but little work in January. However, on the 12th, I made a brief report in regard to the Falls of Saint Anthony, which is printed as House Executive Document No. 118, Forty-first Congress, second session.

I finally was taken sick with pneumonia, which confined me to my bed nearly six weeks and left me in a very enfeebled condition. While I was sick the order came, (General Orders No. 16, February 7, 1870,) directing me to complete my reports, and not later than the first of April proceed to Detroit and take charge of the survey of the lakes. My health, however, would not permit me to do this, and at my request another officer was sent to the Lake survey, and I was allowed till the 31st of May to gain strength and prepare to turn over my duties to my successor, who had been named when the order of February 7 was made.

On April 30 I submitted a report on the subject of reservoirs on the headwaters of the Mississippi, (see House Ex. Doc. No. 285, Forty-first Congress, second session,) and on May 24 a report on the Du Luth and Bois-Fort reservation road, (see Senate Ex. Doc. No. 104, Forty-first Congress, second session.) On turning over my works, on May 31, I made a report on the condition of them and suggesting plans for continuing operations. (See Annual Report of the Chief of Engineers for 1870, pp. 226 and 227, for what relates to the Wisconsin River; pp. 224 to 289 relate to my western works, and pp. 444 to 454 to eastern works.)

My new station was fixed at Newport, R. I., and I was authorized to take with me such notes, drawings, &c., as were needed to complete my final reports. Everything, however, was left with my successor this season for reference, and directions were given to make copies of all needed for continuing improvements, assistants being employed under my direction for this purpose. There had been very little work doing at my new station prior to my arrival, and it promised to afford me an opportunity for uninterrupted employment on the unfinished reports, which related to the Minnesota River, to the Wisconsin River, to the Upper Mississippi River, and to the bridges on the Mississippi River.

Congress, however, made provision for a number of improvements and surveys in my new district, and as this was my first experience in harbor-works on large bodies of water, my time was much taken up in studies of the subject as well as in carrying out the improvements. I also had to report on the proposals for the superstructure of Rock Island bridge, and was engaged a large part of the autumn on the Board of Engineers on the Ohio River bridges, (see Annual Report Chief of Engineers for 1871, pp. 397 to 457,) and the international bridge across the Niagara River, (see Annual Report of Chief of Engineers for 1871, pp. 217 to 221,) which, with my duties at Newport and some minor operations, allowed no time for other work.

Progress in 1871.—The completion of the reports on the bridges on the Ohio River and the Niagara River, and other work, engaged me till March, at which time I had the Wisconsin and other unfinished western river work sent to me. A thorough revision of all the maps and sections was made in this year, and complete tracings made of them and sent to the Chief of Engineers. Some parts of the map, on a scale of two inches to the mile, have been published with Colonel Houston's reports.

The improvement of the Wisconsin by means of wing-dams was begun this season under Col. D. C. Houston, United States Engineers, and he visited me in June, and I gave him my views on the subject. He states in his annual report that he could not commence work earlier than June for want of necessary maps in my possession; but this was not my fault. All the maps he needed for commencing had been copied the summer previous and left with the officer in charge of the work. In some way they were mislaid, and, as soon as I was informed of it, other copies were made. Colonel Houston reported the result of this year's operations with wing-dams as very satisfactory.

Besides my duties at Newport this year, (see Annual Report of Chief of Engineers for 1871, pp. 727 to 828, inclusive,) I was a member of a Board of Engineers to report upon the alterations in the Cincinnati bridge, and of another on the harbor of Chicago.

Progress in 1872.—My attention having been called to the success of the improvement of the Garonne River, in France, by a brief account of it in a report by Major Merrill, United States Engineers, on the harbor of Saint Louis, made to the mayor of that city in 1869, I obtained copies of the reports of M. Baumgarten and M. Fargue, published in the "Annales des Ponts et Chaussées," for the purpose of making an estimate of the cost and probable result of applying a similar plan to the Wisconsin River. M. Baumgarten's work we translated, reducing the measures to English ones, and copied the maps and diagrams, which it seems to me very desirable to have published. This work would convey a great deal of useful information, and correct some important misconceptions of river-improvements. The work will be again referred to when treating of the improvement of the Wisconsin River.

This year, besides my duties at my station, which were very extensive, (see Annual Report of Chief of Engineers for 1872, pp. 815 to 955, inclusive,) I made a report on the subject of bridging the Mississippi at La Crosse, (Annual Report of Chief of Engineers for 1873, pp. 554 to 563,) and one upon the bridge across the Missouri at Saint Joseph, and its auxiliary works. I was, besides, a member of a Board of Engineers on the Mississippi River, between the mouth of the Illinois River and Meramec

River, (Annual Report for 1872, pp. 358 to 366,) and was engaged about one month in Washington as a witness in a suit brought against the United States by the contractors for the masonry of the Rock Island bridge.

Some considerable work, however, was done in preparing the material for the Wisconsin River report, but there was not enough time to write it out connectedly.

Progress in 1873.—Very considerable progress was made in the Wisconsin report in January and February, but a stop was made on the passage of the act for rivers and harbors on March 3, as it was necessary that the work at this station should be at once resumed, (see Annual Report for 1873, pp. 947 to 1051.) The remainder of this year was taken up with these duties and with service as member of the Board of Engineers on bridging the navigable channels between Lakes Huron and Erie, (see Annual Report of Chief of Engineers for 1874, pp. 587 to 636;) as member of the Board of Engineers on the bridge at Saint Louis, (see Annual Report of Chief of Engineers for 1874, pp. 636 to 680;) and of the Board of Engineers on the Fort Saint Philip Canal project, (see Annual Report of Chief of Engineers for 1874, pp. 823 to 854.) The duties on these boards occupied me almost exclusively six months.

Progress in 1874.—Early in this year I prepared, with great care, a report on the previous season's operations near Edgartown, Mass. On the 30th of June I was relieved of about half my duties at my Newport station; and the closing up of the different works, so as to make a proper transfer, consumed a good deal of time. For the duties at Newport, see Annual Report of Chief of Engineers for 1874, pp. 183 to 289, vol. 2. In the summer I was made a member of the commission on the reclamation of the overflowed lands of the Lower Mississippi. I, however, got on my former western river operations and completed the final report on the Minnesota River, (see House Ex. Doc. No. 76, 43d Cong., 2d sess., republished in Annual Report of Chief of Engineers for 1875, pp. 380 to 451.) I also nearly finished the Wisconsin report, and probably would have finished it if I had not had to attend, early in December, the meetings of the commission on overflowed lands, at Washington. This duty was not finished till near the middle of January, (see report printed as House Ex. Doc. No. 127, 43d Cong., 2d sess., reprinted in Annual Report of Chief of Engineers for 1875, pp. 536 to 678.)

During 1874 I had an opportunity for the first time to study the large publication in relation to the construction of the great Gauges Canal in India, written by Colonel Cantley, of the royal engineers.

During the present year (1875) I have spent all the spare time I could get in working up the data on the Upper Mississippi River survey, some of which was applicable to questions arising in the present report, and also in revising and partly rewriting this report. It has been a long and, in many respects, tiresome task, which is now completed. The frequent interruptions, and long intervals at which it was suspended, caused each time a strong mental effort to recover what had passed out of the mind under the pressure of intervening occupation. Much of the interest belonging to the subject was thus wasted or lost. I have had the faithful assistance of a number of engineers, among whom I would especially name Messrs. D. W. Wellman, W. W. Rich, and J. P. Cotton.

The expense of the examinations and surveys in 1866–'67–'68–'69, together with the construction and copying of the original maps, and the preparation of this report and the diagrams to illustrate it, has been about $39,000. This is exclusive of my own labor and that of Major Suter.

CHAPTER II.

EARLIEST HISTORICAL ACCOUNTS OF THE ROUTE OF THE FOX AND WISCONSIN RIVERS.

INTRODUCTORY REMARKS — HISTORY OF DISCOVERY, &C., BY JOHN G. SHEA — Events leading to discovery—Adventures of the Sieur Nicolet, A. D. 1639—Discovery delayed by Indian wars—Discoveries by Father Marquette and the Sieur Jolliet—Captivity of and discoveries by Father Hennepin, 1680–'81—His rescue by Lieutenant Du Luth—EARLY HISTORY OF MICHIGAN, BY C. LANMAN—Condition of the country at the time of English occupation in 1760—Condition not changed by the English occupation, which nominally ended in 1783—Wonderful changes wrought by the American Republic—NOTE BY JONATHAN CARVER, 1766 — RECOMMENDATION OF LIEUTENANT Z. M. PIKE, UNITED STATES ARMY, 1805—REPORT OF MAJOR LONG, UNITED STATES ARMY, 1817 AND 1819—MAP OF THE ROUTE, BY CAPTAIN H. WHITING, FIFTH UNITED STATES INFANTRY, 1819, WITH NOTES.

INTRODUCTORY REMARKS.

A very interesting natural feature is presented by the courses of the Wisconsin and Fox Rivers. They flow toward each other to within six miles of meeting, and then, turning in opposite directions, (although separated only by a low plain across which their floods intermingle,) the waters of the one pursue a southerly course to the distant Gulf of Mexico, and those of the other a northerly direction to the equally remote ocean-receptacle—the Gulf of Saint Lawrence. Each of these termini was a region beyond the bounds of the knowledge of the aboriginals on the banks of the two rivers. While all relating to the distant seas to which these waters flowed was to them a mystery, they could yet readily appreciate the advantages the near approach of the two streams afforded them as an easy route of communicaiton between the Mississippi and the great lakes, and it was but natural that their wonder should ascribe the existing conditions to the work of a deity, and that they should make offerings to him for his favor—acts which appeared shockingly idolatrous to the early missionaries. Every enterprise of man in new regions seeks the paths which nature has provided, and thus in due course of events this route became the path by which white men first reached the great river—the Michi-Sipi—in early periods of American history.

HISTORY OF DISCOVERY, ETC., BY JOHN G. SHEA.

I take the following account of discovery from the work of John G. Shea, entitled "Discovery and Explorations of the Mississippi Valley," published by Redfield, Nos. 110 and 112 Nassau street, New York, 1853. This publication contains a print of the original map made by Father Marquette, (then recently found among the records preserved at Saint Mary's College, Montreal,) a reduced copy of which accompanies this chapter. (Plate 1.) The account which I present is mainly made up of quotations, with merely such minor changes and interpolations as large omissions and a little different arrangement require; the distinction between modified and quoted matter is intended to be preserved by quotation-marks.

Events leading to discovery.—"Quebec was founded by Champlain in 1608. He was soon joined by Recollet friars, and while he entered the Seneca country with his Huron allies, the intrepid Father Le Caron had ascended the Ottawa, and reached the banks of Lake Huron. Subsequently, others joined him there; they invited the Jesuits to aid them, and the tribes in the peninsula were visited from Detroit to Niagara, and from Lake Nipissing to Montreal.

"The capture of Canada by the English, in 1629, defeated any further missionary efforts for a time, but it was restored in 1632, and the Jesuits sent out to continue the mission alone. They now became the first discoverers of the greater part of the interior of this continent. * * * Within ten years of their second arrival they had completed the examination of the country from Lake Superior to the Gulf, and founded several villages of Christian neophytes on the borders of the upper lakes. While the intercourse of the Dutch was yet confined to the Indians in the vicinity of Fort Orange, and five years before Eliot, of New England, had addressed a single word to the Indians within six miles of Boston Harbor, the French missionaries planted the Cross at Sault Ste. Marie, whence they looked down on the Sioux country and the Valley of the Mississippi."

*   *   *   *   *   *

Adventures of the Sieur Nicolet, A. D. 1639.—"As early as 1639 the adventurous and noble-hearted Sieur Nicolet, the interpreter of the colony, had struck west of the Hurons, and reaching the last limits of the Algonquins, found himself among the Ouinepegon, (Winnebagoes.) * * * With these Nicolet entered into friendly relations, and, exploring Green Bay, ascended Fox River to its portage, and embarked on a river flowing west."

And he avers that had he sailed three days more he would have found the sea. The "sea" was the interpretation this traveler, like others, had given to the Indian name "Mississippi," which in their language signified "great water."

Discovery delayed by Indian wars.—The war which broke out in 1641 between the Iroquois (Six Nations) and the Hurons (Wyandots) destroyed the Jesuit missions to the latter, in the extreme West, and drove the Hurons from their lands. A remnant of them located themselves near the place known now as La Pointe, near Bayfield, on Lake Superior, at which a mission called La Pointe du St. Esprit was located in 1658, but soon after abandoned for Macinac on account of the hostility of the Dakotas. Lake Superior receives its name from being the "Lac Superieur," or Upper Lake of the Ottawas. These Indian wars so retarded explorations in these regions that no material advance was made till 1673. But—

"The course of the Mississippi, its great features, the nature of the country, were all known to the western missionaries and the traders, who alone with them carried on the discovery of the West. Among the latter was Jolliet, who in his rambles also penetrated near the Mississippi."

As these Indian wars seemed an obstacle to so hazardous an undertaking on the part of the missionaries, as the exploration of the great river, they—

"Urged the French Court to set on foot an expedition, * * * and at last, on the 4th of June, 1672, the French minister wrote to Talon, then intendant of Canada, 'as after the increase of the colony, there is nothing more important for the colony than the discovery of a passage to the South Sea, His Majesty wishes you to give it your attention.'"

Discoveries by Father Marquette and the Sieur Jolliet.—Just at this time Frontenac succeeded Talon, who returned to France. The Sieur Jolliet was appointed to the charge of the expedition, and the pious Jesuit, Père Marquette, was selected to accompany him. It is from the journal and map of the latter that our best knowledge of the expedition is derived. Those made during the voyage by Jolliet were lost by him in descending the rapids of the Saint Lawrence River, near Montreal, and those subsequently made by him were from memory.

Marquette says:

"It was on the 17th of May, 1673, that we started from the mission of Saint Ignatius, at Michilimakinac, where I then was. Our joy at being chosen for this expedition roused our courage, and sweetened the labor of rowing from morning till night. As we were going to seek unknown countries, we took all possible precautions that, if our enterprise was hazardous, it should not be foolhardy; for this reason we gathered all possible information from Indians who had frequented those parts, and even from their accounts traced a map of all the new country, marking down the rivers on which we were to sail, the names of the nations, and places through which we were to pass, the course of the great river, and what direction we should take when we got to it."

"Above all, I put our voyage under the protection of the Blessed Virgin Immaculate, promising her that if she did us the grace to discover the great river, I would give it the name of Conception."

Marquette was faithful to his promise, and inscribed on his map of the great river, "R. de la Conception." The Algonquin name, however, by which it had become known to the French through the Indians, has prevailed over that given by Marquette, and over that of "Rio del Espiritu Santo," given by the Spaniards to its lower course more than one hundred and fifty years previous, and over that of "R. de Colbert," the name of the great minister of Louis XIV, which Father Hennepin vainly endeavored to fasten upon it a few years after.

The name *Michi-Sipi*, literally Great Water, for a time thought to refer to the Pacific Ocean, has become the name of the great river for all time.

At the time of the expedition of Jolliet and Marquette, the discoveries of the Spaniards on the Lower Mississippi had been forgotten.

"And although explored for at least a thousand miles, known to have at least two branches equal in size to the finest rivers of Spain, to be nearly a league wide and perfectly navigable, it is laid down on maps as an insignificant stream, often not even distinguished by its name—Espiritu Santo—and then we are left to conjecture what petty line was intended for the great river of the West."

Let us resume the journal of Marquette. He says:

"We made our paddles play merrily over a part of Lake Huron and that of the Illinois" (Lake Michigan) "into the Bay of the Fetid," (Green Bay).

Here he remarked the tide at its head, an effect much studied since:

"Which has its regular flow and ebb, almost like that of the sea."

At this point, on the site of the present city of Green Bay, was the mission of Saint Francis Xavier.

The expedition reached Maskontens on the 7th of June, which place was supposed by Marquette to be the limit of the previous discoveries of the French. This was probably the vicinity of the present village of Roslin, as Marquette says it was three leagues from the Wisconsin. According to the narrative of Major Long's expedition to the source of the Saint Peter's River in 1823, the league of Marquette and Hennepin is 2¾ English miles.

On "the 10th of June," Marquette says—

"Two Miamis whom they" (the Indians) "had given us as guides embarked with us, in the sight of a great crowd, who could not wonder enough to see seven Frenchmen alone, in two canoes, dare to undertake so strange and so hazardous an expedition.

"We knew that there was, three leagues from Maskontens, a river emptying into the Missisipi; we knew, too, that the point of the compass we were to hold to reach it was the west-southwest; but the way is so cut up by marshes and little lakes that it is easy to go astray, especially as the river leading to it is so covered with wild oats that you can hardly discover the channel. Hence we had good need of our two guides, who led us safely to a portage of twenty-seven hundred paces, and helped us to transport our canoes to enter this river, after which they returned, leaving us alone in an unknown country, in the hands of Providence."

* * * *

"The river on which we embarked is called Meskonsing," (Wisconsin;) "it is very broad, with a sandy bottom, forming many shallows, which render navigation very difficult. It is full of vine-clad islets. On the banks appear fertile lands diversified with wood, prairie, and hill. Here you find oaks, walnut, whitewood, and another kind of tree with branches armed with long thorns. We saw no small game or fish, but deer and moose in considerable numbers.

"Our route was southwest, and after sailing * * * forty leagues on this same route, we reached the mouth of our river, and * * * safely entered the Missisipi on the 17th of June, with a joy that I cannot express."

I shall not follow Father Marquette farther on in the journal of his voyage in detail, as he says no more about the Wisconsin River and never visited it again. He continued down the Mississippi to about the mouth of the Arkansas River, where he and Jolliet no longer doubted that the Mississippi terminated in the Gulf of Mexico. The object of the expedition as ordered by the French court was thus accomplished, and to proceed farther would endanger the results of their explorations by exposing them to the liability of being captured by the Spaniards on the Lower Mississippi. They therefore turned back and ascended the Mississippi to the mouth of the Illinois River, up which stream they proceeded as far as the portage, near the present site of Chicago, where they crossed over to the shore of Lake Michigan, and coursed along it to the mission at Michilimakinac.

Captivity of and discoveries by Father Hennepin, 1680–'81.—In 1680–'81, Father Hennepin, a Franciscan, a member of one of the religious orders which succeeded the overthrow of the Jesuits, descended the Illinois River to its mouth, and was there made prisoner by the Dakotas. They carried him up the Mississippi, above the Falls of Saint Anthony, which he named, (after Saint Anthony of Padua,) and then up the river he named Saint Francis, (since known as Rum River, from its dark amber-colored water,) to its source in Lake Issati, (now named Mille Lacs,) where he spent the winter. The Dakota traditions still make this lake the ancient center of their nation.

His rescue by Lieutenant Du Luth.—At Lake Issati, Father Hennepin was ransomed by a French officer named Du Luth, and returned with him by way of the Wisconsin and Fox River route to the French settlements. This closes what I have taken from the works of Mr. Shea.

Early history of Michigan, by C. Lanman.—A very good account of the early occupation of Wisconsin is given by Mr. Charles Lanman, in his "History of Michigan," published by E. B. Smith & Co., Detroit, from which I take a few general remarks.

Condition of the country at the time of English occupation in 1760.—Except the noble aims of the missionaries, the only object of the French was to pursue the fur-trade, which was vigorously carried on through every channel which nature presented. Such small settlements as they formed about the trading-posts were prevented from expanding by tyrannical restrictions. Agriculture, instead of being stimulated, was repressed, and the settlers were but the servants of gigantic corporations, royal monopolies, whose rule was solely for their own pecuniary benefit.

The Frenchmen affiliated with the savages, married their women, and their progeny of half-breeds became the main working-force of the fur companies. Their villages were small and confined to limited areas, and they developed a condition of life which here and there still survives, through all the mutations of succeeding events which have swept away the red man, given rise to populous cities of another race, and reticulated the land with railways.

Condition not changed by the English occupation, which nominally ended in 1783.—The victory of the English over the French at Quebec in 1760, which caused, in the same year, the capitulation at Montreal, and the surrender to the English of the control of the whole region, effected little change there. The fur-trade was pursued as before. The Frenchmen and their descendants remained unmolested.

Wonderful changes wrought by the American Republic.—Even the success of the American Revolution, by which the control of a large piece of the fur-bearing regions passed, in 1783, to the control of the United

States, made but little change in the development of the country till the steady approach of the pioneer American settlers caused the gradual extinction of the Indian titles to the land, and the creation of territorial governments, which soon after developed into States. It is almos wholly within the last fifty years that the marvelous transformation oı our Northwest has been brought about, which contrasts so pleasantly with what existed before.

NOTE BY JONATHAN CARVER, 1766.

The village at Prairie du Chien, when visited by Jonathan Carver in 1766, was estimated by him to contain three hundred families. A remnant of this village, as distinct as the aboriginals from the inhabitants of the American city, still occupies the old village site.

RECOMMENDATIONS OF LIEUT. Z. M. PIKE, UNITED STATES ARMY, 1805.

In 1805, Lieutenant Pike, United States Army, in a report of an exploration towards the source of the Mississippi, recommended the building of a fort on the high bluff on the Mississippi opposite the mouth of the Wisconsin River, to control the movements of the Indians along it, and protect the white settlers.

REPORT OF MAJOR LONG, U. S. A., 1817 AND 1819.

The Wisconsin River was visited by Major S. H. Long, United States Topographical Engineers, in 1817 and again in 1823, and he thus describes it:

"The Wisconsin River, from its magnitude and importance, deserves a high rank among the tributaries of the Mississippi. When swollen by a freshet it affords an easy navigation for boats of considerable burden through a distance of more than one hundred and eighty miles. Its current is rapid, and, like the Mississippi, it embosoms innumerable islands. In a low stage of water its navigation is obstructed by numerous shoals and sand-banks. At the distance from its mouth above mentioned " (too great an estimate by sixty miles) " there is a portage of one mile and a half across a flat meadow, which is occasionally subject to inundation, to a branch of Fox River of Green Bay, thus affording another navigable communication which boats have been known to pass. The valley of the Wisconsin is somewhat narrower than those of most other rivers of this region, but in other respects is very similar to them. The high country here assumes a more hilly and broken aspect, and the soil becomes more sandy and meagre." See Long's " Expedition to the source of the St. Peter's River," vol. 2, chapter v.

MAP OF THE ROUTE BY CAPT. H. WHITING, FIFTH UNITED STATES INFANTRY, 1819, WITH NOTES.

In 1819 the Fifth Regiment of United States Infantry made the voyage from Fort Howard, near Green Bay, to Prairie du Chien, via the Fox and Wisconsin Rivers, and Capt. Henry Whiting, of, that regiment, prepared a map of the route on a scale of an inch to four miles, with numerous marginal notes. From these the following description is compiled:

Fort Howard is on the left bank of the Lower Fox River, about two miles from its mouth; about three miles above are rapids and a mill, and between these and the fort was a French settlement occupying both banks of the river, and numbering about sixty families. From the rapids at the mills to the Grand Chute, the current is generally so rapid as to render a tow-line and setting-poles necessary, and the boats are for the most part moved up in that way. In this space were passed, first, the Little Kakalin Rapids, one-quarter of a mile in length, easily surmounted with setting-poles and oars; second, the Great Kakalin

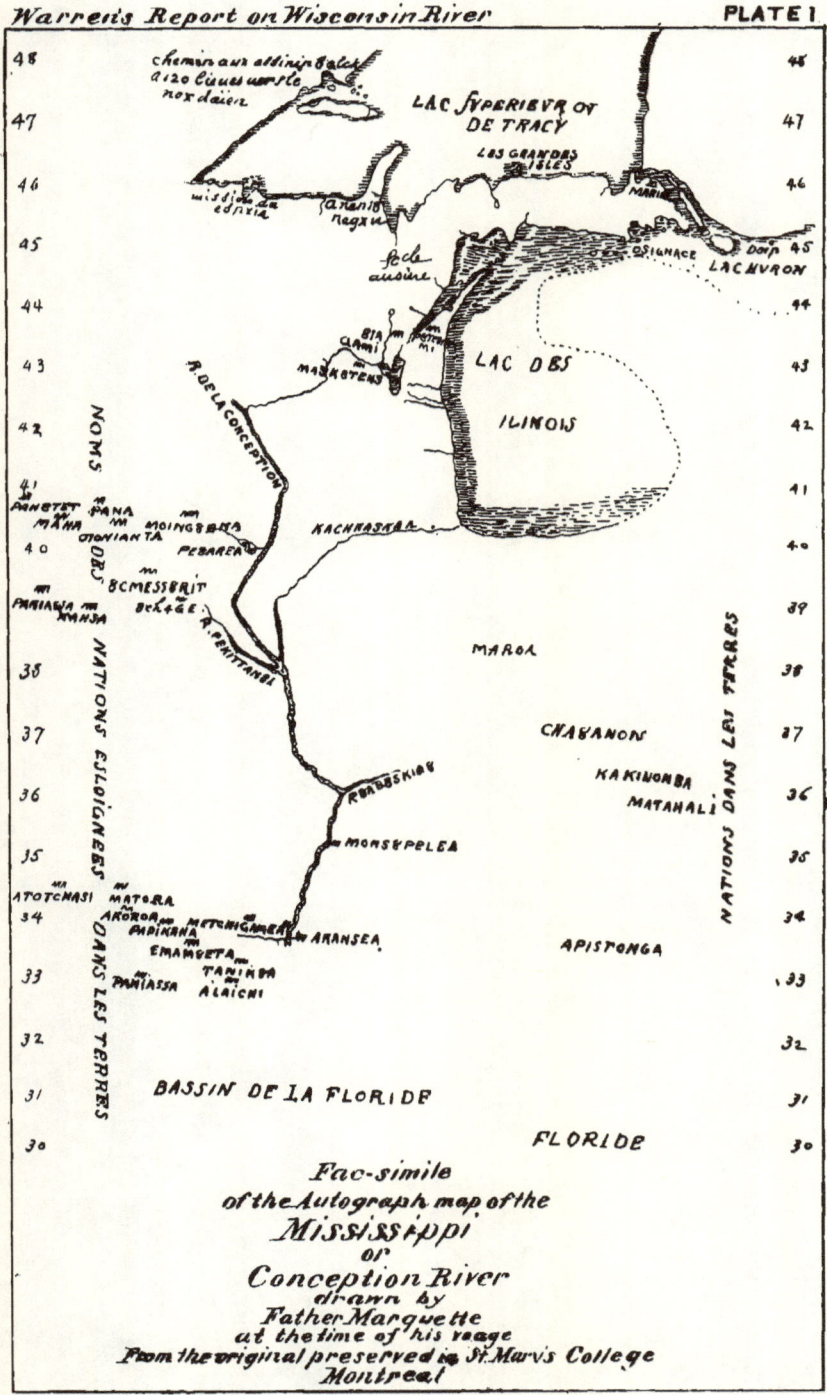

Rapids, one mile in length, very broken and violent, where the boats are unloaded, and the baggage transported one thousand yards by land; third, La Petite Chute, a ledge stretching across the river, making a descent of about twelve inches; fourth, La Grosse Roche, which makes a perpendicular fall of about two feet. Both these two last-mentioned are surmounted with loaded boats.

At La Grand Chute there is a perpendicular fall of about four feet all across the river, and the boats have to unload and the baggage is transported 500 yards. Above the Grand Chute and below Lake Winnebago there are two or three inconsiderable rapids which are surmounted without much difficulty or delay.

The Fox River thence to the portage has always a strong current and is often entirely overgrown with grass and wild rice, but presents no other impediments. It winds through a narrow prairie bordered by oak openings and undulating lands, generally of a beautiful appearance, but probably not remarkably rich in their soil, but wherever the river washes them seems to be a sandy, reddish loam.

The portage between the Fox and Wisconsin Rivers is about 2,500 yards; the road runs over a marshy prairie. There is a Frenchman residing on the rising ground between the rivers. He keeps the proper transportation for boats and baggage.

The limestone bluffs and highlands begin on the Wisconsin about eight miles below the portage. Just above Prairie du Sac appears to be the apex of the highland of the Ouscousin and the head of the great valley through which that river winds. The river is full of islands formed by the sand-bars, which are constantly increasing in number. The general depth of the river is, at the ordinary height of the water, four to five feet, but the sand-bars often extend entirely across the river and have not more than eight or ten inches of water; the sands, however, are quick and oppose but little resistance.

From a peak of the highlands near the river, (Bogus Bluffs,) about 500 feet high, one has a view of the valley and the highlands of the Ouscousin. The valley is four and five miles wide, about half covered with wood, and apparently rich. The highlands appear to be nearly parallel, and eroded ridges cut transversely presenting their broken sections to the valley, and all of them exhibiting more or less marked strata of rocks, which wear the aspect of castles, towers, turrets, &c., dilapidated and desolate. These highlands appear to be the common level of the country, broken into ridges and covered with a scanty vegetation.

The history of the Wisconsin and Fox River route, and the region it traverses, continues to relate principally to Indian traders, military operations, and Indian wars, down to the close of the Black Hawk war, about 1832. It was along the Wisconsin that this heroic chief and his despoiled followers attempted to escape, and near the mouth of which they were all destroyed except a few that were granted quarter.

Wisconsin formed part of the Northwest Territory till the year 1848, when it was admitted as a State in the Union. Much prosperity attended the first settlements along the Wisconsin River on account of the natural advantages for business which it presented. The construction of the railroads from Milwaukee to La Crosse, and from Madison to Prairie du Chien, soon drew the trade and inhabitants away from the banks of the river. The warehouses and many dwellings were abandoned and fell into decay. Long reaches of river became the almost undisturbed homes of wild animals. The Indians, who had been moved farther west, began to straggle back to their old haunts. While we were examining the rivers the smoke of their camp-fires could frequently be seen, and around them they cooked and ate their game in primitive simplicity. Their canoes were often met by us. Almost every feature of the landscape as it was two hundred years ago, seemed in places restored, and it required no effort of the imagination, in the haze and mists of twilight, to picture to ourselves the canoes of Jolliet and Marquette as they glided down the stream on their adventurous voyage of discovery.

CHAPTER III.

HISTORY OF THE IMPROVEMENT OF THE ROUTE ALONG THE FOX AND WISCONSIN RIVERS SINCE SURVEYS AND IMPROVEMENT WERE BEGUN; PROGRESS OF THE IMPROVEMENTS AND CONDITION DOWN TO 1870.

Survey under War Department, in 1836, by Mr. Center, civil engineer—Survey under War Department, in 1837, by Mr. Pettival, civil engineer—Bill for the improvement of these rivers and for a canal to unite them, reported by United States Senate committee in 1839—Survey of the Fox and Wisconsin Rivers, under War Department, by Captain Cram, in 1839—Report upon survey and estimates of Captain Cram, made by committee of House of Representatives in 1846—Survey of Green Bay, under War Department, by Capt. W. G. Williams in 1845—Lands granted to the State, on its admission into the Union, for improving the navigation of the Wisconsin and Fox Rivers and for constructing a canal to unite them; act approved August 6, 1846—Operations in 1848; report of board of public works for 1848—List of rapids on Lower Fox River, with the fall at each—Operations in 1849; report of board of public works for 1849—Character of the Wisconsin and difficulty of improving its channel, stated by Alton—Operations in 1850; report of board of public works for 1850—Operations in 1851; report of board of public works for 1851—Plan of improving the Wisconsin River, by Acting Commissioner Croswell—Operations in 1852; report of board of public works for 1852—Condition of the Wisconsin River improvement and a plan for continuing the same, by Acting Commissioner Richardson—Table of expenditures on the Wisconsin River—Expenditures made in 1852—Table of total expenditures to date—Geological survey of the Wisconsin—Progress of improvement in 1853—Surrender of the works of improvement, lands, &c., by the State to a company, June 1, 1853—Company chartered, with conditions, July 6, 1853—Condition and character of the works in 1854, by C. D. Westbrook, jr.—Reservoir on the headwaters of the Wisconsin as a means to increase its low-water depth, suggested by Mr. Westbrook—Expenditures by the company from August 20, 1853, to November 15, 1854—PROGRESS OF THE FOX AND WISCONSIN RIVER IMPROVEMENT SUBSEQUENT TO 1855-'56—Additional lands granted to the State by Congress—Increased capacity of the improvement required by the State—Condition of the works January, 1859; report of the chief engineer of the company, Mr. D. C. Jenne—Condition of the improvement in 1860; report of the president of the company to a committee of the State legislature—Navigation of the Wisconsin can be improved by running a steamboat; money expended otherwise would be of no avail; from same report of president of company—Expenditures from October 3, 1856, to December 31, 1859—Expenditures from beginning of improvement in 1848 to 1859 — Operations in 1860-'61-'62; report of superintendent of company—Increased capacity necessary for passage of gunboats; estimated cost of, by Mr Jenne, civil engineer, in 1862—RENEWAL OF INTEREST IN THE IMPROVEMENT BY THE UNITED STATES—Report of Committee on Naval Affairs, Thirty-seventh Congress, upon the improvement, with estimates for an increase of capacity so as to pass gunboats, 1863—Company having failed to perform its agreement the works of improvement, land, &c., were sold in 1866—Green Bay and Mississippi Canal Company, incorporated by the State August 15, 1866—Examination and estimates ordered by Congress—Condition of these rivers, improvement, &c., 1866—Condition of the Lower Fox River improvement in 1866—Condition of the Upper Fox River and improvement in 1866—Condition of the Wisconsin River in 1866.—WORKS OF IMPROVEMENT, ETC., IN 1867—WORKS OF IMPROVEMENT IN 1868—WORKS OF IMPROVEMENT IN 1869—CONCLUDING REMARKS TO CHAPTER III.

Survey under War Department in 1836, by Mr. Center, C. E.—On account of the increasing importance of the Fox and Wisconsin route of communication, a survey was made under the instructions of Colonel Abert, chief of Topographical Engineers, United States Army, in 1836, at the entrance of the Fox River and Green Bay. This survey was made by Mr. A. J. Center and Lieutenant Rose, both of the Army, the former of whom made the report after he had resigned from the Army. Mr. Center's report was dated in April, 1838, and I believe it was not published. The survey extended from Fort Howard to Tail Point, a distance of about six miles. The map was made on a scale of 8 inches to a mile.

Great interest was taken in the improvement of this route by the War Department, as it would facilitate the movement and supply of troops operating to protect settlers against hostile Indians.

Survey under War Department in 1837 by Mr. Pettival, C. E.—In April, 1837, instructions were issued from the Topographical Engineer Bureau of the War Department, to J. B. Pettival, civil engineer, to make a survey and examination of the Fox River, for the purpose of determining the best practical mode of improving the navigation. A part of the Upper Fox was meandered while so overflowed that the chain was buoyed up by floats and stretched on the surface of the water. This survey was so hurried that another one was recommended. The report was printed as Doc. No. 102, House of Representatives, War Department, Twenty-fifth Congress, third session. Mr. Pettival's description of, and remarks upon, the physical features of the route are very interesting, and will be referred to by me in treating of the physical features.

Bill for the improvement of these rivers and for a canal to unite them, &c.—On February 11, 1839, the United States Senate "Committee on Roads and Canals," to which were referred the memorials of the legislature of the Territory of Wisconsin (Wisconsin being all that was left of the Northwest Territory after Michigan was admitted in 1837) upon the subject of improvement of the navigation of certain rivers in Wisconsin, reported a bill the first section of which provided "for the improvement of the navigation of the Wisconsin and Neenah (Upper Fox) Rivers, and for their connection by a canal." The report says:

The Wisconsin may be rendered navigable by the removal of the timber from its banks where it overhangs the channel, and occasionally contracting its waters by closing the heads of the sluices or shallow channels around the islands. * * Its general width is about a mile; these improvements, therefore, will permit the steamboats which navigate the Upper Mississippi to ascend this river to the Great Bend nearest to Lake Michigan.

A grant of land was recommended to supply funds for this improvement.

I have quoted in full the method recommended for improving the navigation of the Wisconsin River. It has ever since been regarded with particular favor, and, although it may be made to accomplish as much as was then proposed, it is a work of great difficulty, if it is not impracticable, to make it meet the present wants of a through line of water-transportation between the lakes and the Upper Mississippi. I shall especially quote all the plans proposed for improving the Wisconsin River as we reach them in the following chronological history of the improvements.

Survey of the Fox River, under the War Department, by Captain Cram, in 1839.—The next surveys, for the purpose of improvement on the Fox and Wisconsin route, were conducted by and under Capt. T. J. Cram, Topographical Engineers, in 1839. This report is dated January, 1840, and forms Senate Document No. 318, Twenty-sixth Congress, first session. Its title is "Report on the further survey and estimate of the cost of improving navigation of the Fox and Wisconsin Rivers, and connecting the same by a navigable canal or water-communication."

Report upon survey and estimates of Captain Cram, made by the Committee of House of Representatives, in 1845.—This report of Captain Cram is also embodied in the report of the House Committee on Public Lands, House of Representatives, No. 551, Twenty-ninth Congress, first session, dated April 6, 1846, which is the one I have consulted. There are printed with this report both general and special maps. He refers in the opening of his report to three routes for communication by water between the Mississippi and Lake Michigan, as follows:

Route No. 1. Through the valley of the Wisconsin River to the portage; thence by a canal across the portage into the Fox; thence down this river to Green Bay.
Route No. 2. Through the valley of the Rock River, from its mouth to the head of its natural navigation; thence by canal into the southern extremity of Lake Winnebago; thence through this lake and the lower part of the Fox River into Green Bay.
Route No. 3. Through the valley of the Illinois River, from its mouth to the head of its navigation; thence by means of a canal along the valley of the unnavigable part of the river to the southwestern part of Lake Michigan.

The general features of route No. 1, and the more immediate surveys called for, are stated as follows by Captain Cram:

Those steamers that are in the habit of navigating the Upper Mississippi, in attempting to ascend the Wisconsin in times of low water, meet with sand-bars. These are the only obstructions, and they are of a nature such as to be continually shifting their positions. The same steamers, however, which are unable to ascend in lowest stages of water, meet with no difficulty in ascending the Wisconsin during spring and fall as far up as the portage; and there is no doubt that steamers of sufficient tonnage could be constructed, with a draught sufficiently small to allow of their passage up the Wisconsin, in the present condition of its sand-bars, even in times of ordinary low water; and as the most serious obstacles pertaining to the whole of route No. 1 were known to be in the Fox, it was deemed best to commence the survey upon the part of the Wisconsin in the vicinity of Fort Winnebago, and proceed across the portage into the Fox, and down the same to Green Bay. In pursuance of this plan, not only has a general reconnaissance of the whole Fox been made, but all places demanding improvement have been surveyed in a manner necessary to estimate the cost of improving the navigation, as required in the act of Congress which directed the survey and estimate to be made.

Captain Cram, therefore, made surveys at the portage between the Wisconsin and Fox Rivers; at the Winnebago Rapids at the outlet of Lake Winnebago, and at Grand Chute, Little Chute, Grand Kakalin, Rapide Croche, Little Kakalin and Depère (the parts occupied by rapids) in the Lower Fox. His proposed plans of improvement contemplated canals 40 feet width at bottom, 55 feet at water-line, and 5 feet depth. The lock-chambers were to be 110 feet by 30 feet. Dams were to be built at the rapids; and sharp elbows, bar-deposits, and trees were to be removed from the Upper Fox. The estimate of total cost was $448,470.18, divided up as follows:

1. At Depère, dam and lock	$20,306 79
2. At Little Kakalin, dam and lock	28,978 84
3. At Rapide Croche, dam and lock	19,062 29
4. At Grand Kakalin, dam and locks	107,574 85
5. At Little Chute, dam and locks	99,693 60
6. At Grand Chute, dam and locks	82,382 74
7. At Winnebago Rapids, dam and lock	23,748 50
8. The portage between Fox and Wisconsin Rivers, canal and locks	64,085 81
9. For removing elbows, bar-deposits, trees, &c., along the Upper Fox	6,230 50
10. For superintendence, 6 per centum	25,385 18
Total	448,470 18

Captain Cram made a comparison of the estimated cost of improving the Lower Fox River with the estimated cost of an independent canal, leaving Lake Winnebago at Clifton, and striking the Lower Fox below Rapide Croche. The cost of this latter plan was estimated at three times the other. Captain Cram's report gives a map of this route on a scale of $\frac{4}{5}$-inch to a mile.

The committee reported a bill to grant—

The alternate sections for only two miles on each side of the route, which is estimated to be sufficient for the completion of the work.

It will be seen from the above that Captain Cram made no surveys of the Wisconsin River, nor any estimate for its improvement. That the natural navigation was greatly overvalued, is shown by the little use made of it after the route along the Fox River was subsequently opened, which latter failed mainly of its utility from the inadequacy of the Wisconsin River for navigation. Indeed, this navigation was so little valued, that no serious opposition was raised to the bridging of the river by the Milwaukee and Prairie du Chien Railroad in such a way as to completely prevent its being used by steamboats in low stages.

Survey of Green Bay under War Department, by Capt. W. G. Williams, in 1845.—In 1845 a survey of Green Bay was made by Capt. W. G. Williams, Topographical Engineers, U. S. A., the map of which was published as H. Ex. Doc. (War Department) No. 170, Twenty-ninth Congress, first session, on a scale of two miles to one inch.

Lands granted to the State on its admission into the Union, &c.—The report of the House committee last referred to, made April 6, 1846, recommending a grant of lands, was in accordance with the report of the Senate Committee on Public Lands on the same subject, dated January 8, 1844. An act accordingly was passed, and approved August 8, 1846, which is as follows:

Be it enacted by the Senate and House, &c., That there be, and hereby is, granted to the State of Wisconsin, on the admission of such State into the Union, for the purpose of improving the navigation of the Fox and Wisconsin Rivers, in the Territory of Wisconsin, and of constructing a canal to unite the said rivers at or near Portage, a quantity of land equal to one-half of three sections in width on each side of the said Fox River, and the lakes through which it passes, from its mouth to the point where the Portage Canal shall enter the same, and on each side of said canal, from one stream to the other, reserving the alternate sections to the United States, to be selected under the direction of the governor of the State, and such selection to be approved by the President of the United States. The said river, when improved, and the said canal, when finished, shall be, and forever remain, a public highway for the use of the Government, free from any toll or other charge whatever for the transportation of the mails, or for any property of the United States, or persons in their service passing upon or along the same: *Provided*, The said alternate sections reserved to the United States shall not be sold at a less rate than $2.50 the acre: *Provided also*, That no pre-emption claim to the land so reserved shall give the occupant, or any other person claiming through or under him, a right to sell lands at any price less than the price fixed in this act, at the time of the settlement on said lands.

SEC. 2. *And be it further enacted*, That as soon as the Territory of Wisconsin shall be admitted as a State into the Union, all the lands granted her shall be and become the property of said State, for the purpose contemplated in this act, and no other: *Provided*, That the legislature of said State shall agree to accept said grant upon the terms specified in this act, and shall have the power to fix the price at which said lands shall be sold, not less than one dollar and twenty-five cents the acre, and to adopt such kind and plan of improvement on said route as the said legislature shall from time to time determine for the best interest of the State: *Provided also*, That the lands hereby granted shall not be conveyed or disposed of by said State, except as said improvement shall progress. That is, the said State may sell so much of said lands as shall produce the sum of twenty thousand dollars, and then the sales shall cease until the governor of said State shall certify to the President of the United States that one-half of said sum has been expended upon said improvements, when the said State may sell and dispose of a quantity of said lands sufficient to re-imburse the amount expended, and the fact of such expenditure shall be certified in the manner herein mentioned.

SEC. 3. *And be it further enacted*, That the said improvement shall be commenced within three years after the said State shall be admitted into the Union, and completed within twenty years or the United States shall be entitled to receive the amount for which any of said lands may have been sold by the said State, provided that the title of purchase under the sales made by the State in pursuance of this act shall be valid.

The State of Wisconsin accepted the above grant with its provisions by act of its legislature, approved June 29, 1848. Another act, approved August 8, 1848, containing 47 sections, provided for the conduct of the improvement, from which the following is extracted:

Section 1 provides that the construction of the improvements contemplated by the act of Congress, * * * and the superintendence and repair thereof after completion, shall be under the direction and control of a "board of public works."

Section 5 provides that—

The said commissioners shall first commence the construction of the canal, and after said canal is finished, the improvement of the Wisconsin and Fox Rivers shall be commenced, beginning at both ends of the canal down each stream, so as to make said streams navigable as the improvements progress, with the exception of the improvement of the several rapids on Fox River below Lake Winnebago, which may be commenced at any time said commissioners may think proper. After the construction of the canal the net proceeds of one-sixth of the sales of the grant of land is hereby set apart for the improvement of the Wisconsin River, and five-sixths of said proceeds to the improvement of the Fox River: *Provided,* That no more than ten thousand dollars shall be expended in improving the navigation of the Fox River from the said canal to Lake Winnebago, until further action of the legislature of the State, or until the said river shall be made navigable to Green Bay.

* * * * * * *

SEC. 15. In the construction of such improvements the said board shall have power to enter on, take possession of, and use all lands, waters, and materials, the appropriation of which for the use of such works of improvement shall, in their judgment, be necessary.

SEC. 16. When any lands, waters, or materials, appropriated by the board for the use of said improvement, shall belong to the State, such lands, waters, or materials, and so much of the adjoining lands as may be valuable for hydraulic or commercial purposes, shall be absolutely reserved to the State, and whenever a water-power shall be created by reason of any dam erected or other improvements made on any of said rivers, such water-power shall belong to the State, subject to future legislation.

Sections 17, 18, 19, 20, and 21 make provisions for compensating parties from whom any property is taken under authority specified in section 15.

SEC. 22. As soon as any portion of said improvements shall be completed so as to admit of use, the board shall make rules and regulations from time to time, in respect to the passage of boats, rafts, and other floats, through the canal and locks, and all matters connected with the navigation thereof, and impose such forfeitures for the breach of any such regulations as may be deemed reasonable by them.

The foregoing extracts from this act of the Wisconsin legislature contain all there is in it affecting considerations of engineering and navigation. There is nothing in the act fixing upon the dimensions of the canal and locks.

Operations in 1848—*Report of board of public works for* 1848.—The first board of public works appointed by the legislature of Wisconsin consisted of James B. Estes, Albert S. Story, John A. Bingham, Curtis Reed, and H. L. Dousman. They appointed C. R. Alton the chief engineer. The annual report of operations in 1848 was dated January 19, 1849. Their operations consisted in making surveys and plans of improvement on the Fox River, and of the canal at "Portage," and the expenditures were $1,631.81. In the plan of improvement they adopted, they decreased the depth proposed by Captain Cram, from 5 feet to 4 feet at low water, and enlarged the dimensions of the locks from 110 feet by 30 feet to 125 feet by 30 feet.

Captain Cram, in his measurements of the fall on the rapids of the

Lower Fox necessary to be overcome by dams and locks, was considerably under the mark, and he does not enumerate among the list of rapids the Cedar Rapid just above Little Chute, or else includes them both in one. For convenience of reference in the report of operations following, I will give now a correct list of the several rapids, with their distance apart, and the fall at each as it was ascertained at the time of the examination made by Major Suter, in 1866. It is as well to note here that the map published with our report gives two locations of Rapide Croche; the upper one is the location of the dam, the other is a mistake.

List of rapids on Lower Fox River, with amount of fall and distances apart between head of each.

Name.	Fall.	Distance apart.
	Feet.	Miles.
Depere	8	0
Little Kaukana, (or Kakalin)	8	6
Rapide Croche	8	6
Grand Kaukana	50	4½
Little Chute	38	2½
Cedar Rapid	10	0¾
Grand Chute	38	4
Winnebago Rapid	10	4¼
Green Bay to Lake Winnebago	170	28

During our reconnaissances of the route in 1866, we were permitted by the canal company to make tracings of the diagrams of all the improvements up to that date. These were filed in the engineer headquarters at Washington, with the report dated January 21, 1867, and can there be referred to.

Operations in 1849—Report of board of public works for 1849.—The second annual report of the board of public works is dated January 21, 1850. Contracts were made for guard and lift locks and the two sections of canal at Portage; for improving both channels at Winnebago Rapids; for improving both sides of the river at Grand Chute; for improving the east side of the river at Rapide Croche; and for improvement of west side of river at Depère. The improvements at Depère were contracted for at the nominal sum of one dollar. Those at Winnebago Rapids and the Grand Chute were not begun this year. Fair progress was made at the other points. A steam-dredge was also built at a cost of $12,000, and set to work removing bars in the Big Bend, at and below Mechan Creek, and cutting a new outlet to the lake, (Lake Puckaway.)

Character of the Wisconsin and difficulty of improving its channel, &c.—An examination of the Wisconsin River below Portage was made in 1849 by the chief engineer, Mr. Alton. (His full report is given in the assembly journal for 1850, p. 571.) The following from this report is interesting, and shows views held in regard to the Wisconsin River which ruled at this period in the progress of the improvements. At the time of the examination, the river being at an "extremely low stage, a channel having not less than 2½ feet could be traced the entire distance from 'Portage' to the mouth." He further says:

The general character of the stream is such that it would be extremely difficult, if not impossible, to make any improvement in the channel by the ordinary method. The current is uniformly strong, running at the rate of three or four miles an hour, frequently divided into several channels or sloughs interspersed with numerous sandbars, and, to one entirely unacquainted with it, it would seem to present insuperable obstacles to navigation.

Mr. Alton thought the overhanging trees the greatest obstacle in the way of light-draught boats, and recommended that they should be cut away and a few snags removed. He also thought the steam dredge-boat should be set to work to cut an entire new channel from about half a mile below the lower ferry, " probably Bridgeport," to the Mississippi, following a line of sloughs or pond-holes, as exhibited on a map accompanying the report, and that one of the present channels of the Wisconsin should be closed up. He estimated the entire cost of this at $6,000.

The total expenditures in 1849 were as follows:

Depère, valve-gear	$411 86
Rapide Croche	6,949 62
Upper Fox, steam-dredge, $12,000; operating, $1,463.80	13,463 80
Portage, canal and locks	13,447 19
Wisconsin River, (probably for examining)	333 52
Engineers	6,120 97
Printing	544 85
Contingent	3,972 82
	45,244 63

Operations in 1850—Report of board of public works for 1850.—The third annual report of the board of public works of the operations during 1850, dated January 1, 1851, gives the following information:

The lock at Depère was completed and opened for the passage of boats early in the summer, but the miter-sill was found to be 2 feet too high, and must be lowered that much. Some rocks were removed from the channel between Depère and Rapide Croche.

At Rapide Croche the lock and section of canal were completed at an expense considerably greater than the first estimate. The lock had to be sunk a foot lower, and the section of canal made 1,000 feet longer. A serious breach in the dam at this place occurred in April.

At the rapids of Grand Kaukana, and Little Chute, arrangements for doing the work, though nearly consummated, failed.

At Cedar Rapid the dam was completed, and considerable portion of the lock-pit excavated.

At the Grand Chute the work progressed rapidly, till want of funds compelled a suspension.

At Winnebago Rapids the dam was completed, and about two-thirds of the canal excavated.

The Upper Fox River was remarkably low. The dredge was employed deepening the channel at the outlet of Lake Puckaway and between this lake and Buffalo Lake; also in cutting a new channel at the entrance into Buffalo Lake, and in cutting off a large bend near the junction of the Neenah so as to shorten distance and avoid Mud Lake.

On the Wisconsin River some portion of the overhanging trees that interfered with the navigable channel was cut down and removed last winter. A crane-scow for the removal of snags and to afford facilities for the cutting and removal of such trees as may still interfere with the navigation, was constructed in the autumn.

The following-named expenditures were made in 1850:

At Depère for freight	$10.00
For removing rocks between Depère and Rapide Croche	338.16
At Rapide Croche to contractors	13,222.43

At Cedar Rapids to contractors	$7,549.32
At Grand Chute to contractors	4,656.59
In dredging on Upper Fox and repairs of dredge-boat	4,728.97
On Portage Canal and locks	21,031.58
On Wisconsin River, pay of men and supplies, chopping wood $1,108.17	
On Wisconsin River, for surveying 26.00	
On Wisconsin River for scow and machinery 779.00	
	2,005.17
For stationery, printing, pay of commissioners, engineers, &c.	5,506.49
	59,048.71

The commissioners, at the close of their report, say:

There is a deficiency of about 170,000 acres in the grant of land for the improvement.

Operations of 1851—Report of board of public works for 1851.—The fourth annual report of the board of public works of the work done in 1851, dated January 2, 1852, gives the following information: The operations in 1851 were carried on under a new board, consisting of Caleb Croswell, David M. Lay, and Timothy Burns. Mr. Croswell had the supervision of the operations of the dredge-boat, Mr. Alton, the former chief engineer, resigned, and Mr. J. Kip Anderson, who had been assistant engineer, was appointed in his place. Mr. J. E. Day was appointed consulting engineer, "a gentleman," says the report of the board, "whose labors for the past six years on the Youghiogheny and Monongahela Rivers, made the selection appropriate and acceptable." In all the new contracts made this year, the original plan of the locks was so changed as to make those to be built hereafter 160 by 35, with 5 feet depth on the miter-sills. The contract for the work at the Grand Kaukana and Little Chute provided for payment being made in scrip.

At Depère, the lowering of the old lock two feet was completed in May.

At Rapide Croche, the old dam was of brush, and a breach occurred in it in the spring of 1850. It was entirely unsuited to the location. It was decided to replace it with a spar-dam. The work was commenced and was well under way; the crib-work having been carried across the river, the abutment on the east side finished, and a number of spars in their places. The probable expense of repairs at this point is estimated at $7,494.45.

At Great Kaukana Rapids—

A large portion of the canal was excavated, the protection-wall on the upper section more than one-half finished, and the upper lock-pit ready to receive the walls of the lock. From the lock-pits the earth was removed, and the excavation of the rock was to be carried on during the winter.

At the Little Chute—

But little has been done beyond grubbing and clearing of the line and the delivery of materials.

At the Cedar Rapids—

The dam and section of the canal, as well as the excavation of the lock-pit, are completed, the only work remaining to be performed being the building of the lock, for which the timber, plank, and iron have been prepared and the stone excavated.

The plan "having been changed" from a timber to a composite lock of the enlarged size, "the cost of the work will much exceed the original estimate." Work delayed for want of funds.

At the Grand Chute the contractors were embarrassed in their work by the difficulty of negotiating the warrants with which they were paid. Yet, "the improvement has progressed rapidly." "The timber and other materials for the dam and locks are delivered." At the Winnebago Rapids, since the last report, very little additional work has been done.

On the Upper Fox River—

During the past season the dredge has been in active operation on this stream, having performed much more service than in any previous year. The earth excavated amounted to 145,440 cubic yards; boat at work 170 days; average 855 cubic yards per day; maximum work during long days was 1,768 cubic yards per day.

The Portage Canal and locks were finished and accepted. A breach, however, occurred on the 28th of September.

During the prevalence of a flood, never before equaled in extent at that season of the year, the portage between the Fox and Wisconsin Rivers became so overflowed that the water from the last-mentioned stream broke through the canal-bank a short distance from the guard-lock, washing away at that point from 12 to 15 rods of the embankment.

A breach of about the same extent occurred near the other end of the canal. There was a third breach, of limited extent compared with the others. The report says:

The entire cost of these repairs, so elaborately descanted upon in particular quarters soon after the disaster, does not exceed the sum of $700; and a permanent barrier is now in the course of construction to provide against such an occurrence in the future.

This report contains the regulations and rates of toll adopted for the route, and these were kept in force by the law transferring the works to a company in 1853.

Plan of improving the Wisconsin by Acting Commissioner Croswell.—The following plan of improving the navigation of the Wisconsin River below Portage is proposed in the report of Mr. Croswell, acting commissioner for improving the Wisconsin River this year:

I trust I may be allowed respectfully to allude to the present navigable condition of the Wisconsin River below Portage. On that point, much neglected as it has been, but little has hitherto been said, and much less accomplished, by way of improvement. The opinion has been indulged, and, in my humble judgment, too readily so, that very little, if anything, can be done to aid the navigation of that stream between Fort Winnebago and the Mississippi. According to a former report, the principal obstacles to its improvement were found at the different points on the river where the stream is widest. At such places the depth of water is necessarily less than in the narrower portions, where the current is more rapid. From such observations as my position in the board for the past two years has enabled me to make, and from the experience of those most familiar with the obstructions of the stream, the opinion has been forced upon me that if the whole volume of water at the head of these flats was turned to one of the shores, all the main difficulties in the way of the successful navigation of the Wisconsin would at once be overcome. This, in my humble apprehension, could be easily effected by driving piles from the opposite shore as far into the stream as it might be deemed best to obstruct it, and by sinking a pier at the termination to prevent the current from washing away the work. Against these piles trees should be placed in such manner as to cause the sand to bank and form a dam. This dam would naturally turn the water to the narrow channel, and increase the velocity of the water to such an extent as to create a channel through the flat, and yet not be sufficiently strong to prove of any hindrance to steamboat navigation. At proper points, where these dams might occur, a convenient crossing could be established; and were wing-dams of this description to be thrown out at convenient intervals between Fort Winnebago and the Mississippi River there would seem to my mind no apparent obstacle in the way of the largest steam-vessels passing with ease up and down the stream during the entire season of navigation.

This annual report also contained the report of an examination of the Wisconsin River from Portage up to Beaulieux Rapids, made by William L. Dewitt, civil engineer, during 1851. He submitted an estimate of $52,264.36 for improving this portion of the river.

The following expenditures were made in 1851:

Depère	$928 95
Rapide Croche	1,284 03
Grand Kaukana	915 83

Grand Kaukana and Little Chute, scrip issued*	26,000	00
Cedar Rapids	8,888	93
Grand Chute	4,819	85
Upper Fox, dredging, &c	6,300	77
Portage Canal	12,047	96
Survey of Wisconsin above Portage	1,275	54
Contingent fund, pay of commissioners, &c	6,828	66
	69,290	52

Operations in 1852—Report of board of public works for 1852.—The fifth annual report of the board of public works of the work done in 1852, dated January 1, 1853, is signed by Peter H. Prame, William Richardson, and Andrew Proudfit. The pamphlet contains the reports of the chief engineer, of Mr. Richardson, acting commissioner for the improvement of the Wisconsin River, and Mr. Prame, the commissioner in charge of the dredge-boat. The purpose of the improvement is considered in this report, and its condition and future prospects discussed.

At Depère work was continued on the rebuilding of the lock, and rocks removed from the channel between it and Rapide Croche.

At Rapide Croche, a portion of the west dam having been carried away, an unsuccessful attempt, costing $2,732.28, was made to repair it. It was finally replaced by a spar-dam bolted to the rock bottom.

At Little Kaukana Rapids it was found that a dam and lock were necessary, and a plan was prepared for making them, the estimated expense being $17,022.92.

At the Grand Kaukana the work was nearly completed. At Little Chute the work was carried on vigorously.

At Cedar Rapids the work was nearly completed.

At Grand Chute the work was carried on vigorously.

On the Upper Fox River dredging was continued.

At the Portage Canal the right to use the water-power at the lift-lock was leased for a term of thirty years, at $275 per year.

Condition of the Wisconsin River improvement, &c.—I copy here the report of Acting Commissioner William Richardson, dated January 1, 1853, as it gives an authentic and complete account of all that had been done up to this time on this part of the improvement:

I deem it my duty to make, at this time, a brief statement of the plan, progress, &c., of the works of improvement on the Wisconsin River, which I have had the honor to direct as acting commissioner on said river. The act of our State legislature of the 8th of August, 1848, set apart one-sixth ($\frac{1}{6}$) of the net proceeds of the lands granted by Congress to aid in the improvement of the Fox and Wisconsin Rivers, and to connect the same by a canal (after the construction of the canal) for the improvement of the Wisconsin River, which act I conceive to be yet in force. The acts of April 14 and 19, 1852, provide for the same thing, and make it obligatory on the board of public works to commence the improvement of said river the present season, and to complete the same, as soon as practicable, upon the plans submitted by the chief engineer in his report for the year 1849, or in such other manner as best calculated to open a channel through the several flats on said river. The law making it thus obligatory on the board to commence this work the present season, I took the earliest opportunity (after my appointment upon that part of the improvement) to examine the stream, and determine, if possible, a practicable mode of improvement. I made an excursion on the river, from the Portage Canal to its mouth, for the purpose of ascertaining the cause of the deposits of sand in particular localities, believing a thorough knowledge of this cause necessary to a successful improvement of said river. By repeated observations upon the stream in a low stage of water, I became satisfied that the plan submitted in the engineer's report above referred to was the proper plan, and that brush, earth, gravel, and stone were the proper materials to be used in the construction of the dams.

---

* NOTE.—In the consolidated table given further on, being unable to proportion this from the reports, I divided it equally between the two.

G. K. W.

I am pleased to have it in my power to state in this connection, that, at least one of your honorable body, Chief Engineer Mr. J. Kip Anderson, and Assistant Engineer Mr. S. G. Callaghan, (after accompanying me in a small row-boat from the Portage to the mouth of the stream,) fully concurred with me in opinion upon this subject. The lack of funds applicable to this work I deem a sufficient apology for not commencing earlier in the season. I had the work commenced within two days after the first advertisement of lands, from the sales of which we were entitled to moneys to pay on said works. The character of the work is such that I deemed it impracticable to let the same by contract; consequently I selected good, efficient men as superintendents, and hired men by the day to do the work. I commenced at the Portage Canal and have proceeded down the river, as per act of the legislature of August 8, 1848. I have had seven (7) dams erected, and two now in course of erection. The aggregate length in lineal feet of the nine (9) dams is 4,205, and constructed at a cost of about $11,000. In putting a dam across a branch of the river, where a connection could be made with an island, I have generally located the dam some distance from the head of the island, for the following reasons: *first*, the dam thus located is not subject to a raking effect of the current, as would be the case if the location was at the head of the island; *second*, a large recess is formed for the accumulation of sand above the dam, which will add great strength to it; *lastly*, the fall below the dam to the foot of the island being but little, the water below the dam, during a rise in the river, will keep very nearly upon a level with that above; consequently, when the water flows over the dam there will be no danger of an undermining process. I have had the dams given good width of base, and raised them but little above low-water mark, believing it unnecessary to obstruct the free flow of the water when high. The opinion indulged in by many, that wing-dams should angle down stream, I conceive to be erroneous. If the dam is not at right-angle with the stream, it should (in my opinion) angle up instead of down stream. If angling down, the current will rake it, and naturally tend to fill the channel below the dam with sand. But if angling up stream, both of these effects will undoubtedly be avoided. There has been expended under previous administrations of the board of public works, in surveys, chopping timber, &c., upon this river, the sum of $3,872.73. The contingent expenses properly chargeable to this part of the improvement, $1,500, making the aggregate amount of expenditure or liability incurred for the improvement of this stream, up to the time of finishing the two dams above mentioned, $16,372.73.

Several of the dams are under water, and, from a careful obsevation, I am satisfied that the current will produce no injurious effect upon them. If these dams produce the desired effect, (which I have no doubt of,) I think it is safe to assume that unobstructed navigation from the mouth of the river to Portage City, for steamers drawing two feet water, can be effected for a sum not exceeding $25,000, which, added to the present liabilities, will make the sum total for this part of the improvement $41,372.73, which is certainly a less sum than the law sets apart for the same.

I have employed a small force in clearing overhanging timber from the channel. A statement of their progress, the expenditures on this part of the improvement in detail, the materials, implements, &c., applicable to operations next season, &c., I will present you at an early day after the completion of two unfinished dams.

I am informed by Mr. H. Meriton, civil engineer, that he was employed on this work, and that four of the dams were located between the ferry-bridge, above Portage, and the mouth of the Baraboo River. Some remains of these are yet to be seen, as shown on the map of our survey made in 1867.

Two dams were located near the mouth of Honey Creek; one above on the right bank still standing, connecting an island with the main shore; the other, below the creek on the left bank, running out from the shore, in which logs were used, is still partly remaining, but it has become separated from the main shore by the wearing away of the bank, and now occupies a place well out in the stream, a fate which attends all wing-dams not constantly cared for.

There were no other dams erected on the Wisconsin before or since the year 1852, except by mill-owners, or others, to obtain water-power. I have a letter from Mr. B. J. Stevens, Vice-President of the Canal Company, saying that the Improvement Company did not erect any works on the Wisconsin River for its improvement, since the works were transferred to them.

The other commissioners, in speaking of the work done this year (1852) on the Wisconsin River, say:

If this cheap kind of dam which we recommend to be constructed should be found not to answer the desired end, and as the cost of placing piles for the erection of more suitable wing-dams to confine the water to one channel would far exceed the means at the disposal of the State, we must fall back upon the suggestion of the engineer of 1849, and rely upon the removal of the overhanging trees, and the snags from the river, which can be done at the estimated cost of $5,000. We are inclined to the opinion that the frequent running of the boats up and down this, now, will keep the channel open and make it navigable, as is found to be the case on some portions of the Upper Mississippi and Missouri having a similar current and bottom.

Table of expenditures on the Wisconsin River.—In the foregoing statement Mr. Richardson says that the expenditures properly chargeable to the improvement of the Wisconsin River, up to this time, amounted to $16,372.73.

Of this he says the dams in 1852 cost about	$11,000 00
The report of the board for 1850 gives for scows and chopping	2,005 17
The survey below Portage, by Mr. Alton, in 1849, was	333 52
The survey above Portage by Mr. Dewitt, and report cost, as stated in report for 1851, $1,275.54, and for 1852, $491.16	1,766 80
Chargeable to contingent fund, (says Mr. Richardson)	1,500 00
	16,605 49

Thus $16,605.49 is the largest sum we find in the official reports charged directly to the Wisconsin River. Mr. Richardson states the whole amount to be $16,372.73.

There was expended in 1852 on crib and dock work, for protection of the guard-lock, in the portion of the Wisconsin River contiguous to it, $5,905.47. This was paid for out of the Portage Canal fund, I believe, and charged to that in the Commissioner's report. If added to the other expenses on the Wisconsin River improvement, which it seems hardly chargeable to, we should have the whole expenditure on that river $22,510.96, of which only $13,000 was actually spent in works of improvement, to wit: For scows and cutting overhanging trees in 1850, $2,005.17; for dams in 1852, $11,000. This is the only authority that I can find for the statements of Mr. Westbrook, in his report in 1854, that $25,000 had been expended in the improvement of the Wisconsin River.

There was a difference of opinion as to where the funds were to be obtained for improving the Wisconsin River, and in the expenditures stated in the report of the Board for 1852 the $11,000, which Mr. Richardson says was expended on the Wisconsin, does not appear. I have accordingly, in putting it in the following table of expenditures, increased the amount they reported by that much.

Expenditures made in 1852.

Depère	$15 00
Rapide Croche	4,648 94
Grand Kaukana } Divided equally in the consolidated table.—G. K. W. Little Chute }	47,262 42
Cedar Rapids	9,559 17
Grand Chute	22,993 23
Upper Fox, dredging	2,433 15
Portage Canal	23,227 29
Wisconsin River survey, $491.16; improvement, $11,000	11,491 16
Contingencies, including patent for lock-gates, &c	15,513 19
	137,143 55

I have not seen the report of the Board of Public Works in 1853, closing up their connection with the work, but in the report of Mr. C. D. Westbrook, jr., dated December 1, 1854, made to Isaac Seymour and William J. Averill, trustees of the mortgage-bonds of the Fox and Wisconsin Improvement Company, it is stated, p. 50, that the total expenditure by the State, up to the time the improvement was surrendered to the company, was $428,855.83.

From all the information I can obtain from the reports of the Board of Public Works, the amounts expended on the works in 1848, '49, '50, '51, and '52, amounted to $312,359.22. There must then have been charges for other purposes, connected with the sale of the lands, interest on obligations to pay, &c., amounting at that time to the difference, viz, $116,496.61. I have entered it under the column of miscellaneous expenditures in the year 1853, in the following table, in which all the expenditures heretofore given are consolidated.

Expenditure in improvement of Fox and Wisconsin Rivers, under State management, up to 1853.

	1848.	1849.	1850.	1851.	1852.	1853.	Totals.
Depère		$411 86	$10 00	$928 95	$15 00		$1,365 81
Little Kaukauna							
Rapide Croche		6,949 62	13,222 43	1,284 03	4,648 94		26,105 02
Grand Kaukana				13,915 83	23,631 21		37,547 04
Little Chute				13,000 00	23,631 21		36,631 21
Cedar Rapids			7,549 32	8,888 93	9,559 17		25,997 42
Grand Chute			4,656 59	4,819 88	22,993 23		32,469 67
Winnebago Rapids							
Upper Fox River		13,463 80	4,728 97	6,300 77	2,433 15		26,926 69
Portage Canal		13,447 19	21,031 58	12,047 96	23,227 29		69,754 02
Wisconsin River		333 52	2,005 17	1,275 54	11,491 16		15,105 39
Miscellaneous	$1,631 81	10,638 64	5,844 65	6,828 66	15,573 19	$116,496 61	156,953 56
Total	1,631 81	45,244 63	59,048 71	69,290 52	137,143 55	116,496 61	428,855 83

Geological survey of the Wisconsin.—In the year 1852, the report of the geological survey of Wisconsin, &c., made, under direction of the United States Treasury by David Dale Owen, U. S. geologist, was published by Lippincott, Grambo & Co., Philadelphia. In this, pp. 277 to 293, is the report of an examination made in 1847 of the Wisconsin River, from Portage up to its source, by Col. Charles Whittlesey, and, on pp. 510 to 520, the Wisconsin, from Portage to the mouth, made in 1849, by Dr. B. F. Shumard.

These reports contain valuable information in regard to these rivers, and attention is called to them here in the chronological order of their appearance.

Progress of improvement in the year 1853.—The effort to provide for the expenses of the works of improvement in previous years by the proceeds of the sale of public lands granted by the United States had only partially succeeded. At two places, Great Kaukana and Little Chute, the contractor had so far been paid entirely in scrip, and at other places payments had been only granted by certificates or warrants of indebtedness. The sale of lands had proceeded too slowly to meet current expenses when prosecuting the work in a proper manner, and an interest on the first cost was accruing, to add to the amount at final payment. A further grant of land was also required.

To meet the wants of the case, an issue of State bonds was proposed, but this being held unconstitutional by a majority of the legislature—

It resolved to surrender the whole improvement, the balance of the grant of public lands remaining unsold, hydraulic privileges, &c., to a company, upon receiving guarantees that the work should be accomplished, and the parties interested as contractors or otherwise secured from loss.

Surrender of the works of improvement, lands, &c., Company chartered, &c., &c.—An association styling itself the "Fox and Wisconsin Improvement Company," comprising Otto Tank, Morgan L. Martin, Urial H. Peak,

James G. Lawton, Theodore Conkey, Mason C. Darling, Benjamin F. Moore, and Edgar Conklin, all of Wisconsin, concluded its articles of agreement on June 1, 1853. This association applied to the legislature for an act of incorporation, which was granted, and approved July 6, 1853.

The second, third, and seventh sections of the act required the parties comprising the association to give certain bonds, and file releases of contractors, which conditions were duly complied with, July 20, 1853, whereupon the work was surrendered, and taken possession of by the company.

Section 2 of this act—

* * Conditioned that the said company shall vigorously prosecute the said improvement to completion, and complete the same within three years from the passage of this act on the line located by the Board of Public Works, and as contemplated in the report of the Board of Public Works, and estimated by the chief engineer, on hte 1st day of January, 1853, in a substantial and durable manner, and so as to enable boats of 2 feet draught, and a breadth of 30 feet, during ordinary stages of low water, to pass with facility from Green Bay into the Wisconsin River. * *

Section 2 also provided—

That the said improvement shall in all future time be free for the transportation of the troops of the United States and their munitions of war, without payment of any tolls whatever; and, that no provision of this act shall be so construed as to allow, permit, or authorize the charge or collection of any tolls or transit duties for the passage of any vessel or merchandise, or property of any kind, along or over the main channel of said rivers.

And also that—

The said company shall charge no higher rate of tolls than was established by the Board of Public Works for the years 1851-'2, which rates shall be uniform for each lock, and to all persons and boats passing through them.

Section 8 provides that—

The State may become the owner and proprietor of the works of improvement constructed under this act, and of the whole works of improvement at any time after twenty years upon paying to said association or their assigns the actual costs expended by said association in the construction of said improvement over and above the avails of the grant of land by Congress, and applied or received by said company to aid in said improvement, the said lands to be estimated at the rate of one dollar and twenty-five cents per acre.

For the purpose of completing the work, the company, in 1853, resolved to issue bonds to the amount of $500,000.

In 1853 the legislature of Wisconsin authorized the Milwaukee and Prairie du Chien Railway Company to build three bridges across the Wisconsin River, which authorization provided for draws of 50 feet width, and required that the stream where touched or intersected should be restored to its former usefulness.

The bridges built under this law were, however, located entirely with regard to convenience of the railroad alignment, and so little regard was paid to the stream that not only has navigation been almost cut off, but the very permanence of the bridge-piers has been maintained only by such an excessive use of riprap stone as renders a proper restoration of the navigation almost impossible, without rebuilding the bridges themselves.

Condition and character of the works in 1854, by C. D. Westbrook, jr.—
The very interesting report of Mr. Westbrook, frequently referred to by me before, gives the condition of the work at the date of November 15, 1854, from which the following is taken:

At Depère the work is considered as finished. At Little Kaukana, materials for dam and lock have been collected.

At Rapide Croche, the work is considered finished.

At Grand Kaukana, the work is generally finished, with the exception of swinging the gates and graveling the dam.

At the Little Chute there yet remains 22,500 cubic yards of excavation; the raising of the walls of the upper of the two combined locks; the swinging of the gates and the graveling of the dam.

At Cedar Rapids the work is generally finished, with the exception of swinging the gates and graveling the dam. At the Grand Chute, the walls of one of the locks are yet to be raised; 15,000 cubic yards of excavation and embankment remain; the gates for the locks are to be swung and the dams to be graveled. Winnebago Rapids: At the Neenah, or southern channel of exit from Lake Winnebago, the canal lock and dams have been completed, ready for use when the dam below at the Grand Chute is tightened. A wall will probably be extended from the lower and outer wing of the lock, to deflect the current, which now sets across its entrance into the channel. The improvement here was executed without cost to the State, in consideration of the use of the water-power. The lock and canal, however, are of the original size. The former is 60 feet wide on the bottom and 4 feet deep, and the latter 140 feet in length by 35 feet width in the chamber.

At Menasha, where the second and northern channel issues from the lake, the dam is erected and the channel excavated. The lock-pit was excavated and the foundation in progress at the commencement of November. The contract time for completion extends to the 1st of July. Here, as at Neenah, the contract for the execution of the work without cost to the State was taken in consideration of the use of the water-power thereby created. Subsequently it was determined to enlarge the canal to a bottom width of 100 feet and a depth of 5 feet, and the locks to a size in the chamber of 160 feet by 40 feet. This change, by contract, involved an expenditure of $16,734.40 beyond the original plan. The expenditure yet to be made at this point is $10,916.87.

On the Upper Fox River, the dredge had continued working on the river, principally above the Forks. This dredge was 110 feet long, 28 feet wide, with draught of 30 inches. It has removed, on an average, 850 cubic yards a day for a season of 170 days, excavating at times 1,700 cubic yards a day. Up to the close of 1854 there had been expended on the Upper Fox (including $12,000 for the first cost of the dredge-boat) about $30,000. The present navigation is confined to one steamboat, which ascends daily to Berlin, a distance of about forty miles; and horse-boats and scows, by means of which lumber is carried from the Wolf River, through the Upper Fox, into the Wisconsin, and down the latter stream to different markets on the Mississippi. A steamboat, however, has made weekly trips to Montello, one hundred miles above Lake Winnebago, from Oshkosh, a city of 3,000 inhabitants, at the entrance of the Fox into Lake Winnebago.

Reservoir on the headwaters of the Wisconsin River, &c.—It does not appear that anything was done upon this river in 1853 and 1854. Mr. Westbrook thought a great improvement to the low-water navigation might be made by—

> The location of a dam upon the upper waters of the Wisconsin, where the public lands have not as yet been brought into market, that will create a reservoir in which a quantity may be stored up from the high water in the spring of the year, to maintain an equable supply throughout the dry season, sufficient for the uninterrupted navigation of the stream. * *

Expenditures by the company from August 20, 1853, to November 15, 1854.

At Rapide Croche	$292 00
At Grand Kaukana	32,902 21
At Little Chute	50,950 73
At Cedar Rapids	7,546 17

At Grand Chute		$42,218 17
At Winnebago Rapids, (Menasha Channel)		5,817 53
On Upper Fox, (dredge-boat)		3,833 16
On docks and barges built	$9,621 84	
On expenses, engines, &c	8,132 09	
Interest	9,547 70	
		27,301 63
Total		170,861 60

The cost of completing the work according to the terms of the act of the legislature surrendering the improvement to the company, is estimated, on November 28, 1854, by J. Kip Anderson, the engineer of the company, as follows:

At Grand Kaukana	$2,887 00
At Little Chute	7,673 68
At Cedar Rapids	901 85
At Grand Chute	10,031 65
Total	21,494 18

There were, however, many other improvements contemplated by the company, such as a dam and lock at Little Kaukana and one dam and lock, at least, on the Upper Fox River.

Appended to this report will be found the specifications of the manner of constructing the canal and locks and dams. Following them will be found the bills of timber, of stone, and of iron used in their construction. In the notes attached to the specifications will be found other items embraced therein, which will complete the description of the work.*

In regard to its general character, I would say that, while differing in opinion in regard to a few of its details, the plan of the work and its execution, so far as I have been able to judge, exhibits a full assurance of effecting the purpose for which it was designed and of security against the action of destructive forces.

The dams, with a single exception, are bolted to the bare rock. The one excepted is at the Grand Kaukalin. It rests upon crib-work filled with stone, and is to be further protected with the same material, at one of its wings, at the foot of its spars, and at the break of its overflow, from the undermining action of the water.

The same security, in the character of the foundations, has been had in the construction of the locks. The walls of all at the Grand Kaukalin, two at the Little Chute, one at the Cedars, and three at the Grand Chute, rest upon a smooth surface of limestone, out of which material their walls have raised. One at the Grand Chute has its walls laid in timber and earth foundations. Though the work was executed a year since, not the least sign of their settlement can be perceived, which would readily have been exhibited by the starting of the plank in the flooring course.

Of the additional locks with timber foundations, one at Depère, one at the Rapide Croche, and one at Neenah, have been built and in use for several years. The first is of stone, faced with timber and plank, and the other two of timber filled with clay. The remaining locks, with timber foundations, are two combined at the Little Chute.

Another fact of great importance in regard to the stability of the work, is its exemption from the danger of freshets, inasmuch as no tributary of any size empties into the Lower Fox. Lake Winnebago is an immense reservoir, controlling the rise of the water below, whose fluctuations are never more than between 3 and 4 feet.

Whenever the banks of the canal, which are generally upon the bottom-lands of the river above high-water mark, come in contact with the current, they are protected from its action by heavy walls.

These facts, together with an examination of the specifications, will remove all apprehensions in regard to the stability of the work.

PROGRESS OF THE FOX AND WISCONSIN RIVER IMPROVEMENT SUBSEQUENT TO 1855–'56.

I have no information of the details of the improvement for this period, and I can give only general features.

Additional lands granted to the State by Congress.—In the session of

---

* I have made these specifications an appendix to my report and used them as the basis of my estimate of the cost of locks for a canal along the Wisconsin River.

G. K. W.

1854–'55 acts of Congress were passed by which the State was authorized to select, in addition to the previous grant, two sections per mile for every mile of improvement, &c. The total grant would then amount to five sections per mile for the whole length of the Fox River and lakes, through which it runs, a distance of about 216 miles.

Increased capacity of the improvement required by the State.—In 1856 the legislature of Wisconsin passed another act, requiring an increased capacity to the improvement, so that boats drawing four feet water could navigate the Lower Fox, and those having a draught of three and one-half feet could use the Upper Fox; the locks to be 160 feet long by 35 feet wide, admitting of the passage of boats 144 feet long by 34 feet wide, of a tonnage of from 300 to 350 tons. This work was commenced immediately and prosecuted with energy until the revulsion in the money-market in the fall of 1857, when it was in part suspended. (See Report No. 55, H. Rep., 37th Cong., 3d session, dated March 3, 1863.) I have not positive authority for it, but presume that the increased capacity required by the legislature was in consideration of the additional land-grant made by Congress, which was given to the company on the condition that it should execute its deed of trust, covering all the unsold lands granted by Congress, the works of improvement, &c., to three trustees, who should sell the same in case the company did not perform its part.

As to the expenditures between the years 1854 and August 25, 1856, Mr. John F. Seymour, in his report to the special committee of the legislature in 1860, states that "the amount expended by the company for construction and navigation to August 25, 1856, is reported at $504,806.06." As Mr. Westbrook's report gave the amount expended up to the close of the year 1854 as $170,861.60, we have $333,944.46 as the expenditure for the intervening period. I can only infer what this was expended for by the following extracts from the report of Mr. Jenné, chief engineer, &c., giving the condition of the work in 1856.*

Condition of the works January, 1859; report of the chief engineer, etc.— The report of Mr. Daniel C. Jenné, chief engineer, &c., dated January 7, 1859, made to the governor, says that in June, 1856, the navigation from Green Bay to Lake Winnebago was opened, but, owing to the dam and lock not being built at Little Kaukana, it was suspended in the latter part of the season.

That in 1857 the navigation of the Lower Fox was good until September, and from that time to the middle of October, the time the dam at Little Kaukana was completed, there was some difficulty between this point and Rapide Croche, which ceased thereafter.

That during 1858 there was no interruption of navigation, except for a few days, about the 1st of May, when a break occurred in the canal at Menasha. Steamboats have made their regular trips daily from Green Bay to Oshkosh and Fond du Lac. They have also run regularly from Oshkosh to Berlin, and for a considerable portion of the year from Berlin to Montello and Packwauka, and occasionally to Fort Winnebago. Navigation was opened on the 12th of April and closed on the 27th of November, making seven and a half months, which is nearly one month more than the average of New York canals.

The report of Mr. Jenné informs us also—

That since the passage of the act of 1856, the company have been actively at work at different points on the Fox River.

---

*In the spring of 1857 the Milwaukee and Prairie du Chien Railroad-crossing the Wisconsin River three times, was opened through to the Mississippi River.

Taking the work in the order adopted by me, we learn from Mr. Jenné's report the following in regard to the condition of the works at the close of the year 1858.

At Depère the lock is not yet commenced, but will probably be built the coming year.

At Little Kaukana the dam, lock, and canal section are complete.

At Rapide Croche the lock and section of canal is about four-fifths completed, and will be brought into use by the 1st of June, 1859. At Menasha (Winnebago Rapids) the section of canal is completed.

On the Upper Fox the lock and dam at Montello is over one-half finished, and will be completed by October, 1859. The lock at Fort Winnebago has been completed. The lock at Portage City has not been commenced, but will probably be built during the coming year. The canal at Portage City is not finished, but will progress during the year 1859, and is now in a condition to pass boats up to the city. A large amount of dredging has been done, and by the opening of navigation in the spring there will be no trouble in passing steamboats from Green Bay to Portage City, and barges will be able to pass out into the Wisconsin River.

The company have two powerful dredge-boats, which will be engaged in deepening the upper river at all points which may be necessary during the next year. Two wing-dams have been built in the vicinity of Princeton on the bars, which contract the water and form a good channel over the bars. Several more wing-dams will be built the coming year, between Princeton and Berlin, and these, with the dredging which will be done, will form a good channel for boats drawing $3\frac{1}{2}$ feet of water at all places on the Upper Fox, during ordinary low water on said river.

On the Wisconsin River no work had been done for improving it since the passage of the act of 1856. Mr. Jenné examined the river from Portage City to the mouth, in October, 1857, and says: "I am satisfied that it can be successfully navigated, and that within the next two years steamboats will run direct from Green Bay to the Mississippi River, and thence up and down that river to any points where boats now run."

Condition of the improvement in 1860.—The next report of improvement obtained by me is the printed one of Mr. John F. Seymour, president of the company, made to a select committee of the Wisconsin legislature in 1860.

Mr. Seymour states that he was appointed president of the company in 1858. He states:

At Depère the lock, by a change of plan, sanctioned by the governor in 1857, is to be lengthened, but can be used with some repairs for another year or two. At Rapide Croche the new cut-stone lock and canal, constructed by Messrs. Conkey and Wesley, will be ready for use this spring. The work on the Lower Fox is completed so as to give $4\frac{1}{2}$ feet depth of water in all ordinary seasons; and during the extraordinary drought of last summer, a small amount expended in tightening the dams relieved the navigation from all difficulty except the Menasha Channel. The company is now at work on this channel, and no further serious difficulty is apprehended there, unless there should be a recurrence of a similar drought.

On the Upper Fox River, by a change of plan, approved by the governor in February, 1857, the lock and dam in the vicinity of Princeton have been dispensed with, and the bars improved by means of wing-dams, piers, and dredging, and a large amount of this kind of work has been done between Berlin and Mechan River. It is proposed to put in several other wing-dams, both above and below Berlin, against the recurrence of a season similar to that of last summer.

A dam and lock have been partially built at Montello. A new lock has been built at Fort Winnebago on the site of the one built by the State, and sunk 5 feet lower than the old lock, to give sufficient depth for navigation. It is now anticipated that a lock and dam of low lift may have to be built about four miles below Fort Winnebago in consequence of the trouble experienced in keeping that part of the river open for navigation. The lock into the Wisconsin River at Portage was repaired last year, and with some additional repairs will answer all the purposes of navigation the present year. It is intended that both dredges shall be employed for the most part of the ensuing season on the Upper Fox. In regard to the navigation of this river, W. J. Clemans made affidavit on the 14th of March, 1860—

That he had charge of the dredge-boat No. 2, owned and worked by the Fox and Wisconsin Improvement Company in the year 1859; that, in the month of August last, he came on said dredge from Menasha to Portage; that where he found the depth less than 3¼ feet, he dredged it to the depth of 5 feet, except on the Omro bar, where he dredged 4 feet deep; that he did not find it necessary to dredge from Berlin to within four miles of Portage; that of this four miles two had a depth of 5 feet water; that he did not dredge the remaining two miles, having been ordered to the upper lock to dredge it out, which he did; that these two miles aforesaid had been dredged out by said company, but had filled up with sand during that season; that said Upper Fox is constantly filling up with sand, and will require dredging every year; that the water in Fox River was lower last year than it had been known to be for seven years past.   *   *

Navigation of the Wisconsin to be improved by running a steamboat, &c.—Mr. Seymour says, with reference to this Wisconsin, the Company have been—

Guided in many respects by the opinions of men of experience, such as Hercules, Dousman, and other gentlemen familiar with that stream; that the navigation of the river by steamboat would make a channel as in the Mississippi, and that generally money expended otherwise would be of no avail, although there may be some points where the stream will have to be contracted by wing-dams, &c. A steamboat made regular trips from Portage to Sauk in the latter part of last season, and several other boats ran out of the Fox into the Wisconsin during the season.

Expenditures from October 3, 1856, to December 31, 1859.—The following table shows the expenditures for all kinds of work from October 3, 1856, the time the work passed into the hands of the company, up to December 31, 1859.

MISSISSIPPI RIVER AND LAKE MICHIGAN. 43

Statement of expenditures by Daniel C. Jenné, chief engineer and superintendent, for work done on the Fox and Wisconsin improvement, from October 3, 1856, to December 31, 1859.

Kind of work.	1856.	1857.	1858.	1859.	Total.
Lock, dam, and section at Little Kaukana.		$34,404 96	$10,063 56	$901 59	$45,370 11
Lock and section at Rapide Croche		5,300 00	23,544 47	7,012 55	35,917 02
Dam embank, Grand Kaukana	$100 00				100 00
Enlarging canal at Little Chute		1,579 80	2,508 20	37 96	4,125 96
Rebuilding combined locks, Little Chute				10,625 01	10,625 01
Lock and section at Menasha		1,980 00	3,626 66	208 40	5,815 06
Lock and dam at Montello		14,360 00	5,203 65		19,563 65
Lock at Fort Winnebago	500 00	13,657 57	14,310 00	56 26	28,523 83
Lock at Portage City			897 07		897 07
Constructing dredges	302 99	11,721 22	11 11	253 36	12,288 68
Operating dredges	535 83	5,950 53	3,956 23	5,617 29	16,059 88
Wing-dams at Upper Fox		1,901 93	1,600 00	3,000 00	6,501 93
Lock-houses	20 20	1,050 19			1,070 39
Printing	152 00	107 20			259 20
Miscellaneous	901 94	532 30	2,559 45	788 66	4,782 35
Navigation account				304 40	304 40
Water-power account				68 40	68 40
Land damages			3,093 00	260 00	3,353 00
Engineering	2,212 56	10,294 33	8,635 25	7,354 33	28,496 47
Total construction	4,725 52	102,900 03	80,008 65	36,488 21	*224,122 41
Operating department	1,368 70	12,830 93	12,190 91	9,563 13	35,953 67
Total	6,094 22	115,730 96	92,199 56	36,051 34	260,076 08

* This total foots up $106 less than the footing given in the printed report from which it has been taken.

Expenditures from beginning of improvements in 1848 *to* 1859.—The following consolidated table shows all the expenditures from the beginning of the improvement in 1848 to 1859, distributed among the different parts of the work as far as the published data available will allow us to do it.

Statement of expenditures on the Fox and Wisconsin River improvement from 1848 to 1859, inclusive.

	Under the State prior to 1853.	Under improvement company in 1853-'54.	Under improvement company from 1854 to August 25, 1856.	Under improvement company from August 25, 1856, to 1859.	Totals.	Remarks.
Depère	$1,365 81				$1,365 81	Improvement made by the water-power company.
Little Kaukana	26,105 02			$45,370 11	45,370 11	
Rapide Croche	37,547 04	$292 00		35,917 02	62,314 04	
Grand Kaukana	36,631 21	32,902 21		100 00	70,549 25	
Little Chute	25,997 42	50,950 73		14,750 97	102,332 91	
Cedar Rapids	32,469 67	7,546 17	Distribution of this amount not known.		33,543 59	
Grand Chute		42,218 17			74,687 84	
Winnebago Rapids, (Menasha)		5,817 53		5,815 06	11,632 59	Partly built by water-power company.
Upper Fox	26,926 69	3,833 16		54,414 14	85,173 99	Includes lock and dam at Montello, 1857 and 1858, and a few wing-dams, but mainly dredging.
Portage Canal	69,754 02			29,420 90	99,174 92	
Wisconsin River	15,105 39				15,105 39	Surveys, wing-dams, snags, and trees.
Miscellaneous	156,953 56	27,301 63	$333,944 46	38,334 21	556,533 86	
Totals	428,855 83	170,861 60	333,944 46	224,122 41	1,157,784 30	

MISSISSIPPI RIVER AND LAKE MICHIGAN.

Mr. Seymour further states—

The work still proposed to be done is as follows:

Lengthening lock at Depère	$10,000
Enlarging canals on Lower Fox	2,000
Gravelling dams	1,000
Completing lock and dam at Montello	12,000
Rebuilding lock at Portage	25,000
Building drawbridge at Portage	2,500
Enlarging canal at Portage	2,500
Wing-dams on Upper Fox at Portage	5,000
Dredging Upper Fox at Portage	7,000
Engineering and contingencies	8,000
Total	75,000

By reference to these tables, Mr. Seymour says—

It will be seen that a much larger amount has been expended than was contemplated in the report of September, 1856. There is still about $75,000 worth of work to be done, making the cost about $300,000 instead of $200,000, as specified in the report of 1856. This has occurred in consequence of a better class of work being done than was contemplated, and of many unforeseen contingencies which could not have been anticipated.

Mr. Seymour also states—

The company have paid out for State indebtedness and construction, since October 3, 1856, $181,539 more than they have received from the sales of land and tolls.

The select committee of the legislature reported:

Your committee are of the opinion that the said improvement company have, considering the pecuniary embarrassments of the past two years, and the general depression of all kinds of business consequent thereon, done all that could reasonably be expected.

Operations in 1860–'61–'62; report of superintendent of company.—In these years, as far as I have learned, there was little done. The report of the superintendent of the company, dated August 18, 1862, makes the expenditure from January 1, 1860, to August 18, 1862, only $6,585.92. The amount of lands remaining unsold, belonging to the company August 1, 1862, was $421,201\frac{27}{100}$ acres. This report says that—

The State and the company also insist that they are entitled, under the acts of Congress, to select for the *Wisconsin River* five sections for every mile of its improvement from Portage City to the Mississippi River, a distance of one hundred and thirteen miles, which would still further increase the quantity of lands about 362,000 acres.

Increased capacity necessary for passage of gunboats, &c.—On December 18, 1862, Mr. Jenné, at this time division engineer on the New York canals, made a report to the president, Mr. John F. Seymour, in relation to making the works of improvement of a capacity suitable for the passage of gunboats 144 feet long, 34 feet beam, and 6 feet draught, as follows:

On the Lower Fox:

Excavating dam at foot of the Depère lock	$10,000
Raising eight dams varying from 600 to 1,400 feet in length	30,000
Rebuilding one dam 700 feet at Grand Kaukauna	12,000
Rebuilding four locks	104,000
Raising fourteen locks and new gates	66,000
Raising banks and protecting with wall five miles of canal	83,000
Excavating channel of river at Menasha and Neenah	25,000
Rebuilding guard-gates at Grand Kaukauna and Menasha	10,000
Total	340,000

On the Upper Fox:

Building five locks and dams	$150,000
Dredging channel at different points and other necessary work	120,000
Total	270,000

On canal and locks, Portage City:

Enlarging and deepening canal and protecting banks	$30,000
Rebuilding guard-lock and protecting head, and cutting down breast-wall of lift-lock	30,000
Total	60,000
On the Wisconsin River:	
Building dams for contracting channel of river, and other necessary work	$250,000
Engineering and contingencies	80,000
Total	330,000
Grand total	1,000,000

He says:

Should it be considered advisable to make the locks of sufficient length to pass boats of 200 feet, it would be necessary to increase the length about 60 feet. The location of all the locks now built is such that the change can readily be made at a cost of $10,000 per lock. The whole cost would then be as follows:

Cost of improvement as per foregoing estimate	$1,000,000
Cost of lengthening 25 locks, $10,000 each	250,000
Total for boats 200 feet long	1,250,000

The above estimates are, in my opinion, ample for the work contemplated, which can all be done in two years.

In this report Mr. Jenné says:

The Wisconsin River has a descent of about 1 foot to the mile for one hundred and fifteen miles; is from 500 to 1,000 feet wide, and has a current of two miles per hour. The bed of the stream is of a sandy formation, and in many places has great width. This is a channel in all cases of from 5 to 6 feet in low water, but this being crooked, where the water spreads out, it requires to be reduced in width by means of the wing-dams, when the river will make its own channel as it recedes from high to low water. The work required to increase the depth of water, in all the improvement, so that gun-boats drawing 6 feet of water can navigate the same, will be as follows: * * *

The Wisconsin River would be improved by the continuation of wing-dams located so as to contract the shallow portions of the channel. The desired water-way may be further secured at low water by the constant passage of boats between the points at which sand may be deposited by the variable action of the current.

RENEWAL OF INTEREST IN THE IMPROVEMENT BY THE UNITED STATES.

During the third session of the Thirty-seventh Congress, a resolution in regard to this route was adopted by the House of Representatives, as follows:

Resolved, That the Committee on Naval Affairs is requested to inquire into and report upon the practicability and probable cost and time required to improve the Wisconsin and Fox rivers, so as to give an uninterrupted navigation from the Mississippi River to Lake Michigan for vessels of war 200 feet in length, 34 feet beam, and drawing not less than 6 feet of water; and also to report such other facts relating to the defense of the lakes, and a suitable naval station thereon, as they may deem desirable for the information of the House.

Report of the Committee on Naval Affairs, Thirty-seventh Congress, &c.— Mr. Pike, from the committee, made a report March 3, 1863. They had Mr. Jenné's estimate before them, and, it appears, conferred with Colonel Cram, United States Engineers. The report says:

Colonel Cram adds somewhat to Mr. Jenné's estimate, and gives as follows:
Probable estimate to pass a boat 200 feet long by 34 feet beam:

I would increase Mr. Jenné's estimate for his proposed method of improving the Lower Wisconsin, so as to allow a draught of 6 or 6¼ feet, to	$315,000
And for the canal at Portage City, 6 or 6¼ feet draught, to	70,000
And for the Upper Fox, 6 or 6¼ feet draught, to	340,000
To which add the above estimate for an improvement in the Lower Fox, for a draught of 12 feet, including the dredging of 24,000 cubic yards at the mouth of the Fox, (sic)	1,662,384
	2,387,384

The increase of depth in the Lower Fox to 12 feet was suggested for the purpose of making Lake Winnebago a naval station, which, it was held by some, would not be prohibited by the "treaty of 1817," but the committee regarded the treaty as practically covering this case. The report of the committee closes with the following enlarged views:

> The true ground, as the committee think, upon which to place the propriety of yielding assistance to this Wisconsin enterprise, is its great natural importance in making cheaper and easier the intercourse between the grain-regions of the Northwest and the manufacturing and commercial States of the East. The expenditure of twenty millions in the completion of this work and that of Illinois, with a corresponding enlargement of the means of conveyance in the East, would be many times repaid in the increased general prosperity which would result from it. Whenever some systematic and well-matured plan shall be laid before Congress, which shall compass this result, it is to be hoped that it may be adopted.

Congress took no further action at that time on the proposition.

Company having failed to perform its agreement, the works of improvement, lands, &c., were sold in 1866.—In the summer of 1866 the "Fox and Wisconsin Improvement Company" having failed to perform fully its agreement with the State, the trustees sold the works of improvement, lands, franchises, &c., at public sale, thereby destroying this company.

Green Bay and Mississippi Canal Company, incorporated by the State August 15, 1866.—The purchasers were by act of the legislature permitted to organize themselves into a company, and they assumed the name of "The Green Bay and Mississippi Canal Company." The certificate of their incorporation is dated August 15, 1866.

Examinations and estimates ordered by Congress.—The act of Congress approved June 23, 1866, under which the survey of this route was placed under my charge, contained the following, which may be considered as intended to cover the expectations of that body in directing surveys and examinations of the Fox and Wisconsin rivers:

> And the Secretary of War * * * * shall cause such needful examination of other harbors and places in the fourth section of this act specified upon the sea and lake coasts, and on western rivers, to be made as will enable him to determine what improvements thereof are required to render them safe and convenient for the navigation of the naval and commercial vessels of the United States, and the cost of such improvements; and he shall make full report thereof, and of the plans deemed advisable therefor, to Congress at the commencement of the next session, for such action as may be judged expedient and right.
>
> SEC. 4. * * * * The Fox and Wisconsin rivers, in the State of Wisconsin * * *

Condition of these rivers and improvements, &c., in 1866.—Brevet Major C. R. Suter, to whom I intrusted the details of the examination, made his report, dated January 2, 1867. My report is dated January 21, 1867, and that of the Chief of Engineers and of the Secretary of War transmitting it to Congress are dated January 29, 1867; the whole printed as part of H. Ex. Doc. No. 58, second session of the Thirty-ninth Congress. As this was not repeated in any subsequent annual report, and not readily referred to, I abstract from it the following brief account of the condition of these rivers and the improvements on them at that date, and the new works and repairs required:

Major Suter had assistance from Mr. N. M. Edwards, the chief engineer of the company, and was allowed to trace such copies from the maps of the company as were needed. These were not published with the report, and can now be seen with the files of the engineer headquarters.

Condition of the Lower Fox River improvement in 1866.—The Depère dam is located at the head of natural navigation of the Fox River, five miles above the town of Green Bay and seven miles above the mouth of the river. It is 1,400 feet long and 6 feet high, and in good order. The canal section is 750 feet long and forms a basin. The lock is composite, with wooden bottom, is 140 feet long, 35 feet wide, 17 feet high, 8 feet lift, with 4 feet 3 inches on the lower miter-sill. Four feet three inches is the greatest depth attained on the lower miter-sill, but when the wind blows out of Green Bay, there is sometimes not more than two feet. This lock is very unsatisfactory. It is only 140 feet long, while all the others are 160 feet long. The pit should have been sunk at least 2 feet lower. A large piece of shoal water intervenes between the lock and the channel of the river. The bottom is solid rock.

The upper level has 6 feet or more depth of water to within half a mile of Little Kaukana lock, where it diminishes to five and four.

Estimate.

To make 4 feet draught... $45,000
To make 6 feet draught up to the next lock, with locks 220 by 35 feet, will require 83,300

The Little Kaukana dam is six miles above Depère. It is 550 feet long and 6 feet high. It is quite level but leaks considerably.

The canal leading around the dam is 1,166 feet long, with the lock at the lower end. The lock is composite, 160 feet long, 35 feet wide, 19 feet high, bottom of rock, head-walls of masonry, is in good condition, needing no repairs. It has 8 feet lift, with depth on lower miter-sill of 5 feet 8 inches.

The level above has about 4 feet depth, but the channel is quite crooked, and to be available for vessels of 4 feet draught the dam must be repaired and raised 1 foot; to make 6 feet draught the dam must be raised 3 feet and straightened; the canal-banks and the lock must also be raised and the latter lengthened 60 feet for boats 220 feet long.

Estimate.

For securing 4 feet draught up to next lock............................. $3,000
For securing 6 feet draught, boats 220 feet long........................ 27,736

The Rapide Croche dam is six miles above Little Kaukana. It is 440 feet long, 6 feet high, and in good condition. A canal 1,800 feet long runs from the dam across a point of land. At the lower end is a fine stone lock, the only one in the improvement, all the others being composite. It cost $60,000. The lock is 160 by 35 feet, 19 feet high, with 8 feet lift, and depth of 6 feet 6 inches on the lower miter-sill.

The level above has 5 feet depth to within half a mile of the upper end, where loose stones on the bottom cause the depth to vary between 3 and 5 feet. These stones must be removed.

To get 6 feet draught, the dam, canal-banks, and lock-wall should be raised 1 foot and the upper level cleared of loose stones. For vessels 220 feet long the lock must be lengthened 60 feet.

Estimate.

To make 4 feet draught up to next lock $4,000
To make 6 feet draught for boats 220 feet long up to next lock......... 41,000

The Grand Kaukana dam is four and a half miles above the Rapide Croche. It is 583 feet long and 6 feet high. It is in a very dilapidated condition and should be rebuilt. The canal around the rapids is 7,400 feet long, overcoming, by means of five locks, a fall of 50 feet. The average width of the canal on top is 130 feet, with two basins for boats to pass. These locks are all composite, 160 feet by 35 feet, with bottoms of rock.

First or upper lock: Height, 24 feet; lift, 9 feet; depth on lower miter-sill, 9 feet 4 inches. Needs new wood-work to upper section.

Second lock: Height, 20 feet 7 inches; lift, 10 feet; depth on lower miter-sill, 6 feet 2 inches. Needs new wood-work to the upper section and one pair of new gates.

Third lock: Height, 20 feet; lift, 11 feet; depth on lower miter-sill, 5 feet 1 inch. Needs new wood-work to upper section, and one new pair of gates.

Fourth lock: Height, 21 feet 4 inches; lift, 10 feet; depth on lower miter-sill, 6 feet. Needs new wood-work for upper section and four new gates.

Fifth lock: Height, 21 feet; lift, 10 feet; depth on lower miter-sill, 6 feet. Needs new wood-work for half the upper section.

The upper level up to Little Chute is over 5 feet deep.

The second, third, fourth, and fifth levels have a nearly uniform depth of about 5 feet.

To obtain water enough for 4 feet draught it will only be necessary to rebuild the dam and repair the locks.

For 6 feet draught for vessels 220 feet long it will be necessary to raise the dam and upper lock-walls and canal-embankment above it 1 foot, also the walls of the fourth lock and the canal-banks on the level above so as to make 6 feet on the miter-sill of the third lock. The levels will have to be dredged out and the locks lengthened 60 feet, for which there is sufficient space.

Estimate.

For 4 feet draught up to next rapid $22,800
For 6 feet draught for vessels 220 feet long up to next rapid 111,670

The Little Chute dam is two and a half miles above Grand Kaukana dam. It is 690 feet long and 7 feet high. It has settled on the west end for one-quarter of its length from 1 to 12 inches. The canal is, below the dam, 6,467 feet long. The fall of 38 feet is overcome by four locks 160 by 35 feet, the two lowest ones combined. The least width of the canal is 100 feet on top, and there are several basins in which boats can pass each other.

Upper or lock No. 1 is 14½ feet high; has a lift of 4½ feet, with depth of 6 feet 1 inch on lower miter-sill; bottom, rock. Needs repairs on gates and new wood-work for upper section.

Lock No. 2 is 18 feet 4 inches high; lift, 10 feet; depth on lower miter-sill, 4 feet 10 inches; bottom, rock. Needs new lower gates and repairs on wood-work of upper section.

Lock No. 3: Height, 19 feet 3 inches; lift, 10 feet 9 inches; depth on lower miter-sill, 6 feet 5 inches; bottom of wood.

Lock No. 4: Height, 21 feet; lift, 12 feet 9 inches; depth on lower miter-sill, 6 feet 9 inches; bottom of wood. Upper sections of both 3 and 4 need repairing. The upper level has 6 feet draught or more, except in the mouth of the canal at the Cedars; at that point only 3½ feet. The second level is about 5 feet deep. The third level has 4 feet depth and upward. To make 4 feet draught it will only be necessary to level up the Little Chute dam. To make 6 feet draught, the dam and upper lock-walls and canal must be raised two feet. The three levels will need considerable dredging, and for vessels 220 feet long all the locks will have to be lengthened 60 feet.

Estimate.

For making 4 feet draught $7,530
For making 6 feet draught for vessels 220 feet long.......... 77,200

The Cedar Rapids dam is three-quarters of a mile above that at Little Chute. It is 470 feet long and 7 feet high. It has settled for about half its length from 1 to 18 inches. A canal 1,200 feet long, its banks faced with dry stone, leads around the dam with a lock 160 by 35 feet near its upper end. The lock is 19 feet high; lift, 10 feet; depth on lower miter-sill, 3 feet 11 inches; the bottom is rock; head-walls, dry masonry. It needs new wood-work for the upper section and repairs to two gates. The upper level has a good depth, averaging about 5 feet to within a short distance of the paper-mill at Appleton lower lock. For a distance, say 500 feet below the mill, it is barely 4 feet. To make 4 feet draught, leveling the dam is all that is necessary. To make 6 feet draught, the dam, canal-banks, and lock-walls must be raised one foot and considerable dredging done; and to allow vessels to pass, 220 feet long, will require the lock to be lengthened 60 feet.

Estimate.

For securing 4 feet draught..... .... $3,930
For securing 6 feet draught for vessels 220 feet long............................ 23,400

This Appleton Lower Dam (Grand Chute) is three miles above that at the Cedar Rapids. It is 440 feet long, and quite tight and lower, and could not be raised without overflowing much valuable property. The dike on the Appleton side should be raised.

A canal 1,267 feet long leads around it with the lock at the lower end of it 160 feet by 35 feet. This lock is 19 feet 3 inches high; lift, 8 feet 6 inches; depth on lower miter-sill, 6 feet 8 inches; bottom is of rock; wood-work is good; one gate needs replacing and must be lengthened 60 feet for vessels 220 feet long. The level above will require some dredging to obtain 6 feet draught.

Estimate.

For 4 feet draught................. ....Nothing.
For 6 feet draught for boats 220 feet long................................. $11,000

This Appleton Upper Dam (Grand Chute) about one-third of a mile above the Lower Dam, is 800 feet long and about 7 feet high. It is quite tight, but for about 430 feet of the middle portion has settled from 1 to 10 inches. A bulk-head about 1,000 feet long by 12 feet wide on top extends from the right-bank extremity of this dam and forms the left bank of the canal. It is built, like the locks, of dry masonry, faced with timber, which is decayed, and the whole should be replaced by good stone masonry.

The canal is carried from the lower end of the bulk-head across a point of land a distance of 3,600 feet. In this portion there are three locks, 160 by 35 feet each, having a total lift of 29½ feet.

The first or upper lock is 23 feet high; lift, 7 feet 9 inches; depth of water on lower miter-sill, 8½ feet; bottom is of rock. Needs a pair of gates, new wood-work for upper section, and relaying of right-hand wing-wall. The second lock is 22 feet 2 inches high; lift, 11 feet 9 inches; depth of water on lower miter-sill, 4½ feet. Needs new pair of gates and new wood-work on upper section. The third lock is 22 feet 1 inch high; lift is 10 feet; depth on lower miter-sill 8 feet 8 inches.

Needs one pair of gates and new wood-work on upper section. The upper level has over 6 feet till within about 900 feet of the Menasha lock; for about 300 feet of this distance there is only 3 to 3½ feet. The other levels are designed for 4 feet but have all got somewhat filled up and will need dredging. The lock-walls and canal-banks at the third lock will need raising to secure 6 feet draught on the miter-sill above, and all must be lengthened 60 feet for boats of 220 feet length.

Estimate.

For securing depth of 4 feet.. $18,870
For securing depth of 6 feet for boats 220 feet long............................. 63,870

The Menasha Channel (Winnebago Rapids) is on the right-bank side of Doty's Island, which here divides the stream. The dam is about five miles above the upper dam at Appleton. It is 460 feet long and 6 feet high, and in good order. The canal around the rapid is about three-quarters of a mile long, and the lock is situated at the lower end. Numerous mills, situated along this canal, draw their water from it. These mills now draw more water than they are entitled to, and so lower the depth for navigable purposes; that while there is 6 feet draught at the upper end of the canal, there is but 3 feet at the lower end. The lock is composite, 160 by 35 feet; the lift is 10 feet, and the depth on the lower miter-sill is 6 feet 2 inches. The upper section of planking and timbers need renewing and the gates repairing. The locks will have to be lengthened 60 feet for vessels 220 feet long. The entrance to the canal is obstructed above by two bars. The outer one is composed of sand and can be dredged; but the inner one, being composed of stiff, hard clay, mixed with gravel and covered with bowlders, will require to be coffer-dammed and dug out by hand. This channel, however, is much better than the other or Neenah Channel, and at present is the only one used for navigation.

Estimate.

For making 4 feet draught.. $13,270
For making 6 feet draught with locks 220 feet long.................................. 54,200

The Lower Fox forms the outlet of Lake Winnebago, a body of water thirty-five miles long, from nine to fourteen miles wide, with depths varying in the deepest parts from 12 to 25 feet. Over the fifteen and a half miles of lake navigation, between the Upper and Lower Fox Rivers, there is a depth of over 20 feet. This lake is a great reservoir, and prevents any sudden changes in the volume of the outlet from freshets—the extreme fluctuations in the Lower Fox not exceeding 3 to 4 feet. The level of the lake does not reach more than 3½ feet above the ordinary level maintained by the dams at the outlets, but it is occasionally drawn down by the water-power mills nearly 2½ feet below this level. The total fall from Lake Winnebago to Green Bay is about 170 feet, and the distance thirty-seven and a half miles. The minimum volume of the Lower Fox is given by Mr. Westbrook at 2,320 cubic feet per second.

The following table is made up from the figures of Major Suter's report, as modified by me in arrangement in the foregoing abstract:

Table in regard to Lower Fox River in the autumn of 1867.

Place.	Intermediate distance.	Distance from mouth of river.	Number of locks.	Elevation overcome.	Height above Green Bay.	Cost of making navigation from one dam to next above. For 4 feet draught, locks 160 x 35.	For 6 feet draught, locks 220 x 35.
	Miles	*Miles.*		*Feet.*	*Feet.*		
Depére, dam	7	7	1	8	8	$45,000 00	$83,300 00
Little Kaukauna, dam	6	13	1	8	16	3,000 00	27,730 00
Rapide Croche, dam	6	19	1	8	24	4,000 00	41,000 00
Grand Kaukana, dam	4½	23½	5	50	74	22,800 00	111,670 00
Little Chute, dam	2½	26	4	38	112	7,530 00	77,200 00
Cedars, dam	0¾	26¾	1	10	122	3,030 00	23,400 00
Appleton, lower dam	3	29¾	1	8½	130½		11,000 00
Appleton, upper dam	0¼	30¼	3	29½	160	18,870 00	63,870 00
Menasha, dam	5	35½	1	10	170	13,270 00	54,200 00
Lake Winnebago	2	37¼			170		
Total	37½		18	170		118,400 00	493,370 00

Condition of the Upper Fox River and improvement in 1866.—The present traveled route between Oshkosh and Fort Winnebago is one hundred and four miles, the air-line being fifty-four miles. As near as can be estimated, there have been made 18,000 feet of cut-offs by dredging, making a saving of about three-fifths of the distance. The total fall is about $33\frac{1}{10}$ feet. In most places there is a fall of a foot in two and a half miles, but there are long reaches where the fall is scarcely perceptible. Several lakes occur on the course of the river, which are generally shallow and full of wild rice.

The mouth of the Fox River at Oshkosh is very deep; the channel has upward of 20 feet of water, which continues along the whole riverfront of the town; thence to Lake Buttes des Morts, and through that lake there is over 12 feet of water; the river is broad and deep, with no perceptible current. About ten miles from Oshkosh the Fox is joined by the Wolf River, a stream of nearly its own size. This river is navigable for about fifty miles; it penetrates into the lumber regions in the northern part of the State, and a great quantity of logs and sawed lumber is floated down the river to Oshkosh.

After passing the mouth of Wolf River 6 feet is the least depth until we reach Omro Bar, half a mile below the town of that name; thence to the town, 4½ feet of water. This portion of the river is quite crooked, but this is of no great importance to small vessels, on account of the depth of the water. Two miles below Omro a cut about a mile long, carrying the waters of the Fox straight to Lake Buttes des Morts, would save seven or eight miles of distance. From Omro to Delhi there is about 5 feet of water; never less, except in small spots. Above Delhi there is the same depth to Eureka Bar. From here to the town of Eureka, one and a half miles, there is only from 4 to 4½ feet, with occasional deep spots. In front of the town there is 6 feet of water. At Eureka there is a permanent bridge, the only one between Berlin and Oshkosh. There are several floating bridges, however, where country roads cross the river. From Eureka to Sacremento there is an average depth of 6 feet. The river is quite narrow.

Above Sacremento there is an average depth of 5 feet half-way to

Berlin; then from 4 to 4½ feet as far as a floating bridge three-quarters of a mile below Berlin. Above this bridge, and also in front of the town of Berlin, there is about 5 feet of water. Between Sacremento and Berlin there is not much marsh along the river, and the banks are generally high. Above Berlin, the average depth is from 5 feet to 6 feet for eight miles. At this point there is a short bar on which the water is only 3½ feet deep. The average depth above here is from 5 feet to 6 feet, until the mouth of the Puckeyan River is reached. Just above the mouth of this stream is a short bar with 3½ feet of water. At the lower end of Willow Bend is another short bar with 3½ feet of water. At the mouth of White River is a bad bar 300 yards long, and having only 3 feet of water on it. In the west side of the first bend above White River is a flat bar caused by a sudden widening of the stream. It is 200 yards long, and has 3½ feet of water on it. (The lowermost wing-dam is about two miles below State Centre.) There is a bar below this lower wing-dam with 3 feet of water. Above this wing-dam there is from 3½ feet to 4½ feet of water; usually 4 feet and often more. The banks of the stream from Berlin to the lower wing-dam are generally low and marshy, but above this point they are quite high, and continue so to the mouth of the Mechan River. There is a second wing-dam at State Centre. At Saint Mary are the ruins of a bridge. From Saint Mary to Princeton the river is quite shoal. The average depth is 4 feet, but on the bars there is less than 3 feet. There are two more wing-dams at Princeton. There is also at this point a good, permanent bridge across the Fox.

Between Princeton and the mouth of Mechan River there are three wing-dams. In this portion of the river the water is quite shoal, not more than 3 feet deep. From Omro to the mouth of Mechan River the fall is about 1 foot in two and a half miles, and there is quite a strong current. Above Mechan there is slack-water to Lake Apuckaway. The river is very wide, with 6 feet or 8 feet depth of water or more. Within the Big Bend, above Princeton, the ground is quite high, about 30 feet above the level of the river. If a canal could be cut through here about ten miles would be saved, as the neck is only a mile wide.

Lake Apuckaway is a sheet of water eight and a quarter miles long and from one to two miles wide. The lower end of the lake is very shallow and full of reeds and wild rice. A channel, running northeast from Marquette, has been cut through for steamers. It is from 3 feet to 3½ feet deep. A channel, having 4 feet of water, leads along the eastern shore of the lake. The bottom of the lake is very soft, black mud, through which a channel of any depth can be easily dredged. For about a mile to the westward of Marquette the lake is filled with rushes. A channel exists, however, which has about 4½ feet of water. After getting out of the rushes, there is from 5 feet to 6 feet of water to the end of the lake.

At the mouth of the Fox, that is, where it enters Lake Apuckaway, there is a bar half a mile long, where there is only from 3 feet to 3½ feet of water; above this there is 5 feet or 6 feet for about three miles. Just below the large bend there is about 4½ feet; then for a mile from 6 feet to 7 feet. The rest of the way to Montello the river is shallow. Three and a half feet is the average depth, and 3 feet is the least. There are a good many sand-banks just below Montello which wash into the stream and cause bad bars. The current between the lakes is quite rapid.

At Montello, a lock and dam are being constructed to raise the water above Lake Buffalo. As shown by the plan, it is designed to cut the canal through into a bayou, which has a depth of about 7 feet. The Montello River has also been turned into this bayou.

The dimensions of the lock, dam, and canal, when finished, will be as follows: Dam, 151 feet long; canal, 650 feet long and 90 feet wide; lock-lift, 3 feet; depth on lower miter-sill, between 8 feet and 9 feet; height of lock, 15 feet; length, 160 feet; width, 35 feet; composite lock with head-walls of masonry.

Above the mouth of Montello River there is from 4 feet to 4½ feet of water as far as the lower end of Lake Buffalo. Lake Buffalo is a large rice-field, about thirteen and one-half miles long and half a mile wide. The Fox crosses it in a very tortuous but deep channel. After entering the lake there is from 6 feet to 9 feet as far as Packwaukee, and even as deep as 15 feet. There is a pile-bridge across the lake at Packwaukee. From Packwaukee a good channel leads to the end of Buffalo Lake. The water runs from 7 feet to 9 feet in depth. Between Lake Buffalo and Lake Menomin there is a channel of about the same depth, and also through Lake Menomin. This channel is exceedingly crooked. Lake Menomin is a large wild rice-field, like Lake Buffalo. It is one and one-half miles long by half a mile wide. After leaving this lake, and especially after passing Merritt's Landing, just above Moundville, a series of small but bad bars are met with. They are caused by the washing of a high sand-bluff on the river-bank. These bars have barely 3 feet of water on them. The worst of them could be avoided by a cut-off. In the last mile below Roslyn the channel is, as a general rule, quite deep, from 6 to 8 feet; but shoal spots occur, where only 4½ feet is to be found. The channel is exceedingly crooked and narrow. A great many cut-offs should be made in this portion of the river.

From Roslyn to the first cut-off there is from 5½ feet to 7 feet of water. Just below this cut-off is a short bar with only 3 feet of water. In the cut itself, there is about 4 feet. Above the cut is another bar with 3 feet depth. This first cut-off is only about 40 feet long, but it saves nearly a mile of distance. From the first to the second cut-off the depth is about 4½ feet. In the cut-off there is a bar with about 3 feet of water; the rest of the cut has a depth of about 4½ feet. From the second to the long cut-off there is from 6 feet to 9 feet of water. At the lower end of the long cut-off there is 5 feet of water; at the middle, 4 feet; at the upper end, 3 feet, with a short bar having from 2 feet 8 inches to 3 feet. From the end of the cut-off to Governor's Bend lock there is about 5 feet of water. Between Governor's Bend lock and Roslyn the stream is very crooked, and several long cut-offs should be made. The cut-off just below Governor's Bend is about a mile long, and saves about three miles. Governor's Bend lock, dam about 4 feet high and 60 feet long. Canal 570 feet long and 57 feet wide. Lock, composite; lift, 4 feet; depth on lower miter-sill, 5 feet 6 inches; height, 15 feet; length, 160 feet; width, 35 feet; new and in good order. From this lock to Winnebago lock there is slack-water. The channel leads almost entirely through cut-offs, and is quite free from sharp bends. The width of these cut-offs is about 60 feet. The depth will average 4½ feet to within a mile of Winnebago lock. In this last distance the channel is full of sand-bars; the water gradually shoals from 4½ feet to 2½ feet. At the foot of Winnebago lock there is 8 feet of water.

At Winnebago lock the lift is 7 feet; depth on lower miter-sill, 6 feet 1 inch; height, 17 feet; length, 160 feet; width, 35 feet. Composite lock with masonry head-walls, all in good order.

The canal which connects the Fox and Wisconsin Rivers is quite shoal. At the lower end it is 5 feet deep for about 200 feet; then 3 feet deep to within 500 feet of the first railroad-bridge ; then 2½ feet deep to the second railroad-bridge ; then 2 feet deep to the town of Portage. At the upper or Wisconsin end it is about 18 inches deep. The mill at the lower end draws the water down about 1 foot. At the upper end of the canal is a guard-lock, which is used as a lift-lock when the Wisconsin is high. It is in a very dilapidated condition, and should be rebuilt. It is two and a third miles (12,400 feet) in length, and 75 feet in width. It is cut through a flat, sandy plain which separates the waters of the Fox from those of the Wisconsin. The Fox River is about 5 feet lower than the Wisconsin in ordinary stages of water. During high water the Wisconsin overflows this neck of low ground at Portage, and also five or six miles above, and a large portion of its waters are thus diverted to Green Bay. The spring rise in the Fox is principally owing to this cause, for the Fox itself fluctuates very little. About seven miles below Portage a stream called Big Slough comes into the Fox. During high water this connects with the Wisconsin and becomes a very considerable stream, bringing a large volume of water into the Fox. In fact, the greater part of the low country between the two rivers is overflowed by the Wisconsin at this time. It will be seen that the canal is not straight, but makes a considerable bend to the westward. The object of this was to place the mouth of the canal on the Wisconsin side, above an island. It was afterward proposed to give it a different direction, but the idea has never been carried out. At present the main bulk of the Wisconsin runs through the inshore channel, and the whole of it can be diverted through there if desirable. It is also much easier to protect the mouth of the canal in the proposed position than in the one it occupies at present. But the change is not a matter of any great importance.

The canal at present is almost filled up with sand, but it is being dredged out.

The only plan of improvement of the Upper Fox River which gives promise of permanency is to create slackwater navigation throughout the whole length of the stream by means of locks and dams. As a great deal of valuable property would be overflowed and ruined by putting in high dams and locks of great lift, it appears preferable to use low dams, say three feet high, and then lower the bed of the stream above and below the dam by dredging sufficiently to destroy the current. Further dredging will give the requisite depth for navigation, and the channel thus made will remain permanent.

Three locks appear necessary between the mouth of Mechan River and Omro. Above the former and below the latter point there is slackwater already, or will be when certain improvements in progress are finished ; notably the Montello lock and dam.

The total fall between Mechan River and a point one and a half miles above Eureka is 12.87 feet, which it is proposed to distribute as follows : One lock at Princeton, 4 feet lift; one lock at Fiddler's Bend, 4 feet lift ; and one lock one and a half miles above Eureka, 5 feet lift.

Ten feet of this total lift is included in the 12.87 feet, the remainder of that sum being allowed for backwater and flowage.

Details from Winnebago lock to Governor's Bend lock : distance, 5½ miles ; fall not accurately known, as the bed of the stream has been much lowered by dredging since the last survey was made. The lock has about 4 feet lift, so that the fall is probably between four and five feet. Slackwater exists above Governor's Bend dam.

Governor's Bend lock to Montello lock : distance, 21 miles ; fall, 5.95

feet, as nearly as can be computed. This is thought to be too much. The Montello dam is to raise the water three feet; and it is proposed to lower the bed below Governor's Bend lock one foot by dredging. This will, it is hoped, give slackwater back to Governor's Bend lock; but, in case it does not, the Montello dam can be raised one foot more. It will probably be necessary to lower the bed of Governor's Bend lock two feet to enable a vessel drawing six feet of water to get through it; but this cannot be stated positively until a new set of levels has been run to ascertain the exact amount. The Montello dam can be raised, if necessary, without overflowing a great extent of country.

From Montello lock to head of Lake Apuckaway: distance, 7 miles; fall, 4.93 feet. Bed of stream to be lowered 4 feet by dredging below the Montello lock, leaving .93 foot fall in 7 miles, or about .13 foot to the mile. From the head of Lake Apuckaway to the mouth of Mechan River there is slackwater.

From mouth of Mechan River to Princeton lock: distance, 5¾ miles; fall, 2.57 feet. Water to be raised 2 feet by a dam, and lowered below the dam 2 feet by dredging. Lock 4 feet lift; flowage, $\frac{57}{100}$ foot.

Princeton lock to Fiddler's Bend lock: distance, 12 miles; fall from foot of Princeton lock, 2.92 feet. Water to be raised 2 feet by the dam, and lowered 2 feet below the dam by dredging. Lock, 4 feet lift; flowage, $\frac{92}{100}$ foot.

Fiddler's Bend lock to Eureka lock: distance, 15¼ miles; fall from foot of Fiddler's Bend lock, 3.38 feet. Water to be raised 2 feet by a dam, and lowered below the dam 3 feet by dredging. Lock, 5 feet lift; flowage, 1.38 feet.

From Eureka lock to Oshkosh: distance, 24 miles; fall, 5.80 feet. Water to be lowered 3 feet at upper end of level by dredging, as stated for Eureka lock. This will reduce the fall to 2.80 feet in 24 miles, or a little less than $\frac{12}{100}$ foot to the mile, which is practically slackwater.

The volume of the Upper Fox at low water is not stated by Major Suter, nor have I seen it stated for any point of its course. At the lock near Fort Winnebago it is a very small stream at low water, merely sufficing as a feeder to slackwater navigation. Its amount is of no practical importance in this view, for any needed supply can be drawn from the Wisconsin River, which is the feeder for the canal connecting the two streams.

Major Suter states the lift of the lock at Fort Winnebago to be 7 feet, and the height of the Wisconsin above the Fox at this point to be 9½ feet. This fall of 2½ feet in 2⅛ miles is inadmissible in a canal for navigation, and is only allowable for supplying water-power. The guard-lock at the head of the canal communicating with the Wisconsin is also a lift-lock even at low water, and enables vessels to pass into the Wisconsin. To the preceding amount of elevation between the Wisconsin and Lake Winnebago, as stated by Major Suter, must be added 2½ feet for the Portage Canal guard-lock, and he makes this allowance in his table of total elevations.

MISSISSIPPI RIVER AND LAKE MICHIGAN.

Table of estimates given by Major Suter, United States Engineers, for the improvement of the Upper Fox River and Portage Canal, with distances and elevations.

	Distance apart.	Total distance.	Fall of water between places.	Elevations above Lake Winnebago.	For draught of 4 feet locks 160 feet by 35 feet.	For draught of 6 feet locks 220 feet by 35 feet.
	Miles.	*Miles.*	*Feet.*	*Feet.*		
Oshkosh to Eureka	22½	22½	5.20	5.20	$9,400	$31,400
Eureka to Fiddler's Bend	16½	39	5.98	11.80	71,673	151,873
Fiddler's Bend to Princeton	12¼	51¼	4.92	16.10	67,400	114,888
Princeton to Mechan River	5¾	57	2.57	18.67	57,654	105,506
Mechan River to head of Lake Apuckaway	6½	63½	0.95	19.62	....	32,852
Head of Lake Apuckaway to Montello	15¼	78½	4.93	24.55	35,202	79,005
Montello to Governor's Bend lock	21	99½	5.95	30.50	40,000	88,466
Governor's Bend lock to Fort Winnebago	5½	105	2.60	33.10	4,693	50,505
Fort Winnebago to Wisconsin River, (Portage Canal)	2¼	107½	9.51	42.61	40,000	80,600
	....	....	....	....	326,022	75,09

Condition of the Wisconsin River in 1866.—Major Suter's report says:

On reaching the Wisconsin River the season was so far advanced that I was obliged to limit myself to a cursory examination of the stream, with a view of determining its general characteristics, the feasibility of rendering it navigable, and the best means of attaining this end. The river when I started from Portage City was about a foot above low-water level for this season. During the time occupied by my examination, it fluctuated between this height and six inches lower. The soundings and cross-sections taken can therefore only be relied on as giving a general idea of the volume of water in the river and the depth of its channel. No reliable survey has ever been made of this river. Its exact length, even from Portage to its mouth, is not known, but is given differently by various authorities, who all base their conclusions on the Land-Office maps. The length which I have assumed is believed to be nearest the truth. The total fall between the same points is also a matter of conjecture. I took twelve observations at intervals of about ten miles, to determine the fall per mile, and the mean of these observations is probably very nearly exact. I give here the length, total fall, and fall per mile, as given by different authorities.

To avoid repetitions, and to enable comparisons to be made here of the value of these determinations and those given by others, the following table has been made. The exact measurements made by our survey in 1867 are added:

Table of different estimates and measurements of length, slope, and total fall of the Wisconsin River below Portage.

Authority.	Length in miles.	Fall per mile.	Total fall.
		Feet.	*Feet.*
Mr. C. D. Westbrook, civil engineer, from levels furnished by railroad companies in 1854	137	0.95	131.00
Silliman's Journal, altitude by barometer	....	.63	....
Mr. D. C. Jenné, civil engineer, chief engineer of Fox and Wisconsin Improvement Company	115	1.00	115.00
Levels furnished Major Sutor by railroad companies in 1866	....	....	179.00
Lengths taken by Major Sutor from latest editions of State sectional maps, the fall per mile a mean of twelve observations, from which the total fall is deduced	112	1.34	150.08
Determined by our survey made in 1867	118½	1.50	178.00

The result of our survey in 1867 thus appears to be nearly the same as that given by the railroad company—the most unfavorable of all for an improvement of the navigation.

This being the case, we must be prepared to make some allowance for the favorable view of the navigation held by Major Suter, and a still greater one for the views advanced by the canal company's engineers and officers, under the influence of the idea that the slope was so much less on the average than it really is.

It is not my intention to quote connectedly from Major Suter's report on the Wisconsin, as the data obtained by him was necessarily very imperfect, and he recommended that a thorough survey should be made. The views he expressed were derived from imperfect data, and although they may be quoted by others hereafter as more favorable than those entertained by me, I refrain from doing it, because I think it would be unjust to him. He submitted an estimate for a thorough survey, but none for any improvement. He thought that with low wing-dams 6 feet draught could be had.

In my report submitting Major Suter's, I said:

I have not as favorable an opinion as Major Suter has of the beneficial effect of dams, and I have estimated for the expense of applying boats to operate directly on the bars, to ascertain the improvement susceptible by that means. This was one of the means suggested by him. The sands of the Wisconsin River bars are easily moved by the water, they being free from any cementing material. I believe a low-water navigation of 3 feet throughout would be all that at present can be promised.

The survey that I made in 1866 at the mouth of the Wisconsin gave a depth over the bar of only 16 inches.

With the low-water depth of the Wisconsin secured at 3 feet, we might rely much of the time on 4 to 6 feet for average stages.

The locks on the Fox River improvements are designed for 4 feet draught, and it seems questionable whether it would do to undertake increasing this depth before its availability on the Wisconsin was demonstrated. Products passing from the Mississippi to the east through the Lakes must break bulk before reaching its destination. No vessel suitable for these upper rivers would be able to navigate Lake Michigan, nor could the lake vessels in ordinary river-stages float on the Upper Mississippi. Therefore, for the through traffic it would seem best to adapt the improved connecting channel to the size of the grain-barges of the Mississippi. The dimensions of tow-boats need not exceed them.

WORKS OF IMPROVEMENT, ETC., IN THE YEAR 1867.

In accordance with the recommendations of my report an appropriation of $40,000 was made and approved March 2, 1867. An allowance was also made from the item for survey of western and northwestern rivers, to enable me to make a survey from Portage to the mouth of the Wisconsin River.

The procurement of a boat especially designed for the Wisconsin was deferred till a better knowledge of it was gained, and until the result of operations with similar boats on the Mississippi River could be obtained. This was all that was attempted on the Wisconsin River.

The Green Bay and Mississippi Canal Company, during the year, executed several needed works of repair, and continued dredging the channel on the Fox River and the canals around the dams. I have not seen their annual report, but learned from the chief engineer that the dam and lock at Montello were completed, the lock being composite, and costing $19,000. The dams in connection with it cost $9,000.

WORKS OF IMPROVEMENT IN THE YEAR 1868.

This year the Green Bay and Mississippi Improvement Company continued their works of repair and dredging on the Fox River. I personally examined the line of the Fox River, and purchased at Oshkosh the small side-wheel steamer Winneconne, which was supplied with a powerful engine and a spool geared to connect with it, thought to be of great service in pulling snags and warping the boat across shoals. Her dimensions were: length, 84 feet; breadth, 24; draught, light, 2 feet. This vessel had but little difficulty in passing up the Upper Fox, although drawing all the water there was on the bars; but it took a great deal of trouble to get her down the Wisconsin River at all, and she was unable to pass Prairie du Bay till after a rise took place. We were unable to make any use of her worth naming that season.

In October an attempt was made to employ the Caffray (one of the Mississippi dredge-boats) on the lower part of the Wisconsin, she having been satisfactory on the Mississippi. It was found, however, that she could not get into the Wisconsin. She drew about 32 inches, and was 150 feet long by 30 wide, with side-wheels. Only 2 feet water on the bars could then be found for six miles up the Wisconsin. (See pp. 203 and 204 Annual Report of Chief of Engineers for 1869.)

Much additional information about the valley of the Wisconsin River was gained this year by Capt. D. W. Wellman, after he had submitted his report, which is printed with that of the Chief of Engineers for 1868. (See pp. 351 to 356.) In this report he favored a canal along the valley more than any other method of improvement.

WORKS OF IMPROVEMENT IN 1869.

During September and October the Winneconne was employed (with two barges to carry fuel and working-apparatus so as to secure least possible draught) in removing snags from the Wisconsin between Portage and Sauk, and this enabled two small stern-wheel vessels to make trips on this portion of the Wisconsin.

I again made a thorough personal examination of it in company with Mr. Jacob Blickensderfer, jr., an experienced canal engineer, and with his assistance planned the estimate for a canal along the valley, submitted with this final report. I believe no work was done by the canal company beyond repairs immediately needed.

CONCLUDING REMARKS TO CHAPTER III.

My views in regard to the improvement of the Wisconsin differ so much from those generally held heretofore, that I have felt called upon to write this chapter, so that others can see by it the reasons for those previous views, and compare it with my own; and as the Wisconsin forms only part of the route, I have thought it necessary to give an account of the other portion and how its improvement has been carried on, so that in adopting a final plan for a through route of water transportation the whole subject may be presented for consideration. The endeavor has been to make this presentation as complete as possible, because the documents from which it is mostly obtained are not available for general consultation.

CHAPTER IV.

REPRESENTATION OF SURVEYS MADE IN 1867–'68–'69; THEIR OBJECT AND EXTENT; MAPS AND DIAGRAMS CONSTRUCTED FROM MEASUREMENTS; TABLES OF HYDRAULIC DATA; ANOMALOUS PHYSICAL FEATURES CONSIDERED, AND REFERRED TO A GENERALIZATION OF SIMILAR EXHIBITIONS ELSEWHERE.

Preparations for the survey—Instructions for conducting the surveys—DESCRIPTION OF THE MAPS AND DIAGRAMS MADE FROM THE SURVEYS—Continuous plot, scale 200 feet to an inch—Cross-sections of the valley, scales 400 feet horizontally and 40 feet vertically to the inch—Longitudinal profile of the valley—Plots of current measurements for volume—Map of river on a scale of two inches to the mile—General map of the route from Green Bay to the Mississippi River—Sheets of river-gauge curves—GENERAL DESCRIPTION OF THE BASIN OF THE WISCONSIN RIVER—Form of basin, geographical position, &c.—General elevation above the sea—Geological formations in the basin—Climate—DESCRIPTION OF FEATURES OF THE VALLEY—Definition of term valley, &c.—Slopes and terraces not overflowed at high water—Marginal lands and islands overflowed at high water—THE RIVER-BED—Sand-bars, &c.—Their formation—Action at low water—Very bad sand-bars in the Mississippi below the Wisconsin—Very bad sand-bars on the Wisconsin at the junction—Movement of sand-bars down stream—Sources and qualitiy of the sand—Comparison of the Wisconsin sand with other water-moved sands—Gravel and bowlders in river-bed—Falling of trees and snags—Bed-rock—BRIDGES—HIGH AND LOW WATER STAGES AND THEIR DURATION—ICE—SLOPE OF WATER-SURFACE—Table of measured slopes at low water—BEND EFFECT—VOLUME OF DISCHARGE—Method of measuring volumes—Table of measured and low-water volumes—Explanation of construction of table—Volumes at a stage one foot above the low water of 1867—Volumes at Skinner's Bluff for all stages—ANOMALOUS PHYSICAL FEATURES OF THE WISCONSIN AND FOX RIVER BASINS—The near approach of the streams without uniting—Peculiarities in the course of the Wisconsin—Peculiarities in the course of the Upper Fox River—Lower Fox River—Analogies between the Lake Winnebago Basin and the Lake Winnipeg Basin in British America—Probable former extent of Lake Winnebago, with diagram—Hypothesis consistent with above-noted conditions—Previous attempts at generalization in regard to Fox River—PROBABLE CHANGE OF DRAINAGE OF THE FOUR LAKES NEAR MADISON—Explained by the same hypothesis which is applicable to an extensive area.

Preparations for the survey.—The examination of the Wisconsin and Fox River route in 1866 had shown that we were very well informed in every respect concerning the portion in charge of the Green Bay and Mississippi Canal Company, along the Lower and Upper Fox Rivers, and the canal at Portage; but that we had no good survey of the part along the Wisconsin River. It was designed, therefore, to make as thorough a survey as possible of that river from the Portage Canal to the Mississippi during the season of 1867.

Early in August gauges were set up and observers engaged to constantly record the height of the water at the following-named places: At Kilbourn City, about twenty miles above Portage; at Portage; at Sauk City, 29 miles below Portage; at upper railroad-bridge, 25 miles below Sauk City; at Muscoda, 23 miles below the upper railroad-bridge; at the lower railroad-bridge, 21 miles below Muscoda; and at Bridgeport, 14 miles farther down.

This last place is but six miles above the junction with the Mississippi, and within the range of backwater from floods in this latter river. These gauges were observed till the river was closed by ice about the 1st of December. They were also continued at Portage; upper and lower railroad-bridges, in 1868, from April to December, and at the upper and lower railroad-bridges in 1869 till December. In these years the river was open from the first part of April to the first part of December. These gauge observations, as plotted, accompany this report. Observations on the Mississippi, at Prairie du Chien, Winona, and Saint Paul, and on Lake Winnebago, are shown at the same time for comparison. These three years (1867–'68–'69) gave an average volume of water above the promise of years in general, as to the amount of water flowing along the Wisconsin and neighboring streams.

As it was desirable to conduct the survey at low water, the first part of the summer of 1867 was used in preparations, such as fitting up a large, flat scow with a cabin, to serve as a quarter-boat for the surveying party, and in obtaining instruments, note-books, &c.

Instructions for conducting the survey.—The work was executed so nearly in accordance with instructions that I cannot better describe it than by inserting the instructions issued by me August 10, 1867:

UNITED STATES ENGINEER OFFICE,
Saint Paul, Minn., August 10, 1867.

The survey of the Wisconsin River will extend from Kilbourn City to its junction with the Mississippi. It is designed to have the maps and report exhibit all the information required for a thorough consideration of the subject of improving its navigation at low stages, and determining the best plan of executing it.

If this improvement may be made by deepening the water on the bars by means of scrapers in excavating, or by wing and longitudinal dams to prevent such bars from forming, or cause their removal when formed, if by closing up one or more of the channels we can produce a sufficiency in the desired one; or, if these must all fail and resort be had to slack-water by dams with locks, or by continuous canal with locks along the valley, must also be determined, if possible, from the survey; and also the relative advantages of different methods in economical construction and practical value, when made.

The quality of navigation sought is such as will adequately meet the wants of a great line of communication from the Mississippi River to Lake Michigan along this river, the Upper Fox River, Lake Winnebago, Lower Fox River, and Green Bay. The existing information contains but very little that is conclusive concerning the engineering question involved. Nothing, therefore, must be relied on from other sources than this survey, and nothing left undone that circumstances of time and ability will enable the surveying parties to do.

The general features of the valleys of the northwestern rivers must be always kept in mind by the different engineers employed, and they are readily appreciated by reference to the following section and map, Plate II.

The main features observable are, first, a high bluff on each side of the river-valley, from one to ten miles apart, and from 100 to 400 feet high, composed mainly of horizontally stratified rock, and, in the case of the Wisconsin, of magnesian limestone of the Silurian formation. The slopes, however, are often covered with earth and grass, so that the rock is discernible to common observation only at places where quarries have been opened.

The second feature is a level or nearly level terrace mainly composed of sand, though occasionally having a rich surface-soil. Towns are frequently located upon it. This terrace is from 20 to 60 feet above the level of the water; it is never continuous throughout the valley on either side, and rarely of much extent on but one side at a time. It is, probably, the shallow parts of an ancient water-course which once occupied the valley from bluff to bluff. It is now generally above overflow.

The third feature is the bottom-lands of the river, generally overflowed at highest stages, and having the high bluff or terrace for their margin. This bottom contains many lakes and marshes, and is cut up by sloughs forming islands which sometimes divide the main stream into nearly equal parts. The margins of these bottom-lands are, in the natural state, generally wooded, and form the banks of the stream at moderate stages when the sand-bars are covered.

The fourth feature is the bed of the stream, which includes the part covered at medium stages, but large portions of which become dry sand or gravel bars at low stages.

There are thus four different prominent benches or levels in the river-valley:
1. The level forming the main bluff.
2. The sand-terrace generally above overflow.
3. The bottom-land generally overflowed at highest water.
4. The bed of the stream.

It is desirable that the topographical survey shall give the limits of each of these and their elevation. This may be in a very general way for all but the fourth level, to which the details of the survey should be mainly directed.

The sketch of the valley given above assumes a simple case where the river is divided by a single island, but the bottom-lands are often much more complicated in structure.

There is generally, however, as in the case given, one main channel, and to this the more thorough work of sounding may generally be confined. Experience, good judgment, and a knowledge of a special case, when it occurs, must govern the engineer as to what is to be done.

The survey will be conducted as follows:

A continuous transit-line will be carefully measured and staked off on one bank or the other of the main river, as may be most easy, and all the topography sketched along it. The opposite shore must be located by triangulation.

The topographical note-book must show both edges of the bottom-land, and the edge of the water at the time must fix the position of the stakes used by the sounding parties, and must locate all prominent buildings by measurements, angles, or bearings, when practicable.

When passing prominent points marks must be left, on which back sights can be taken as the work progresses, and distant points on bluffs and buildings should be similarly used.

Accompanying this transit-line must be a careful line of levels, in which should be noted frequently the height of the bottom-lands or sand-terrace when near, the height of the water of the river at the time, that of the last high water, and the most noted high or low water mark that may be ascertained. Both these instrumental surveys should establish marks, at least once a mile, on trees, rocks, or permanent buildings; carefully describe them in the notes, and select such as may be readily found after the lapse of years for future surveys to connect with, as well as for the detached portions of this survey.

There will be, besides this main line, two subordinate compass-parties to survey the minor channels, which will connect their work as often as possible with the main line, and must always do so at the point of beginning and ending of such subordinate line.

These parties will note, besides, the topographical sketches and horizontal dimensions, the height of the banks, either bottom-land or sand-terrace, wherever they see them, and will make an occasional section by sounding across the slough or chute they are surveying.

In case one of these parties is surveying a channel as large, or nearly so, as the main channel, it must be sounded with the same care as the main channel, especially if there is any question about which one it would be most desirable to close up.

There will be a separate level-party to run level-lines transversely of the valley as often as the progress of the survey will permit, and where there are steep bluffs the hand-level can be used to level up to their summits.

In all cases side distances for locating important objects must be measured with a tape-line; pacing will frequently ascertain them with sufficient accuracy, and if circumstances prevent this, the estimated distance must be noted.

The sketches must be made to a scale on the ground, must give the kind and quality of the trees, marshes, sand-bars, and rocks; and when objects cannot be entered on the page by using the regular scale, the distance must be noted or estimated by angles or bearings from fixed points. Connections will be made as frequently as may be with the railroad-line, and all the bridges and piers will be carefully measured and located, and notes made of all obstructions.

The sounding-lines will be run obliquely across the stream from 300 to 600 feet apart, more or less closely as the correct understanding of the river-bed may require. The soundings will be taken with a pole at as nearly uniform intervals of time as practicable, with the boats rowed at uniform rates of speed, and practice must be acquired so that the same line can be sounded forth and back with approximately the same result. Occasionally it would be well to sound them both ways, especially at important points.

Where the grounding of the boat prevents the boat reaching the shore, the distance to the stake on the shore must be noted. The sounding-pole should be uniformly 12 or 15 feet long, and "no bottom" recorded where this will not reach.

The cadence of time is lost by changing one pole for another or for a sounding-line at deep places. These deep holes must be determined separately after the regular lines have been sounded. The engineer in charge of the sounding-party must keep a sketch of the river and lines sounded, and must locate, as far as he can with his eye, the position of the bars beneath the water.

At intervals of about ten miles, there should be two sections 200 feet apart carefully sounded, and a series of floats at mid depth observed for velocities, so that the discharge can be accurately computed after the manner it is now being done at Saint Paul.

If possible, the main line should be kept plotted as the survey proceeds, on the scale of 200 feet to an inch, so that no confusion can occur in the system of lines kept in the note-books. A short time in the evening, and times of bad weather, will suffice for this. It, will, besides, serve at once to show the directing engineer if the surveys made leave out any desired information. The quarter-boat is designed of ample size to furnish convenience for this work.

At the quarter-boat, whenever it is lying still, a gauge should be set up and the rise

Warren's Report on Wisconsin River — PLATE II

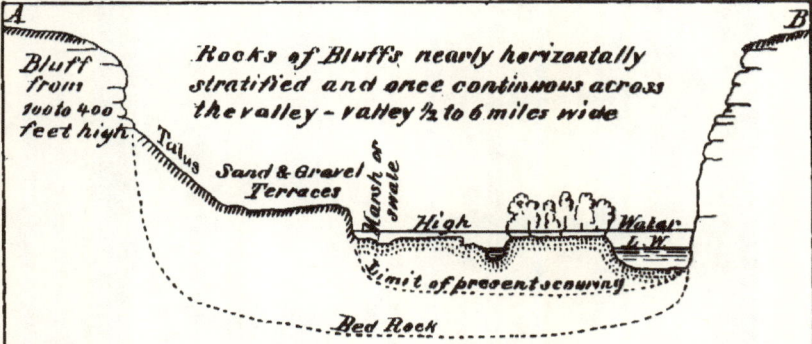

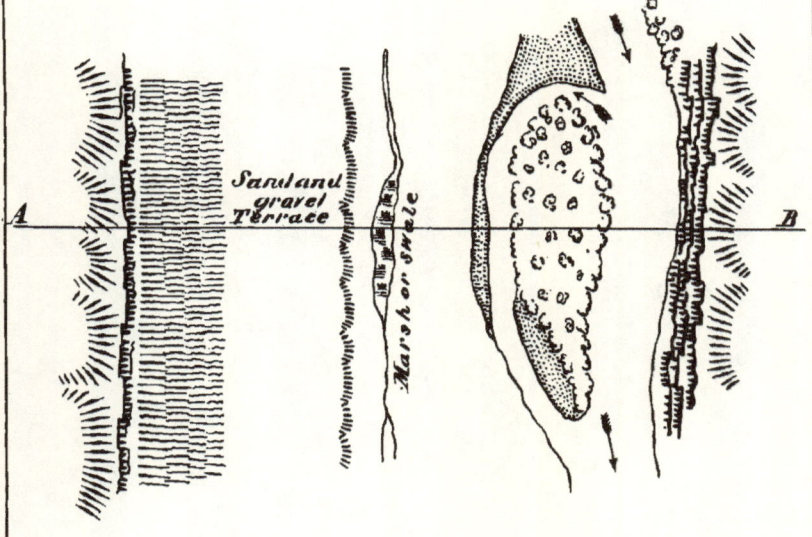

Generalized map & section
of a portion of
The Wisconsin River & Valley
illustrating instructions
for surveys in 1867-8-9
no definite scale

and fall of the river carefully noted. It will be of service, in connection with the regular river-gauges, in reducing the levels to a uniform stage of the river during the time of the survey, so that the slope can be constructed for any stage observed.

In procuring subsistence for the parties, the quantities allowed per man will not exceed the allowance for a soldier in the armies of the United States. And the material procured will be limited to articles thus allowed, unless an equivalent of other materials can be obtained at an equal or less cost than these.

It is directed that no regular meal shall be served on the quarter-boat in the middle of the day, and arrangements must be made for sending a sufficiency of food from the boat to the place where the parties are at work. Small parties working at some distance from the boat must take this meal with them in the morning. In the evening a full dinner-meal will be served on the quarter-boat, and also in the morning before going to the work; and every exercise of authority must be used that this does not delay the commencement of the day's work.

The following party, beside the principal engineer, will be employed on this survey, but the engineer in charge is authorized to change the men from one party to another in any manner he thinks best, according to the nature of the work of each. For main transit-party, one engineer and six men; for main level-party, one engineer and three men; for cross-section level-party, one engineer and three men; for two compass-parties, each, one engineer and three men; for one sounding-party, one engineer and five men; cook and steward, two men; care of quarter-boat, two men.

The engineer in charge will endeavor to inform himself fully of the character and resources of the country for building dams of stone, timber, or brush, and for locks and other masonry. He must also keep a regular journal, detailing the operations of the different parties, and other information. The survey will be conducted in the manner above described, from Portage to the mouth, and if, on arriving at the latter point, it should be found that additional surveys were required in special localities, as undoubtedly it will be, detached parties may be made to execute them.

A weekly report of progress will be made to this office, and further information given from time to time, if required.

G. K. WARREN, &c.

Some minor modifications only were made in conducting the survey. Instead of the edges of submerged bars being sketched in, the method was improved as far as practicable by fixing them by means of bearings to a level-staff, with a telescope having a micrometer, by which the distance was obtained. The very complicated net-work of channels and wooded islands demanded so much work that the boundaries of the bottom-lands next to the high bluffs and terraces could not all be determined in 1867, and such as were not were obtained in 1868–'69. It was impracticable to secure information complete enough to give more than an approximate idea of proper location for a canal, and to furnish a guide for a final survey for location.

The levels, though very carefully made, did not give the surface of the water as often as might be desired.

This slope was constantly varying, although for distances of five or six miles it is nearly uniform throughout. The assistant with the leveling-instrument, Mr. J. Z. Osborn, a gentleman much esteemed by all who knew him, was taken with a fever on the latter part of the survey, and died on the work. His place was filled by Assistant Wellman.

The hydraulic measurements were designed to get the volume of the water as nearly as possible, by the method of Humphreys and Abbot, which was accepted without any attempt at verification on this survey. More careful hydraulic measurements were at the time being conducted at Saint Paul, under similar conditions of flowing water, and it was found there that, as far as anything could be inferred from observations in streams of this character, the laws obtained from the authors referred to were confirmed.

The original surveying-party was composed as follows:

Mr. E. T. Ellsworth, transit-party, on right bank.
Mr. E. L. Billings, compass-party, on left bank.
Mr. I. D. McKown, compass-party, on islands.

Mr. W. W. Rich, cross-sections of valley and location of sand-bar crests.
Mr. J. Z. Osborn, leveling-party.
Mr. R. J. Dukes, soundings and hydrography.
Bvt. Maj. Charles R. Suter was present, in charge. Mr. D. W. Wellman was general assistant, studying the subject and supplying temporary disability of any other assistant, or looking up any matter outside of their specialties. Mr. J. P. Cotton, who had acquired experience of my method of river-surveying during the autumn of 1866, assisted in setting the survey going at Portage.

The field-work was begun in August, and was completed down to the mouth on the 6th of November. A line of levels was also run above Portage to the "Dalles" at Kilbourn City.

The summary of field-work in 1867 is as follows:

	Miles.
Measured transit-line on river-bank	119.3
Measured compass-line on river-bank	117.1
Measured compass-line on islands	116.2
Measured cross-section lines of valley	53.0
Measured survey-lines near Portage and Prairie du Chien	10.0
Total measured lines	415.6
Measured main-line levelings	122.0
Approximate length of lines sounded over	375.0
Number of measurements of volume of Wisconsin	12
Number of measurements of volume of tributaries	5

This does not include the additions made in 1868 and 1869. In the above summary no mention is made of a multitude of triangulations, by which the surveys of opposite banks and at the head and foot of islands and bars were united together.

DESCRIPTION OF THE MAPS AND DIAGRAMS MADE FROM THE SURVEYS.

An account of the labor of mapping this survey and the delays attending it has already been given in an introductory chapter, so we will proceed at once to enumerate the maps and diagrams.

Continuous plot-scale, 200 feet to an inch.—The first plot has been constructed from the field-notes, on a scale of 200 feet to the inch, on white paper backed with cloth. This forms twenty-four sheets, with a uniform length of 10 feet each.

It has been the effort to put upon this map all the notes of the field-books, so that no further reference to them should ever be necessary. These sheets show the measured and triangulated lines, and thus indicate by their proximity to objects represented, the accuracy which belongs to the representation. The appearance of the sand-bars as thus given was made with special care, and is intended to show this important feature as it was there presented. Although every part of this sandy bed changes from year to year, this representation will give a reliable idea of what it is in general—as much alike from year to year as are the leaves of a mature tree, although never exactly the same.

Improvements had accomplished nothing in changing them, and this map, therefore, shows these river sand-bars as seen by Marquette and Joliët in 1763; by Major Long, United States Army, in 1817; by the Fifth United States Infantry in 1819, and by all subsequent examiners. In the future study of them, by such as may desire, it must be kept in mind that these bars are all mutually related. A change in one affects the flow of water, (which caused the change,) and this effect is felt above and below. The elevation of the river surface referred to on assumed datum-plane, and that of the deduced low-water surface, are shown on these plots by figures inclosed by brackets.

Cross sections of the valley—scales 400 feet horizontally and 40 feet vertically to the inch.—Besides this map—scale 200 feet to the inch—there are seventeen cross-sections of the valley on different sheets, made on a scale of 400 feet to the inch horizontally and 40 feet to the inch vertically.

Longitudinal profile of valley.—There was made a longitudinal profile of the river and the immediate banks where the line of levels was run, on scales of two inches to the mile horizontally, and one inch to 40 feet vertically, and all the data that could be shown on a profile in regard to height of bottom-lands, terraces, &c., and slopes of water-surface and distances are given.

Plots of current-measurements for volume.—The measurements of sections and velocities of current, to obtain the volume of water passing, are plotted on manila paper, on scales of 100 feet to the inch horizontally and 20 feet to the inch vertically. On these plots are given the plotted courses of the current and all the calculations used in obtaining the volume. They are fastened together and properly designated, so that this important matter can be readily revised by any one.

All of the foregoing are suited to a study of special localities or subjects.

Map of river on a scale of two inches to the mile.—For the general consideration of the improvement a reduced map has been made on a scale of two inches to the mile, which is as small as will enable the important features to be shown. This scale was chosen because it is that of the United States land-survey township-plots, as filed on their records. This map shows the main bluffs, (which were often too distant to be included on the larger-scale maps,) the terraces, bottom-lands, islands, dry-bars, and under-water bars. The seventeen cross sections of the valley are reduced and placed marginally along it, and the height of the water-surface is noted. This map is designed for publication with this report, if the report be published. It is divided into eight sheets for photolithographing.

General map of the route from Green Bay to the Mississippi River.—We have also prepared a general map and profile of the route from Green Bay to the Mississippi River. The map is on a scale of six miles to the inch, and shows the line of provisional location for a canal. The profile is on a scale of eight miles to the inch horizontal and 40 feet to the inch vertical.

Sheets of river gauge curves.—There have also been prepared for publication, in one sheet, diagrams on curves of rise and fall from the gauge-readings on Lake Winnebago, on the Wisconsin River, and on the Mississippi River, for the years 1867, 1868, 1869.

GENERAL DESCRIPTION OF THE BASIN OF THE WISCONSIN RIVER.

Form of basin, geographical position, &c.—The basin drained by this river is of a comparatively narrow, triangular form, bounded by the water-sheds between it and Lake Superior on the north, Lake Michigan on the southeast, and the Mississippi River on the southwest. From the source to Portage City the general course of the main river is south, the distance in a straight line being about one hundred and ninety miles.

Thence to its mouth the general course is west-southwest for a distance, in direct line, of about ninety miles. The whole basin lies within the parallels of 43° and 46° 10' north latitude and the meridians of 88° 45' and 91° west from Greenwich, and covers about eleven thousand eight hundred and fifty square miles.

General elevation above the sea.—At the junction of the river with the Mississippi the surface at low water is about 625 feet above the level of the sea, which is about that of Lake Superior; Lake Michigan being 589 feet. The level of the country in this vicinity, at the top of the main high banks, (or "bluffs," as they are generally called on western rivers,) is from 400 to 500 feet higher, making the level of the high prairie-land or plateau from 1,000 to 1,100 feet above the sea. Ascending the river from the mouth to Portage the low-water river-surface rises 180 feet, making the low-water surface at Portage 805 feet above the sea. The high plateau rises nearly at the same rate, being just south of Portage about 400 feet above the river, or 1,500 feet above the sea-level. This high prairie is very much cut up by ravines and river valleys, so that considerable areas are but little elevated above the surface of the river. The whole of the basin has been the scene of vast glacial denudations and deposition. At the sources the face of the country is characterized by lakes and swamps, (a feature common to the sources of most of our northwestern rivers,) and is elevated from about 1,400 to 1,600 feet above the sea, or from 100 to 300 feet above the highest lands near Portage. The water from the sources, therefore, descends from 600 to 800 feet in reaching Portage.

Geological formations in the basin.—The lake region about the source is represented on Owens's[*] geological map as composed of heavy drift-deposits, 800 to 1,000 feet above the level of Lake Superior, underlaid with crystalline rocks, with occasional outcrops of granitic and igneous rocks. This is the character of the basin as far down as Whitney's Rapids, a distance from the sources in a straight line of about one hundred and thirty miles. The width of the basin here does not exceed sixty miles. South of Whitney's Rapids the rocks of the Lower Silurian formation appear, generally showing an increased height above the river as it descends. The stratification is but little inclined, the general dip being to the southwest, with some few irregularities and reversals of dip.

From Whitney's Rapids to Honey Creek, (thirty-four miles below Portage,) a distance by the river-valley of about ninety miles, the rock is generally a soft siliceous sandstone, easily crumbled. It has suffered great degradation, the *débris* supplying immense quantities of sand to recent terraces and river formations. The valley of the river from Whitney's Rapids to the Dalles is mainly a broad expanse of sand, with the sandstone rising out of it in detached hills. It is probable that this was formerly a lake-bed before the gorge at the Dalles was cut through, and that a waterfall formed the outlet of the lake, which cut away the barrier and drained the lake. The waves of such lake must have continued to abrade the sandstone, and to spread the sand over the bed through which the Wisconsin now flows.

Below Honey Creek a magnesian limestone of the Lower Silurian begins to form the tops of the bluffs. As the stream descends the valley, the thickness of this limestone increases, and that of the underlying sandstone diminishes, the latter disappearing at the mouth of the river. This soft sand-rock, therefore, forms the bed-rock all the way down from Portage, and there can be but little doubt that under the influences to

---

[*] Report of a geological survey, &c., by David Dale Owen, published by Lippincott, Grambo & Co., Philadelphia, 1852.

which it was subjected while the valley was forming, the excavation into this bed was carried to great depth. It is, at best, but the poorest of foundations for any structure like a dam, even if reached at reasonable depth. The magnesian limestones furnish good building-material, remarkably easy to quarry and cut into shape.

In the basin there are no considerable formations of a geological age between the Silurian and the Post Pleiocene, but almost every variety of glacial drift, modified and unmodified, is found, and many terraces dating from the glacial period to the present time.

Climate of the basin.—The meteorological observations made by the Surgeon-General's Department United States Army,* at Fort Winnebago, near Portage, and at Fort Crawford, on the Mississippi River, three miles above the Wisconsin, are the only ones in my possession in regard to the climate. The observations at Fort Winnebago and Fort Crawford were made at places "elevated 70 feet above the river." The elevations above the sea were at the first locality 870 feet, and at the second 695 feet. The river-valleys in which these observations were made are about 300 to 400 feet below the high lands in the neighborhood. The temperature observations included the period from 1822 to 1845; those for measuring the rain-fall, from 1836 to 1845. The following are the average results obtained:

Table of mean temperature and rain-fall at Fort Winnebago and Fort Crawford, 1822, 1845, and 1836–1845, respectively.

	Fort Winnebago.	Fort Crawford.
Mean spring temperature	45°.49 Fahrenheit	46°.66 Fahrenheit.
Mean summer temperature	67 96 Fahrenheit	72 28 Fahrenheit.
Mean autumn temperature	45 96 Fahrenheit	48 34 Fahrenheit.
Mean winter temperature	19 78 Fahrenheit	21 25 Fahrenheit.
Mean annual temperature	44 80 Fahrenheit	47 63 Fahrenheit.
Mean spring rain-fall	5.58 inches	7.63 inches.
Mean summer rain-fall	11.46 inches	11.87 inches.
Mean autumn rain-fall	7.63 inches	7.90 inches.
Mean winter rain-fall	2.82 inches	4.00 inches.
Mean annual rain-fall	27.49 inches	31.40 inches.

The subject is considered of sufficient importance to require these tables of monthly means to be given in full in this report, and they are accordingly copied below.

* Published as Senate Ex. Doc. No. 96, first session Thirty-fourth Congress, 703 pages-quarto, with an outline map, and entitled "Statistical report on the sickness and mortality in the Army of the United States, compiled from the records of the Surgeon-General's Office, embracing a period of sixteen years from January, 1839, to January, 1855. Prepared under the direction of Bvt. Brig. Gen. Thomas Lawson, Surgeon-General United States Army, by Richard H. Coolidge, M. D., assistant surgeon United States Army, 1856."

Table of temperature at Fort Winnebago, Wisconsin.

Latitude, 43° 31'; longitude, 89° 28'; altitude, 870' feet.

	January.	February.	March.	April.	May.	June.	July.	August.	September.	October.	November.	December.	Spring.	Summer.	Autumn.	Winter.	Year.
1829	25.49	9.64	33.77	46.83	64.01	68.40	70.08	70.36	61.11	55.45	31.00	33.75	48.20	69.61	49.19	22.96	47.49
1830†	17.43	28.90	38.40	57.35	61.97	71.38	83.65	76.20	63.83	60.21	47.62	23.94	52.57	77.08	57.22	22.96	52.46
1831	13.77	18.94	40.12	49.18	50.34	73.55	74.49	72.46	61.37	51.97	33.85	9.88	50.25	73.50	49.06	14.16	46.74
1832	24.40	16.52	41.58	53.52	61.44	72.75	76.04	71.38	64.95	51.69	37.02	32.63	50.83	73.39	52.55	24.32	50.32
1833	29.82	28.31	42.90	54.06	57.40												
1834				43.08	58.94	64.10	67.99	64.35	59.73	47.35	39.00	22.51					
1835	21.13	7.38	30.83	40.34	56.65	62.06	67.56	61.67	51.18	45.75	27.14	18.62	44.28	65.48	41.36	15.71	41.71
1836	15.95	17.66	20.49	36.44	50.34	61.73	68.29	64.12	54.33	36.75	31.25	16.98	39.16	63.76	40.76	13.53	39.31
1837	16.67	19.68	23.30	37.50	49.35	66.57	73.01	64.22	55.77	46.31	35.05	20.77	36.69	64.71	43.71	19.04	41.54
1838	17.95	6.04	37.89	53.97	54.78	60.57	68.56	64.02	51.22	39.21	21.63	12.93	41.58	69.27	39.11	12.31	40.57
1839	22.36	22.79	30.47	44.76	58.95	65.38	66.52	64.49	54.45	52.42	28.16	22.33	46.41	64.38	43.93	22.49	44.30
1840	12.78	22.97	31.52	39.69	55.99	66.27	67.97	63.96	54.50	43.82	30.00	1.45	45.08	65.46	42.76	17.40	42.67
1841	12.03	15.08	28.98	50.58	57.63	57.66	66.16	65.39	57.63	43.28	31.67	23.49	45.29	66.07	42.89	16.87	41.84
1842	20.52	21.95	39.70	44.31	52.88	64.96	70.59	67.04	54.50	47.80	26.76	1st. 31	47.72	63.10	44.09	20.26	43.79
1843	22.03	8.75	12.38	55.17	53.22	63.21	71.10	66.43	61.83	39.89	29.88	27.94	36.64	67.30	43.67	19.34	41.84
1844	16.57	24.47	35.02	48.40		60.57	72.22	63.06	59.10	43.69	32.11	20.87		66.91	43.93	20.64	41.74
1845	23.53	27.54	34.96		57.41								46.92	60.38	44.93		
Mean, 16 years	19.52	18.50	32.60	47.90	56.66	65.63	70.95	67.31	57.83	47.90	32.14	21.33	45.49	67.96	43.96	19.78	44.80

*Changed from 770 ?—G. K. W.   † The summer months of this year are reported as unprecedently hot and dry in Wisconsin.

Table of temperature at Fort Crawford, Wisconsin.

Latitude, 43° 5'; longitude, 91° 00'; altitude, 693* feet.

	January	February	March	April	May	June	July	August	September	October	November	December	Spring	Summer	Autumn	Winter	Year
1823	14.86	23.73	38.01	43.99	60.45	69.25	73.66	72.70	61.16	44.37	34.26	9.53	47.48	71.87	46.60	16.04	45.30
1824	24.59	20.14	26.96	43.86	58.46	67.90	71.34	70.12	61.84	46.53	41.86	26.36	43.09	69.79	46.74	23.76	45.84
1825	18.55	30.43	40.96														
1829																	
1830	20.21	27.94	38.42	56.76	64.10	73.53	71.00	73.76	63.05	54.81	30.26	31.93	53.09	77.35	49.37	22.44	51.81
1831	9.22	18.90	36.80	47.26	61.90	72.69	81.46	77.07	61.45	55.97	43.90	19.98	48.65	73.73	54.44	11.60	45.30
1832	18.42	0.96	31.43	54.84	35.92	72.75	70.56	71.93	60.17	52.00	29.54	5.97	49.40	72.40	47.24	19.09	47.66
1833	27.57	23.94	34.85	58.86	64.92	70.49	74.40	70.06	62.08	52.01	35.18	28.90	52.88	75.26	49.76	19.09	51.84
1834	7.96	34.16	34.74	57.44	51.07	68.88	78.72	76.57	70.27	43.79	39.47	32.93	48.29	75.64	51.18	28.06	46.06
1835	26.27	9.47	35.74	46.45	64.57	68.77	80.49	77.55	59.56	48.58	41.90	27.93	50.04	70.95	45.25	23.35	49.19
1836	17.72	20.03	24.28	45.73	63.91	67.45	73.83	70.85	56.45	49.57	41.99	21.69	45.68	69.22	45.68	19.14	46.06
1837	18.43	25.84	28.86	42.56	56.71	64.08	73.74	67.26	60.49	41.71	29.74	21.57	47.25	69.60	58.29	19.42	45.58
1838	22.03	6.92	43.43	45.16	56.63	72.40	78.22	73.95	61.14	50.06	34.83	50.51	48.92	74.86	45.77	21.95	46.16
1839	27.38	28.88	35.65	61.56	63.44	69.51	78.71	72.05	63.99	45.87	39.66	21.57	44.62	73.42	58.29	15.60	45.96
1840	16.21	20.46	37.15	51.34	65.97	73.89	73.31	70.30	58.81	45.96	27.45	17.86	42.02	72.57	45.77	21.46	46.16
1841	16.79	21.78	36.92	44.99	59.64	71.43	74.25	69.16	59.45	47.94	33.55	25.49	46.41	71.61	47.67	22.03	48.44
1842	20.31	22.71	43.95	59.68	56.28	67.02	73.78	71.13	59.49	47.61	35.63	23.42	51.49	70.85	48.46	21.46	48.74
1843	30.17	7.70	8.99	45.60	56.00	67.12	74.00	71.10	62.74	53.39	36.87	23.69	48.90	70.75	45.56	20.83	48.64
1844	17.25	24.70	37.68	57.24	60.68	66.12	74.19	71.00	65.18	40.32	29.14	19.47	54.42	70.10	47.65	18.83	42.96
1845	24.43	28.06	38.27	52.57	61.01	68.07	75.23	72.33	60.43	46.74	31.27	17.61	36.70	71.88	47.65	20.81	47.61
												20.47	51.57				
Mean 19 years	19.43	21.67	34.53	50.88	60.58	69.55	75.26	72.03	61.51	48.92	34.56	22.65	48.66	72.28	48.34	21.25	47.63

* Changed from 642.—G. K. W.

Table of rain-fall at Fort Winnebago, Wisconsin.

	January	February	March	April	May	June	July	August	September	October	November	December	Spring	Summer	Autumn	Winter	Year
1836	0.48	0.91	.....	2.41	3.18	4.80	5.66	0.16	4.53	0.77	1.28	1.77	5.88	.....	6.87	2.74	31.32
1837	2.03	0.20	0.25	2.98	0.86	2.40	7.67	2.89	5.39	0.79	3.23	1.35	3.92	13.35	9.41	2.64	27.88
1838	0.92	0.47	0.08	1.84	3.59	4.53	0.83	5.35	2.64	1.49	3.71	0.41	6.22	15.42	5.90	2.02	28.95
1839	0.80	1.17	0.79	1.46	2.03	3.71	6.83	4.36	1.43	8.14	1.27	0.76	3.97	9.74	10.84	2.15	28.12
1840	0.18	0.43	0.48	1.40	1.51	5.45	5.79	3.47	1.45	4.03	2.65	0.03	4.54	12.97	8.16	2.59	29.43
1841	0.84	0.56	1.54	1.95	1.17	5.04	3.70	3.79	6.58	1.25	0.55	1.98	4.73	12.94	8.78	2.58	29.48
1842	0.72	0.62	1.71	1.52	1.17	4.07	3.24	2.14	3.45	0.21	3.16	1.14	4.78	10.42	6.78	1.92	24.51
1843	1.51	0.58	2.39	3.52	4.18	4.07	1.20	1.92	4.41	0.60	2.67	0.58	6.71	6.49	7.66	3.84	22.60
1844	1.07	2.49	1.33	2.67	1.46	4.09	5.40	5.16	2.73	0.73	3.12	1.75	7.33	14.63	5.02	.....	.....
1845	.....	.....	3.10	.....	.....	.....	4.37	1.53	.....	.....	1.56	.....	.....	9.99	.....	.....	.....
Mean	0.91	0.82	1.07	2.26	2.25	4.24	4.21	3.01	3.62	2.00	2.01	1.09	5.58	11.46	7.63	2.82	27.49

Table of rain-fall at Fort Crawford, Wisconsin.

	January	February	March	April	May	June	July	August	September	October	November	December	Spring	Summer	Autumn	Winter	Year
1836	0.40	.....	2.90	3.00	3.60	1.10	3.20	2.30	6.40	1.30	0.50	1.60	7.30	6.60	8.20	6.02	34.05
1837	1.30	2.70	0.45	3.57	1.40	4.40	1.83	3.65	7.18	1.16	2.51	2.92	5.05	9.88	10.55	1.62	21.96
1838	1.72	0.09	1.96	2.07	1.03	2.17	1.58	5.68	2.76	1.66	1.44	0.32	3.87	9.43	5.86	.....	21.46
1839	.....	1.00	0.29	3.62	0.54	5.10	1.57	6.30	4.93	5.05	1.90	1.00	6.57	11.90	11.90	2.32	31.25
1840	1.40	0.47	5.76	2.04	2.15	2.57	2.97	0.91	1.90	5.81	1.96	0.12	9.55	12.45	9.71	2.94	31.05
1841	0.19	1.13	2.09	4.04	1.75	2.36	7.75	2.45	3.58	1.21	0.14	3.28	12.26	13.79	3.80	4.42	38.34
1842	1.29	0.93	0.58	4.60	6.90	7.08	1.00	6.43	3.90	0.06	3.47	2.00	5.00	14.51	7.13	2.10	25.58
1843	2.70	0.67	1.42	3.56	4.71	3.10	8.81	4.13	4.90	1.33	2.82	0.47	9.69	9.43	9.05	5.85	39.06
1844	2.60	2.70	2.73	3.36	2.40	4.01	3.90	4.06	2.46	0.76	1.42	2.38	8.49	18.88	4.64	.....	.....
1845	1.10	.....	.....	.....	.....	5.50	.....	1.35	.....	.....	.....	.....	.....	10.75	.....	.....	.....
Mean	1.19	1.24	1.92	2.99	2.72	3.74	3.48	4.05	4.06	2.04	1.90	1.57	7.63	11.87	7.90	4.00	31.40

From these tables it will be seen that the annual rain-fall is some years 20 per cent. below the average and occasionally as much as 25 per cent. The summer rains, on the average, are earlier by two months at Portage than at the mouth of the river, and somewhat heavier, although the annual average is a little the greater at the mouth.

We have no series of observations of the rain-fall in the upper part of the basin, but as far as we can infer from our river-gauge observations in 1867, '68, and '69, the region seems not so well supplied with summer rains as the adjoining basins east and west of it. The upper part of the basin lies in the belt of coniferous trees—pine, spruce, hemlock, and larch—and there is a large business done in making lumber from them. The lower portion of the basin is partly open prairie, partly covered by forests of trees common to this latitude; oak, chestnut, beech, birch, maple, elm, cottonwood, willow, cedar, &c. Where the soil is not too sandy, wheat, barley, oats, maize, hops, &c., grow well, so that although the climate is comparatively dry, artificial irrigation is not needed.

DESCRIPTION OF FEATURES OF THE VALLEY OF THE WISCONSIN.

Definition of term valley, &c.—By the valley is meant that portion of the basin inclosed within the visible outline of the high banks as seen from the river. On this river the high banks are mainly composed of stratified rocks, but in some instances of high terraces, of drift material. It will be sufficient for the purposes of this report to limit our attention to the portion of the valley from the "Dalles," 20 miles above Portage, to the mouth. The "Dalles" are a narrow gorge formed by a cut through the sandstone rock about five miles in length, and in the narrowest place only 54 feet wide. The effect of this contraction is such as to restrain the floods, so that they are said sometimes to rise 50 feet above low water in the valley above, while the same flood will rise not to exceed 10 feet in the valley below. The valley attains its greatest width in the neighborhood of Portage, where it varies from six to twelve miles. Here the Fox and Wisconsin Valleys are the same, not being separated by any high ground. The valley becomes narrower at Dekorra, eight miles below Portage, not there exceeding a width of three miles. The river washes directly against the sandstone at Dekorra, where this rock does not rise higher than about 60 feet above the water-surface, while the more distant bluffs on the other side rise about 400 feet above the water. From Dekorra down to the mouth, the valley varies in width from one to six miles. The course of the outline of the main bluffs and the valley between them is very direct below Portage. The central line of the valley plotted from near the mouth of Baraboo River runs about S. 47° W. for 20 miles; then S. 15° W. for 8½ miles; then N. 89° W. for 39 miles; S. 47° W. for 10 miles; then S. 71° W. for 10 miles; then S. 49° W. for 7 miles; and then W. for 5 miles to the junction with the Mississippi. The total distance by these courses is 99½ miles. The distance in a straight line between the junction of the Baraboo with the Wisconsin and the junction of the Wisconsin with the Mississippi, is about 90 miles, and the course about S. 67° W. The windings of the main valley, therefore, only increase the direct distance by about 10 per cent.

Slopes and terraces not overflowed at high water.—A large portion of the part included as valley is made up of the foot-slopes of the high banks, which, by the addition of glacial and alluvial deposits, became terraces above the present high-water level of the river, and were not formed by it under existing conditions. The terraces are quite a feature of the valley. Some are composed of modified glacial drift, some of river gravel, and some of fine sand. The river, sometimes, in its course, washes directly against these terraces, which thus continually contribute to the material in the river-bed. At other times broad strips of bottom-lands, only submerged at high water, separate the river from the terraces. These terraces are not continuous along the valley but in detached parts. The larger of these are usually, in their natural state, prairies covered with grass and oak openings. One of them is Sauk Prairie, lying upon the right bank on which Sauk City stands. It is three to five miles wide, and ten miles long. This is one of the most valuable agricultural tracts in the Wisconsin Valley. Such places may furnish good canal location. Ten miles below this, on the left bank, is another such terrace, about 20 feet above the river, two or three miles in width, and six or eight miles in length. Two miles farther down Spring Green Prairie begins on the right bank, elevated 30 to 40 feet above the river, three miles wide and ten miles long. About three miles below, on the left bank, is the English Prairie, one to three miles wide and fourteen miles long. Five or six miles lower down, on the left bank, is another, two miles wide and six or seven miles long, on which is the site of Boscobel. There are many other terraces, generally at a higher level above the river, composed of coarser materials than sand and usually wooded.

Marginal lands and islands overflowed at high water.—All along the river, with but few exceptions, is a strip of low land, commonly called "bottom-land," from three to six or eight feet above low water. These lands are generally highest next to the river, and slope away from it, often terminating in lakes or marshes. Where it is not occupied by lakes, marshes, or sloughs, it is covered by a dense forest of trees and undergrowth. The wooded islands are of the same origin and nature as the bottom-lands, and in many instances they are scarcely to be distinguished or separated; in others they divide the river into several distinct channels, being sometimes as much as three miles long. There is a great number of these channels and islands, the shore-lines of which more than double that which a single channel would have. The width of the flood-plain, that is, the width from one edge of the overflowed lands to the opposite edge, including river and islands, below the Baraboo River, is from three-quarters of a mile to three miles. The course of the flood-plain is nearly that of the valley, and, as given before, is 99½ miles from the Baraboo River to the Mississippi. The distance by the course of the main river between the same points is 113 miles, so that the increase of length, by the windings of the river, over that of the flood plain to which it is confined is less than 15 per cent. This directness of flow is a peculiarity of clear-water streams with sandy beds and high slopes. In muddy streams with low slopes it is not an uncommon thing for the meanderings of the river to be double the length of the flood-plain. There seems to be a relation between these two cases pointing to a common cause and effect. The banks of the muddy stream having more firmness cause the river to scour the bed and preserve a single channel, while the gradual yielding of the concave bends increases the curvature and folds, and thus establishes resistance by increased surface of friction, and by diminishing the slope as the course lengthens. In the case of the sandy stream, the banks yield more readily than the bed, and thus the stream spreads and islands form on dry sand-bars dividing the river into separate parts. This increases the frictional surface and diminishes the velocity until a limit is reached. One accommodates its bed to slope and volume by lengthening, the other by widening. The water of the Wisconsin is very free from sediment, and at ordinary times quite clear, with a tinge of amber color from decaying vegetation.

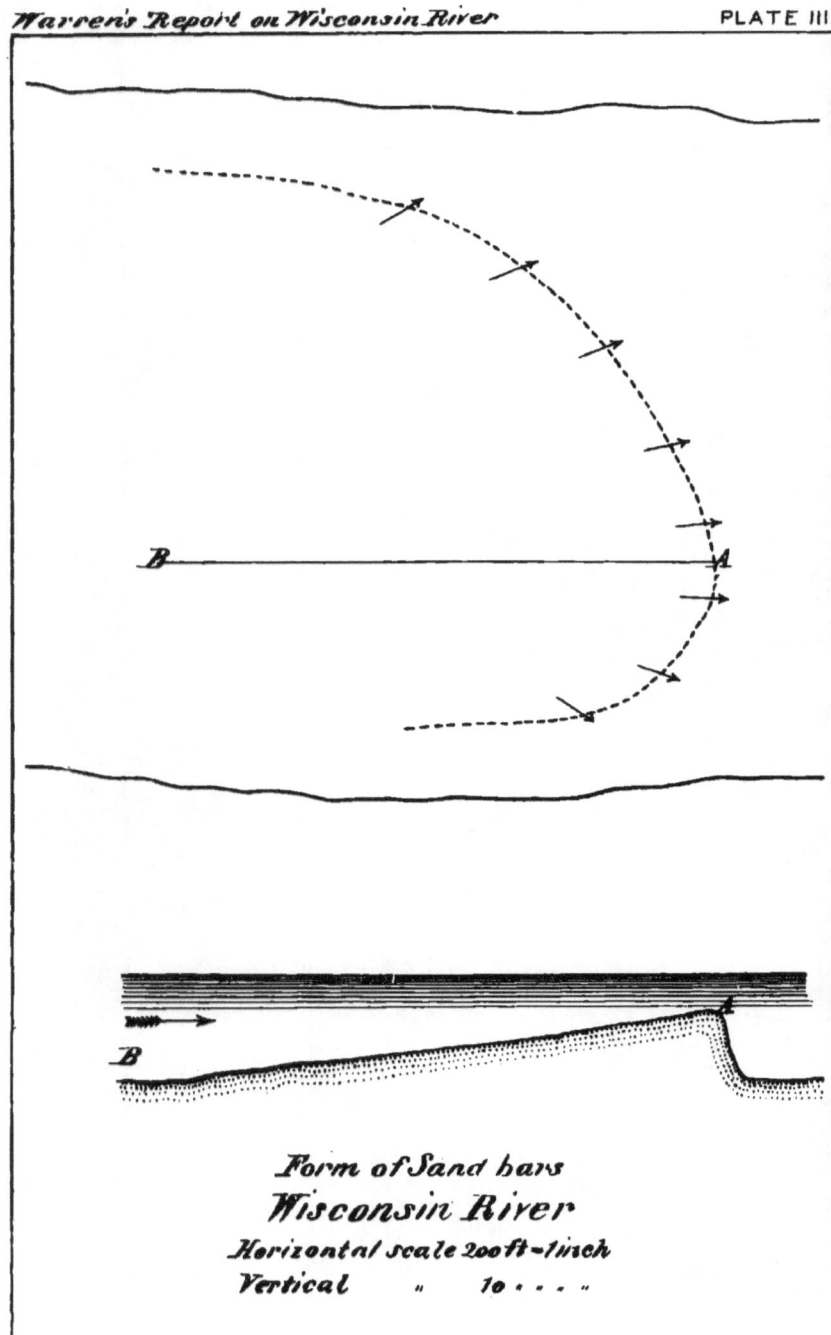

THE RIVER-BED.

Sand-bars.—In the ordinary practical point of view, these form the most important feature of our subject as regards direct effect upon navigation. They were noted by the first explorers in their canoes, and no one treating of the river since has failed to give them prominence. Between Portage and the mouth of the river these shoals are numbered by hundreds. They are composed of grains of almost pure siliceous sand.

Formation of sand-bars.—The sand is moved down stream on or near the bottom. Part of it is deposited in slack or still water where this occurs along the shores, while the greater part is dropped in the still water on the down-stream edge of the bars, in both cases to be again taken up at some future time, under the varying conditions, and moved still further down.

The most important bars are those which are formed by accessions at their lower edges. This kind of bar forms most rapidly where the current is the strongest, and thus the lower edge, which is the shoalest part, is convex down steam, the most advanced part being where the main thread of the stream is flowing. The sand is moved along the gentle slope of the upper side till the crest is reached, when it falls over and stops in the still water below. As the bar thus grows down stream, it becomes more convex, and the water alters its course gradually so as to pass the crest nearly in the direction of the normal lines. The effect of the extension is, therefore, to widen the overflow over the crest (which acts as a weir) and the bar becomes more shoal as it advances, as shown in Figs. 1 and 2, Plate III; the dotted line represents the crest of the bar, and the arrow-heads indicate the direction of the current over it.

The upper surface of the bar slopes toward the water-surface down stream, in a few cases that we measured, at a rate of 0.6 of a foot in a hundred. How far this action would go on in an unchanging condition of the river is not ascertainable, for a rise or fall changes the conditions, gives new courses to the current, and allows the formation of new bars occupying positions different from those of previous ones, but all having the same general law of growth. They are thus superposed on one another at different stages. Some of them have a depth of water just below the crest of ten feet or more, and others of only a few inches. Where one bar thus forms over a previous one, they frequently do not cohere along their lines of junction, and the weight of a man in case of a small bar, or of a descending vessel in case of a larger one, a little way above the crest, is often sufficient to move the upper bar bodily down stream; these bars can thus be passed with considerably more water by a descending than by an ascending boat. When a bar moves down to near a small island, the current is checked so that no more sand passes over the crest. It therefore does not close on to the island unless at flood-stages, when the current passes over the island. The bar, however, often continues to form down the channel on each side of the island. It should be stated, too, that the crest of the moving bar, for the same reason, does not unite with the shore on either side, but leaves a narrow deep place between the bar and the shore, forming what is known as a "pocket" on account of the inability of getting out of the upper end. This upper end of the pocket is closed with a flat sand-shoal, such as forms on the sides of the shores from the material which the current leaves behind in the slack-water, due to the retardation by friction along the banks, or in the still water at the lower ends of islands or points. There is a whole class of bars which forms in this latter way in slack-water along the shores. The effect of these is to narrow the river as it declines to low stages, the action being similar to that of a wing-dam. The moving sand-bars, by spreading and shoaling the water, are the ones that cause the greatest difficulty to navigation.

Action of sand-bars at low water.—All sand-bars have the effect of retarding the flow of the water, and thus producing short stretches of deeper water above them. This effect is well known to the raftsmen, who are warned by finding an unusually good pool at one place that they must meet with a proportionally bad series of bars below. Considering the large slope of the Wisconsin, it may be that this sandy bed is, on the whole, a benefit to natural navigation, such as rafting, by preventing a more rapid flow of the water; this more rapid flow would take place if the river could free itself from sand, and we would probably have a stream composed of pools and shallow rock-rapids. In the extreme low-water stages of the Wisconsin, bars will be very frequently met whose crests cannot be passed with anything drawing more than 15 to 18 inches. There are persons who say that when the river begins to rise the crests of the bars rise with the water-surface, so that there will be no more draught of water over them when the river shall have risen a foot or more along the shore. Although there may be some cases which appear to confirm such statement, I do not think it can be generally true, even if experience does show that every foot of rise in the stream is not realized in an equal increase of depth over the crests of the bars.

In very low stages of long continuance the bars formed at high water become dry; the stream cuts out narrower channels among them, withdrawing itself into a narrower compass, and materially lengthening the water-course while proportionately decreasing its slope. All this tends to improve navigation as long as the low stage lasts, but a rise, by changing the direction of the water, sends it across the low-water channels and fills them up, so that the rise itself, if small and temporary, is regarded as an injury on all the sandy-bed rivers of the Upper Mississippi basin.

Very bad sand-bars in the Mississippi below the Wisconsin.—The sand moving down the Wisconsin and falling into the Mississippi causes the worst of shoals to be formed in the latter stream for several miles below the junction. At the confluence of these two rivers the Wisconsin bars protrude into the Mississippi, narrowing it and forcing its channel across to the high banks of its right or west shore, and acting as a dam. A very considerable diminution of the slope of the Mississippi above is thus produced, and the river is, for many miles, comparatively deep, flowing quietly and lake-like, with excellent channels for navigation. These benefits are obtained at the cost of very bad navigation for many miles below. The Wisconsin sands, moved down by the Mississippi water, form massive bars or shoals, similar in every respect to those on the Wisconsin, over which the water flows with increased velocity and slope. This effect, as just noted in the Mississippi above and below its junction with the Wisconsin, is common to all streams in this region where they receive a tributary, viz, good navigation above this point and bad below. One of the most noted instances of this is the deep Lake Pepin, in the Mississippi above the mouth of the Chippeway River, (a stream the exact counterpart of the Wisconsin,) and the extremely bad shoals extending for miles below.

Very bad sand-bars in the Wisconsin at the junction.—The bars that form in the mouth of the Wisconsin are also very shoal. This river comes from a region of much less summer-rain than the Mississippi. The latter, therefore, has rains and floods when the other has not. The

Wisconsin is often at low stage when the Mississippi is high, and the waters of the former are thus backed up for several miles above its mouth. Special deposits, at such times, take place in the Wisconsin, which its own water is unequal to clearing away when the Mississippi falls again. It is something of a similar feature to this that occurs in the Cumberland at its junction with the Ohio, and which has led to the extensive works of amelioration which have been resorted to there.

Movement of sand-bars down stream.—The movement of the sand-bars down the Wisconsin and the Mississippi is well established. We have observed it in both, sometimes as it progressed, and sometimes afterward by the survey of the same bar in different years. This motion is slow. We have noted it as much as 800 feet a year, but it was only the slowly-moving bars that we could then measure. Generally the same bar cannot be recognized the second year. This is easily understood. Each bar expresses a certain relation between resistances and moving forces. Though this be maintained through considerable changes of volume, it nevertheless will soon happen that the bar will pass into a portion of the river wider, or deeper, or of changing curvature, beyond which its individuality will be lost. This individuality, however, has enough vitality and persistence to cause the forces producing it to repair any artificial change rapidly, and thus to render the operations of dredging or scraping very unsatisfactory.

Sources and quality of the sand.—This sand, disregarding the inequalities of the bars, is spread with much general uniformity over the bed of the Wisconsin, and constitutes the principal ingredient of the bottom-lands and islands. It is derived from sand terraces along its banks, belonging to a former condition of the valley. It originated largely from the breaking up of the sandy rocks of the Silurian formation, through which this river mainly flows, during the glacial period. Its repeated handlings and movings by water have made this sand very clean, and it contains nothing but silex except a little admixture of iron and black magnetite iron-sand. These iron ingredients undergo further oxidation on exposure, and tinge the sand generally of a yellow hue, so that terraces formed of it are frequently named "yellow banks." The accumulation of this iron oxide is sometimes sufficient to partially cement the material together, so that it may be broken, presenting the appearance of a crumbling sandstone. As found in the river this sand is easily moved by waves and currents, and presents the very worst of foundations for any engineering constructions. The presence of the heavy black magnetite sands which are not easily moved, and which are found so difficult of separation from gold-dust in placer-mining, shows that the power which is exerted in moving these sands is considerable, otherwise it would have left this heavy sand behind.

Comparison of Wisconsin sand with other water-moved sands.—The sand of the Wisconsin has been frequently spoken of as easily moved. So far as this is true I think it is due to the force of the water on such a heavy slope, and not to any special nature of the sand. In order to set this matter at rest, I procured sand from several localities on the Wisconsin and the Mississippi and from other places, and had a comparison made of them, as shown in the following tables.

Table of the sizes of sands from different locations.

Location.	Would not pass a sieve 20 mesh to 1 inch.	Passed 20 sieve; would not pass 40.	Passed 40 sieve; would not pass 60.	Passed 60.	Total.	Magnetite, per cent.	Remarks.
Portage, Wis	.0278	.4277	.4313	.1130	.9998	.0005	} Wisconsin River.
Spring Green, Wis	.0400	.3371	.5004	.1220	.9995	Inapp.	
Saint Paul, Minn	.2143	.6561	.1073	.0219	.9996	.0049	
Nininger, Minn	.2920	.5823	.1185	.0074	1.0002	.004	
Beef Slough, Wis	.0811	.5598	.2969	.0596	.9994	.0021	} Mississippi River.
Fountain City, Wis	.0558	.3798	.4341	.1302	.9999	.004	
Rock Island, Ill	.0068	.1101	.4723	.4104	.9996	.0004	
Saybrook Bar, Conn	.0383	.5470	.3600	.0514	.9967	Inapp.	Long Island Sound, mouth of Connecticut River.
Block Island, R. I	.0804	.6218	.2673	.0302	.9997		Ocean beach.
Newport, R. I	.0000	.0553	.5948	.3499	1.0000	Inapp.	Do.

Table of the changes in volume in different sands due to wetting when loose and when packed.

Location.	Loose sand, shrinkage.	Packed sand, shrinkage.	Packed sand, expansion.	Remarks.
Portage, Wis	.0146		.0113	The sand was packed by submitting each half-inch layer in a gill measure, to the pressure equivalent to one-half an atmosphere, for 20 minutes.
Spring Green, Wis	.0107	.0042		
Saint Paul, Minn	.0695		.0262	
Nininger, Minn	.0432		.0160	
Beef Slough, Wis	.0563		.0044	
Fountain City, Wis	.0350	.0150		
Rock Island, Ill	.0296	.0000	.0000	
Saybrook Bar, Conn				
Block Island, R. I	.0788		.0381	
Newport, R. I	.1352		.0439	

Table of specific gravities of sands from different locations.

Location.	Unsifted sand, loose, including voids.	Unsifted sand, packed, including voids.	Unsifted sand, loose, excluding voids.	20 mesh, coarse, loose, excluding voids.	20 fine, 40 coarse, loose, excluding voids.	40 fine, 60 coarse, loose, excluding voids.	60 fine, loose, excluding voids.	Weight of cubic foot, loose and dry.
								Pounds.
Portage, Wis	1.5766	1.7333	2.6392	2.5861	2.6256	2.6392	2.6670	98.66
Spring Green, Wis	1.6376	1.7471	2.6667	2.6391	2.6597	2.6806	2.6806	102.35
Saint Paul, Minn	1.5923	1.7240	2.6397	2.6583	2.6381	2.6378	2.6258	99.51
Nininger, Minn	1.6504	1.7480	2.6184	2.6095	2.6200	2.6220	2.6316	103.15
Beef Slough, Wis	1.5716	1.7080	2.6348	2.6493	2.6427	2.6286	2.6556	98.22
Fountain City, Wis	1.6690	1.6860	2.6400	2.6480	2.6408	2.6396	2.6420	104.31
Rock Island, Ill	1.5579	1.7364	2.6166	2.5946	2.6259	2.6122	2.6259	97.36
Saybrook Bar, Conn*	1.5407		2.6406					96.29
Block Island, R. I	1.4650	1.6860	2.6392	2.6431	2.6392	2.6256	2.6448	91.56
Newport, R. I	1.3895	1.5547	2.6563		2.6500	2.6563	2.6600	86.84

*Quantity too small to make all the determinations. The sand in every case was dry.

Gravel and boulders in river-bed.—In a few cases the bed of the river, where it flows next to gravelly banks, is composed of compact gravel. This is notably the case for a mile or more below Sauk City, and here the river shows the most contracted channel found on the survey. At other places, as just below Dekorra, the gravel forms a broad, shoal bar.

It is probable that works of contraction that will cause the movement of the sands will develop considerably more gravel-deposits than are now visible. Along the bluffs at Merrimac and at some other places bowlders are now seen, and many others would probably be found in deepening channel.

Falling trees and snags.—All along the Wisconsin River the erosion of the bottom-lands at the concave bends undermines the trees and causes them to fall, sometimes into the river and sometimes shoreward. In the latter case the roots often afford protection to the banks against further erosion; in the former, they finally wash out and sometimes stop in the channel forming snags. In very narrow places these inclining trees form serious obstructions to the navigation of boats and occasionally to that of rafts. Scarcely a year passes without some of these trees being cut or dragged away by the rivermen, and once or twice there has been a considerable public expenditure made in this way. (See Chapter III.) I employed a party on this work between Portage and Sauk City in 1869. The removal of these snags with the banks in their natural state is but a temporary remedy, as other trees are continually falling into the stream. As an obstruction, however, they are a matter quite insignificant compared with the shoals.

Bed-rock.—Rock-in-place is found at a few points in the bed of the river. In the vicinity of Dekorra the sandstone which crops out on the left bank forms the river-bed for some distance from the shore. At Muscoda sandstone appears in the bed of the river near the left bank, and four or five miles above, this same rock forms the bottom for a distance of from one-half to three-fourths of a mile.

The piles for the piers of the Muscoda bridge were driven to the rock, which was found at a depth of 20 to 30 feet from the surface of the water. No examination was made at the time of the survey to ascertain the thickness of the sand overlying the rock in the bed of the river. This rock is generally sandstone, easily broken up, and there are many reasons for believing it to have been deeply abraded in former times. Even when reached it would generally furnish a very poor foundation to resist the overflow from any dam constructed in the river-bed.

BRIDGES.

Below Portage City there were at the time of the survey, in 1867, four wagon and three railroad bridges over the Wisconsin. The first is a wagon-bridge at Prairie du Sac; it is a rickety old structure and needs rebuilding. It has two spans, of about 100 feet each, of lattice-truss, combined with a rough arch, and a draw with two openings of 42½ feet each in the clear. The remainder of the bridge is made up of eighteen spans of trussed girder, each from 45 to 60 feet in length; total length of bridge, 1,237 feet. The main spans stand on timber cribs, once filled with stone, with a foundation of piling. The other spans rest upon trestle-work.

The second bridge is at Sauk City. This is a wagon bridge similar to that at Prairie du Sac, though more recently built and in a more substantial manner. There are five spans of lattice truss from 120 to 123 feet each in length. The draw has two openings, each 47 feet wide in the clear. The remainder of the bridge is made up of shorter spans of trussed girder.

The third wagon-bridge is at Muscoda. The superstructure of this bridge is first class. The main bridge consists of two spans, on the Howe-truss plan, 150 feet in length each, and of the draw, which has two openings of 56 feet each. One end of the draw rests upon the sand-rock on the left bank. The remainder of the bridge rests on pile trestle-work, and extends to the terrace on the right bank. The total length of the bridge is 1,683 feet. The piers are cribs of square timber, nicely framed together and filled with stone, resting upon a foundation of piling protected by riprap. The pile trestle-work, above mentioned, is filled with riprap up to low-water mark, so that at that time most of the water is thrown through the three spans near the left bank, giving at all times probably five or six feet of water under the draw.

The fourth wagon-bridge is at Bridgeport. It has two lattice-truss spans, each 160 feet in length, and a draw with one end resting on the right bank. Only one opening of the draw span—54½ feet in the clear—is available for navigation. The remainder of the bridge is on trestle-work.

The three railroad-bridges are similar in their construction, all being built on the Howe truss plan, with spans of about 100 feet in length. The upper bridge has eight spans besides the draw. The total length of the bridge, including trestle-work, is 1,930 feet. The draw-piers make an angle of 64° with the axis of the bridge. The draw-openings, on the line of the bridge, are 53.6 feet and 56.8 feet wide respectively, and on a line perpendicular to the piers about 47 and 50 feet.

The middle bridge has seven spans besides the draw. The draw-piers of this bridge make an angle of 60° with the axis of the bridge. The clear span in each opening, measured on the axis of the bridge, is about 54 feet, and about 50 feet on a line at right angles with the piers.

The lower railroad-bridge has two spans of 125 feet each, one of 95 feet, and the draw in the principal channel, and four spans of 100 feet each over the other channel. These two channels are about one-half a mile apart. The draw-piers of this bridge are perpendicular to the axis of the bridge, with openings of 54.6 feet on the right hand and 55.6 feet on the left.

The piers of the railroad-bridges and of the wagon-bridge at Bridgeport are of stone, resting upon a foundation of piling filled with and protected by riprap. So much riprap has been used in protecting the piers that the steamboat-channel has been contracted to less than 30 feet at low stages, practically filling it up and throwing the main part of the river through other portions of the bridge.

The draws of these bridges are badly located, in most cases being placed near the middle of the river instead of near one shore, where the channel could be directed by artificial means at a much less expense than in the middle of the stream.

Table of widths of draw-openings in the bridges on the Wisconsin River.

Location.	Width at low-water line.		Width at top of piers.		Top of piers above low water.
	Left opening.	Right opening.	Left opening.	Right opening.	
	Feet.	*Feet.*	*Feet.*	*Feet.*	*Feet.*
Prairie du Sac bridge	42.5	42.5	42.5	42.5	....
Sauk City bridge	47.0	47.0	47.0	47.0	....
Upper railroad-bridge	(*)	(*)	53.6	56.8	12.0
Middle railroad-bridge	(*)	(*)	54.5	54.0	12.1
Muscoda bridge	....	56.0	(†)	56.0	....
Lower railroad-bridge	(*)	(?)	55.6	54.6	10.1
Bridgeport bridge	....	No water.	54.5	No water.	....

* Batter of piers unknown.   † End of draw on shore.

HIGH AND LOW WATER STAGES AND THEIR DURATION—ICE.

Observations at the gauges at Portage and at upper and middle railroad-bridges were begun in August, 1867, and, when not interrupted by ice, were continued at those places during 1868 and, excepting at Portage, during 1869, (see diagrams accompanying this report.) The zero is one-half a foot below the low water of 1867. The following tables are summarized from these observations.

Table showing the duration of different stages of water in the Wisconsin River at Portage

Year.	Depth 0–1 foot.	Depth 1 to 2 feet.	Depth 2 to 3 feet.	Depth 3 to 4 feet.	Depth 4 to 5 feet.	Depth 5 to 6 feet.	Depth 6 to 7 feet.	Depth 7 to 8 feet.	Remarks.
	Days.	Days.	Days.	Days.	Days.	Days.	Days.	Days.	
1867	93	58	30	26	19	7			River closed December 9, 1867; opened April 12, 1868; closed December 1, 1868.
1868	104	46	33	36	2				
1869									

Table showing the duration of different stages of water in the Wisconsin River at upper railroad-bridge, begun August 1, 1867.

Year.	Depth 0–1 foot.	Depth 1 to 2 feet.	Depth 2 to 3 feet.	Depth 3 to 4 feet.	Depth 4 to 5 feet.	Depth 5 to 6 feet.	Depth 6 to 7 feet.	Depth 7 to 8 feet.	Remarks.
	Days.	Days.	Days.	Days.	Days.	Days.	Days.	Days.	
1867	36	83	3						River closed December 1, 1867; opened March 28, closed December 3, 1868; opened April 1, closed December 1, 1869.
1868	2	122	36	19	24	25	17	1	
1869		19	28	77	51	41	26	2	

Table showing the duration of different stages of water in the Wisconsin River at lower railroad-bridge, begun August 3, 1867.

Year.	Depth 0–1 foot.	Depth 1 to 2 feet.	Depth 2 to 3 feet.	Depth 3 to 4 feet.	Depth 4 to 5 feet.	Depth 5 to 6 feet.	Depth 6 to 7 feet.	Depth 7 to 8 feet.	Remarks.
	Days.	Days.	Days.	Days.	Days.	Days.	Days.	Days.	
1867	38	82	3						River closed December 3, 1867; opened April 1, closed December 2, 1868; opened March 28, closed December 4, 1869.
1868	74	79	21	18	44	10	4		
1869		35	65	67	45	22	18		

The years 1867 and 1868 were each marked by three rises in the river. These occurred in 1867, on April 20, June 7, and September 28; in 1868, on April 3, June 21, and November 6. These changes of level are common to all the northwestern rivers. The first rise is known as the "ice freshet," and lasts but a few days, usually. The second is known as the "June rise," and upon it the lumbermen chiefly rely to get their logs down the tributaries into the main streams, where they can be rafted. This rise usually occurs in the early part of June, simultaneously with the breaking up of the ice in the lakes, and the melting of the snows at the headwaters, and with rains; it sometimes does not come until much later, and occasionally there is a season when there is no rise at this time. The next usual rise is in the beginning of autumn, from the 20th of September to the middle of October; sometimes, however, it does not occur until near the close of the season.

The year 1869 seems to have been an unusual one on the Wisconsin, from its continued high water. The usual ice freshet came in the early part of April, and was followed by another high water of longer duration on the 28th of April. From this time the river continued to fall until the 15th of June, when it commenced to rise again, and continued to rise until the 30th of the month, when it was between 6 and 7 feet. This was followed by frequent rises, so that the river fell but once below 3 feet on the gauge; from the end of September the river continued to fall until the middle of November, when there was a small rise of a few days' duration.

SLOPE OF WATER-SURFACE.

Our leveling did not touch upon the river-surface oftener than at intervals of 700 to 1,500 feet; the slopes thus obtained vary from 0.095 feet to 3.696 feet per mile. While the survey was in progress, the river rose and fell within the limit of $1\frac{1}{10}$ feet above the low water of 1867, for which changes a correction was made in the levels taken, so as to get the approximate low-water slope for that year. In getting the slope, the distances as measured along the main surveyed line were taken, which may not in all cases correspond with the distance along which the water flowed; the latter could not be well determined, and as there were no deductions based on these slopes, no attempt has been made to correct for this difference in distance as given in the succeeding table. The irregularities of slope as shown by this table convey but a feeble idea of the ever-varying low-water slope corresponding to the irregularities of the bed. In some places the sudden pitch, as at the crests of bars, was visible to the eye, and at others, where a high local velocity from a steep slope was taken up in a pool, the slopes would be found reversed.

In the same section at right angles to the general course the water was found moving in different directions, each part having a slope of its own. The general average throughout the river, when taken for distances of five or six miles, is very uniformly about $1\frac{1}{2}$ feet to the mile, corresponding to the uniformly sandy bed.

The high-water slopes were obtained from the high-water marks of the flood of 1866, the highest known for many years. This slope is very nearly the same as the average low-water slope, and this may therefore be taken as the average slope for all stages.

MISSISSIPPI RIVER AND LAKE MICHIGAN.

Table of measured low-water slopes in the Wisconsin River.

Distance.	Fall.	Fall per mile.	Total fall.	Total distance.	Distance.	Fall.	Fall per mile.	Total fall	Total distance.
Feet.	*Feet.*	*Feet.*	*Feet.*	*Feet.*	*Feet.*	*Feet.*	*Feet.*	*Feet.*	*Feet.*
1,500	.561	1.97	.561	1,500	5,500	2.567	2.46	83.889	280,300
2,800	.967	1.82	1.528	4,300	4,000	1.023	1.35	84.462	284,300
2,000	.036	.095	1.564	6,300	4.300	.921	1.14	85.383	288,600
900	.052	.31	1.616	7,200	6,200	2.143	1.82	87.526	294,200
1,400	.274	1.03	1.890	8,600	4,200	1.688	2.12	89.214	298,400
2,000	.855	2.26	2.745	10,600	6,600	2.152	1.72	91.366	305,000
1,300	.556	2.26	3.301	11,900	5,000	1.454	1.53	92.820	310,000
3,000	1.195	2.10	4.496	14,900	4,700	1.608	1.80	94.428	314,700
1,600	.394	1.22	4.890	16,600	6,100	2.004	1.73	96.432	320,800
1,300	.177	.72	5.067	17,800	5,800	1.303	1.18	97.735	326,600
1,400	.345	1.30	5.412	19,200	4,700	1.354	1.52	99.089	331,300
2,900	.938	1.71	6.350	22,100	7,700	1.426	.98	100.515	339,000
1,100	.173	.83	6.523	23,200	1,500	.395	1.39	100.910	340,500
2,800	.897	1.69	7.420	26,000	3,700	1.010	1.44	101.920	344,200
1,800	.623	1.80	8.043	27,800	7,200	2.828	2.07	104.748	351,400
1,600	.647	2.13	8.690	29,400	4,100	1.420	1.83	106.168	355,500
2,300	.780	1.79	9.470	31,700	5,800	1.591	1.45	107.759	361,300
3,200	1.303	2.15	10.773	34,900	5,000	1.326	1.40	109.085	366,300
7,200	1.989	1.46	12.762	42,100	14,300	3.795	1.40	112.880	380,600
1,900	.813	2.26	13.575	44,000	4,400	1.595	1.91	114.475	385,000
1,300	.678	2.75	14.253	45,300	2,600	.987	2.00	115.462	387,600
3,400	.935	1.45	15.188	48,700	5,400	1.269	1.24	116.731	393,000
5,600	1.024	.96	16.212	54,300	6,300	1.240	1.04	117.971	399,300
700	.490	3.696	16.702	55,000	5,900	1.667	1.49	119.638	405,200
4,000	.696	.92	17.398	59,000	6,200	1.441	1.23	121.079	411,400
2,400	.552	1.21	17.950	61,400	6,400	1.756	1.43	122.835	417,800
6,300	3.053	2.56	21.003	67,700	3,500	.904	1.36	123.739	421,300
5,300	.975	.97	21.973	73,000	4,100	1.299	1.67	125.038	425,400
1,500	.207	.73	22.184	74,500	3,400	.644	1.00	125.682	428,800
2,600	.935	1.90	23.119	77,100	14,700	3.836	1.38	129.518	443,500
5,200	1.913	1.94	25.032	82,300	10,800	2.951	1.44	132.479	454,300
1,600	.210	.69	25.242	83,900	11,900	3.314	1.47	135.783	466,200
3,800	.840	1.17	26.082	87,700	8,800	2.312	1.39	138.155	475,000
3,000	.845	1.48	26.927	90,700	3,400	.710	1.10	138.805	478,400
2,900	.609	1.11	27.536	93,600	6,900	1.834	1.40	140.639	485,300
4,400	1.607	1.93	29.143	98,000	5,466	1.743	1.68	142.382	490,766
3,850	1.064	1.46	30.207	101,850	10,600	2.766	1.38	145.148	501,366
5,050	2.085	2.18	32.292	106,900	5,100	1.383	1.43	146.531	506,466
3,200	.842	1.39	33.134	110,100	3,700	.700	.99	147.231	510,166
2,300	.781	1.79	33.915	112,400	2,700	.476	.93	147.707	512,866
4,400	1.419	1.70	35.334	116,800	4,800	1.816	2.00	149.523	517,666
6,200	1.494	1.27	36.828	123,000	2,800	.879	1.66	150.402	520,466
3,000	.635	1.11	37.463	126,000	1,100	.093	.446	150.500	521,566
4,000	1.006	1.33	38.469	130,000	3,500	.841	1.27	151.341	525,066
2,200	.450	1.08	38.919	132,200	2,100	.621	1.56	151.962	527,166
3,100	.919	1.56	39.838	135,300	2,700	.651	1.27	152.613	529,866
4,000	1.016	1.34	40.854	139,300	2,100	.322	.81	152.935	531,966
1,700	1.047	3.25	41.901	141,000	4,300	1.016	1.25	153.951	536,266
8,100	1.851	1.20	43.752	149,100	2,900	.623	1.13	154.574	539,166
2,950	.618	1.11	44.370	152,050	2,600	.471	.95	155.045	541,766
6,850	2.596	2.00	46.966	158,900	2,500	.694	1.46	155.739	544,266
6,100	2.166	1.87	49.132	165,000	2,700	.602	1.14	156.341	546,966
7,600	2.290	1.59	51.422	172,600	2,700	.598	1.17	156.939	549,666
7,100	1.756	1.30	53.178	179,700	2,650	.392	.78	157.331	552,316
4,000	1.302	1.72	54.480	183,700	2,550	.757	1.41	158.086	554,866
5,700	1.737	1.61	56.217	189,400	4,600	1.168	1.34	159.254	559,466
5,700	1.722	1.59	57.939	195,100	2,600	.656	1.33	159.910	562,066
4,900	1.271	1.37	59.210	200,000	2,700	1.195	2.34	161.105	564,766
1,500	.443	1.56	59.653	201,500	3,000	.571	1.00	161.676	567,766
5,400	.927	.906	60.580	206,900	2,600	.810	1.62	162.486	570,366
5,300	2.177	2.17	62.757	212,200	3,100	1.029	1.75	163.315	573,466
2,000	.313	.826	63.070	214,200	1,800	.130	.38	163.445	575,266
4,900	1.829	1.97	64.899	219,100	4,900	.868	.93	164.313	580,166
11,700	3.871	1.75	68.670	230,800	5,700	1.461	1.35	165.774	585,866
4,700	1.597	1.79	70.267	235,500	5,200	1.597	1.60	167.371	591,066
10,900	2.686	1.30	72.953	246,400	6,300	1.518	1.27	168.889	597,366
4,200	1.218	1.53	74.081	250,600	6,200	2.122	1.81	171.011	603,566
4,100	1.313	1.69	75.394	254,700	2,300	.868	1.99	171.879	605,866
6,600	1.877	1.50	77.271	261,300	6,800	1.562	1.21	173.441	612,666
3,000	1.069	1.88	78.340	264,300	6,000	2.442	2.15	175.883	618,666
5,600	1.700	1.60	80.040	269,900	3,900	.858	1.16	176.741	622,566
4,900	1.272	1.37	81.312	274,800	800	.448	2.95	177.189	623,366

BEND EFFECT.

For the purpose of ascertaining something of the effect of the bends upon the river between Portage and the mouth, we employed Dubuat's formula with the Humphreys and Abbot numerical coefficient, ("Physics and Hydraulics, p. 315,") $h = \frac{v^2 \sin^2 a}{134}$. To get the $\sin^2 a$, a curved line was drawn on the 24 large sheets along the course of deepest water, and tangents were drawn to this, making angles varying from 40° to 15° with each other, as follows: 97 of the tangents thus drawn made angles of 40°, 37 made 35°, 364 made 30°, 124 made 25°, 133 made 20°, and 6 made 15°. The total amount of deflections from the straight line as thus measured amounted to 21,945°; or an equivalent of 60 complete circles. From this data we obtained $h = v^2 \times 1.353$. If we take $v = 1.75$ feet per second, which is as near as we can approximate to the mean low-water velocity, we have $h = 4$ feet. This shows that, as far as we are able to measure the bend effect, the fall of the river's surface from Portage City to the mouth would only be 4 feet less with the same mean velocity if the river were straight. The length of this curved line along which the curvature was measured was about 124.7 miles. The total fall is 178 feet. Subtracting the bend effect from the total fall, we shall have the average slope along this curved line 1.428 feet per mile. If it were practicable, by rectification of the river, to give the low-water channel this development and curvature, we might adopt this slope as the one for the improvement; but it will be seen when we come specially to consider this matter that we shall be unable to make the new low-water channel vary much from the high-water one. The length of the high-water channel from Portage City to the mouth is 115.8 miles.

The curvature is much less at high water, as is shown by the diminished distance, (nearly eight miles,) but we did not specially measure it, as its effect is at most so small.

From what has been said before, in speaking of the limiting bluffs and course of the valley, it will be readily perceived that the course of the river at high water, if rectified, cannot be materially increased in length over what it now is. We are, therefore, within limits when we take the average length of the river at 118 miles, which we do in all our calculations. There is no practical point that I know of in the consideration of the subject that is not independent of any error that might be thus made in a limit so narrow.

VOLUME OF DISCHARGE.

Method of measuring volumes.—The method of gauging the stream was as follows: The float used was a paint-keg about 9 inches high, which was suspended at mid-depth whenever the depth was great enough to admit it. At places the river was so shoal that this small float occupied a very considerable portion of the depth. In computing the discharge given in our tables, we have regarded this measured velocity as the mean velocity of the vertical longitudinal section or prism through which the float moved. The volume from this determination may be from 3 to 5 per cent. too great, but the correction to be applied is uncertain, and there were other sources of irregularity which rendered a very precise determination of volume impossible, although near enough for any practical purposes. The places selected for gauging were such as gave the stream in a single channel, or nearly so, and nearly free from sand-bars. These places are rare at low stages of the river, and only twelve were found suitable during the whole survey. At such places the conditions were all very exceptional.

Table of measured and low-water volumes.—The following table contains the actual measurements made of the volumes of the Wisconsin and its tributaries at and below Portage City, with columns showing the areas drained and the low-water volume adopted for 1867:

[The minus sign after gauge-reading signifies that the river was falling; no sign, that it was on a stand.]

Wisconsin River and tributaries.	Distance from Portage, miles.	Date.	Nearest gauge-reading.	Measured volume, cubic feet, per second.	Area drained, square miles.	Total area drained, square miles.	Adopted low-water volume.
Wisconsin River at Portage, above canal	0	Aug. 24	0.6	3,360	8,200	8,200	2,800
Wisconsin River at Portage, below canal	0	Aug. 24	0.6	3,152	8,200	8,200	
Do	2	Aug. 29	0.55	3,679		8,200	
Duck Creek	3		0.5		100	8,300	
Baraboo River	5	Aug. 31	0.5	431	675	8,975	
Rocky Run	7		0.5		25	9,000	
Wisconsin River at Dekorra	8	Sept. 2	0.5	3,558		9,010	3,175
Merrimac Creek	17		0.5		20	9,030	
Ockee Creek	18		0.5		130	9,160	
Creek at Skinner's	21		0.5		20	9,180	
Wisconsin River at Skinner's Bluff	22	Sept. 10	0.5	3,275		9,180	3,275
Wisconsin River at Sauk City	29	Sept. 17	0.5			9,200	
Creek at Yellow Banks	32				15	9,215	
Honey Creek	34				185	9,400	
Three Mile Creek	38				10	9,410	
Black Earth Creek	41				190	9,600	
Mill Creek	51				120	9,720	
Dodge Valley Creek	52				35	9,755	
Wisconsin River at Lone Rock	54	Oct. 2	1.6	6,557		9,820	
Rush Creek	58				40	9,860	
Otter Creek	59				120	9,980	
Wisconsin River at Middle Railroad Bridge	61	Oct. 4	1.4	5,942		10,080	3,660
Bear Creek	63				80	10,160	
Pine River	66	Oct. 8	1.2	241	270	10,430	
Eagle River	73				100	10,530	
Port Andrew Creek	79				15	10,545	
Wisconsin River at Port Andrew	79	Oct. 18	1.4	5,944		10,555	
Blue River	82	Oct. 19	1.4	220	190	10,745	
Kraps Creek	88	Oct. 23	1.4	70	100	10,845	
Wisconsin River near Boscobel	89	Oct. 23	1.4	6,568		10,865	4,170
Trout Creek	90				20	10,885	
Saunders Creek	91				20	10,905	
Boyd's Creek	95				10	10,915	
Green River	98				70	10,985	
Kickapoo River	100	Oct. 29	1.4	700	730	11,715	
Wisconsin River near Wauzeka	102	Oct. 30	1.4	8,111		11,775	4,750
Warner's Creek	106				20	11,795	
Grand Gris Creek	107				25	11,820	
Bridgeport Creek	111				20	11,840	
Wisconsin River at Bridgeport	112	Nov. 4	1.2	6,977		11,850	4,790
Wisconsin River at mouth	118						

Explanation of the construction of the table.—Special importance attaches to the low-water volume in considering the method of improving the natural channel of the river. This importance is greatest at Portage City, where the volume is less than elsewhere in the portion whose improvement is to be considered. Near this place several measurements were made, which serve as a check upon each other. On the 24th of August a measurement was made above and below the guard-lock of the Portage Canal, into which there was probably flowing at that time 150 cubic feet a second, which amount, added to the volume as measured below, makes a very near agreement with that obtained above. A third measurement, made five days afterward, a little lower down, seems to be from 300 to 500 feet too large when compared with the others. There was a slight rise in the river about this time. The next measurement made was at Dekorra, 8 miles below Portage, after the river had fallen $\frac{1}{10}$ of a foot. It gave the volume 3,558 cubic feet per second. In this intervening distance the Baraboo River, Duck Creek, and Rocky Run had somewhat swelled the volume, to the amount probably of 500 cubic feet per second. This amount, taken from the Dekorra measurement, makes it a little less than that measured just below the guard-lock at Portage; such should be the case, as the river had fallen a little at the gauge at Portage. We cannot make any close comparison, for the amount drawn off by the canal was variable, and its influence at Dekorra could not be exactly measured.

The next measurement was at Skinner's Bluff, at which time the river was at the lowest stage reached in 1867; there the volume was 3,275 cubic feet per second. The small streams coming in between this place and Dekorra drain one hundred and forty square miles, and may have brought in about 50 cubic feet per second, which we will allow, to compensate for the diminished volume of the Baraboo since it was measured. Taking the low-water volume of all tributaries between Skinner's Bluff and Portage at 500 cubic feet per second, and deducting this amount from the lowest water-volume measured at the first-named place, would give us, as the lowest water-volume at Portage, 2,775 cubic feet per second.

This would accord well with our measurement at Portage, by allowing that a fall of two-tenths of a foot diminished the discharge at that point from 250 to 300 cubic feet per second.

We have, therefore, adopted in the table 2,800 cubic feet as the low-water volume of 1867 at Portage. This is as far down the river as we can regard the measured results as checking each other. The volume at Sauk City would seem to indicate even a less volume than above adopted, but at that place, unfortunately, our result was impaired by neglecting a small chute whose capacity was not determined.

The low-water volumes increase as we descend, showing that the additions more than compensate for evaporation, and, consequently, if there is a sufficient amount at Portage there will be enough lower down the river. Still, it is desirable to ascertain the low-water volumes throughout so that we may dispose of the consideration of the question, which may arise, whether, if necessary to continue the canal below Portage, we may not reach a point where the river-volume will admit of its being suitably improved for navigation.

During the progress of the survey below Sauk City the river had begun to rise somewhat, and continued fluctuating, so that the volume measured was greater than the low-water volume. The application of river formulæ to deducing the volumes of discharge is but a rough approximation, in so shallow a stream, with such variable local slopes and obstructed sandy bed. This is specially the case near low water, when a slight rise or fall greatly changes the width and area of the section. Our slope-measurements are generally over considerable distances. The river is one in which the conditions of uniform motion are entirely absent. The only course was to take the Chezy formula $v = B\sqrt{rs}$ in its general form, and, by applying it to all places where our measured volumes were taken, deduce local values for B. This, when done, we assume will enable us to get an approximate result for a rise or fall not exceeding one foot from the stage at which the volume was measured.

The values of B thus obtained are given in the following table. The sectional area used is the mean area of the sections within the space for which the slope was measured.

Locality.	Above low water.	Mean of measurement.						B.
		Volume per sec.	Area.	Wet. per.	r.	v.	Mean slope.	
	Feet.	Cubic feet.						
Portage	0.2	3256	1861	724	2.432	1.749	.000343	61
Dekorra	0.1	3539	2288	697	3.283	1.547	.000229	56
Skinner's Bluff	0.0	3275	2105	1160	1.808	1.691	.000285	60
Upper railroad bridge	1.1	6557	2014	364	5.655	3.185	.000287	79
Middle railroad bridge	0.9	5942	2911	798	3.648	2.041	.000254	68
Port Andrew	0.9	5944	2701	647	4.174	2.201	.000273	65
Boscobel	0.9	6568	3328	972	3.424	1.973	.000275	64
Bridgeport	0.7	6977	4158	1094	3.797	1.698	.000205	61
								64¼

With these values of B at the different localities we deduce the low-water volume at the middle railroad bridge and at Bridgeport. The manner of calculating was as follows: For these small changes of stage the slope was regarded as constant. The wetted perimeter and width the same, and the change in area of section was obtained by multiplying the width by the amount of rise and fall, and adding the product to or subtracting it from the mean sectional area as measured. This method neglects the small amount of decrease and increase of sectional area which results from a decrease or increase in the width, but this was small in amount and not to be obtained with accuracy, and would but little affect the result.

Thus, to find a low-water volume at the middle railroad bridge we multiply 798 by 0.9=718.2, and subtract this amount from 2,911, obtaining 2,192 square feet as our low-water new area of section. The new value of r is 3.648−0.9=2.748. Substituting these quantities in the formula

$$v = 68\sqrt{2.748 \times 0.000254} = 1.796,$$

hence volume will be

$$2,192 \times 1.796 = 3,938 \text{ cubic feet per second.}$$

A similar application of the formula to the case at Bridgeport gives us the low-water volume for 1867, 5,200 cubic feet per second. Both of these low-water volumes appear too large to be in harmony with the low-water volumes actually measured higher up the river, when considering that the low-water volumes must in a measure be proportional to the area drained. We have therefore reduced these amounts about 8 per cent.

Volumes at a stage one foot above the low water of 1867.—For the last five places named in the preceding table for values of B, the Wisconsin was measured when near the stage one foot above low water of 1867.

Applying the Chezy formula with the new constants in the same manner we did when deducing low-water volume, we obtain the volume for the stage one foot above low water, as shown in the first column of the next table.

Locality	Calculated volume per second.	Cubic ft. per second per square mile drained.	Adopted result.
Upper railroad bridge	6,233 cubic feet	.634	6,170
Middle railroad bridge	6,275 cubic feet	.622	6,2·0
Port Andrew	6,142 cubic feet	.582	6,630
Boscobel	6,824 cubic feet	.628	6,825
Bridgeport	8,032 cubic feet	.677	7,435
Mean		.628	

Not feeling sufficient confidence in applying the Chezy formula to get the volumes at the stage one foot above low water to the places above the upper railroad bridge, we have preferred to get it by taking the measured quantity at the upper railroad bridge, and diminished it above in proportion to the diminished area of drainage.

Table of volumes at low water, and at a stage one foot above.

Locality.	Distance from Portage.	Area drained.	Low-water volume, 1867.	Volume 1 foot above.
	Miles.	*Square miles.*		
Portage	0	8,200	2,800	4,950
Dekorra	8	9,010	3,175	5,440
Skinner's Bluff	22	9,180	3,275	5,530
Sauk	29	9,200	3,275	5,530
Upper railroad bridge	54	9,820	3,575	6,170
Middle railroad bridge	61	10,080	3,660	6,280
Port Andrew	79	10,555	3,980	6,630
Boscobel	89	10,865	4,170	6,825
Wauzeka	102	11,775	4,750	7,360
Bridgeport	112	11,850	4,790	7,435

Volumes at Skinner's Bluff for all stages.—For obtaining these volumes we make use of the Humphreys-Abbot formula for mean velocity, (equation 40, page 312, Physics and Hydraulics of the Mississippi.) Knowing by measurement the volume at low water of 1867 at this place, the area of section, hydraulic mean depth and width, we take the Humphreys-Abbot formula for the value of s, (equation 36, page 312,) and deduce the slope which would produce this low-water discharge through this known section. It is 0.0000067420.

Our next step is one of some uncertainty, as we have no other measured volume to deduce the corresponding value of s at this point, which we have selected because we have the sectional area pretty well determined for all stages, which is not the case elsewhere. This natural section being a contracted one for medium and high stages, it is probable that the value of s (which for the low-water discharge is but little more than one-fourth of the average slope) quite rapidly approaches the average as the river rises, and may exceed it in highest stages. We have, however, assumed that the slope in the river at this place reaches the average at a stage 4 feet above low water, and thereafter remains constant up to the highest flood, 10 feet above low water. Between the low-water and the stage four feet above we have assumed that the value of s increases uniformly with each foot of rise. With these values of s and the known dimensions of the section, we deduce the value of v; which, multiplied by the corresponding sectional area, gives the volume. The volume thus determined for the stage one foot above low water is about 170 cubic feet per second less than what we previously obtained by proportioning the volume at the upper railroad bridge to the diminished drainage area at Skinner's Bluff. These determinations of volume, however, have but little practical value in the future discussion of river improvement, being only used in considering the plan of reservoirs at the sources. We have taken the low-water volume as that actually measured at Portage, and the high-water volume is not so important, as we have taken the new high-water channel to be at least equal in dimensions to this natural one; and if this will not accommodate the river the current will increase the sectional area by deepening. We have used these volumes, in discussing improvement by reservoirs at the source, to determine what reservoir-capacity it would be necessary to provide to maintain the natural river at different stages above low water. It is well to remark here that it is highly probable that the low water of 1867 was not an extreme one, and that in such years as 1864 the extreme low-water volume is not greater than 1,500 cubic feet per second at Portage.

Table of volume at Skinner's Bluff for all stages of the river.

Stage of water.	Width.	Area.	Hydraulic mean depth.	v.	Volume.	s.
Low water	1160	2104	1.808	1.556	3275	.000067420
1 foot above	1162	3265	2.798	1.695	5530	.000121815
2 feet above	1164	4427	3.785	2.1544	9540	.000176210
3 feet above	1166	5589	4.766	2.680	14980	.000230605
4 feet above	1168	6751	5.744	3.110	21000	.000285
5 feet above	1170	7913	6.708	3.387	26800	.000285
6 feet above	1172	9075	7.684	3.625	32900	.000285
7 feet above	1174	10237	8.648	3.849	39400	.000285
8 feet above	1176	11399	9.607	4.062	46300	.000285
9 feet above	1178	12561	10.561	4.259	53500	.000285
10 feet above	1180	13723	11.510	4.460	61200	.000285

ANOMALOUS PHYSICAL FEATURES OF THE WISCONSIN AND FOX RIVER BASINS.

The near approach of the streams without uniting.—The example presented by these two streams in their near approach at Portage, thence flowing in opposite directions—forming a channel of communication between distant waters—is one of the most remarkable to be found in the West, although not standing quite alone. It is this feature which gives to the route its most apparent advantage, and that has led to its use and improvement. In regard to its relations to physical geography it is also interesting, for an attempt to account for the relations of present conditions cannot fail to give us a clearer general idea of the structure of the country.

Peculiarities in the course of the Wisconsin.—This stream approaches Portage from the northwest, and, turning to the right, bends through an angle of 130° and pursues a course a little south of west to the Mississippi. After passing Portage it enters a valley between nearly horizontally stratified rocks, once as high at least as 500 feet above the present stream and continuous across its course. The present river could not have eroded this course while the valley of the Fox was open, and this deep valley must date back to some former time, probably preceding the glacial period. Along the valley below Portage the terraces indicate a much higher level of the water than at present, as is the case in most of the northwestern valleys.

Peculiarities in the course of the Upper Fox.—This river approaches Portage from the northeast, and then, turning to the right, doubles back and pursues a northeast course to Lake Winnebago. There is a general absence of high banks in proximity to its course, although low alluvial terraces are common. It winds through broad savannas, with gentle slope and sluggish current, occasionally passing into lakes. Three of these lakes—Mud Lake, Buffalo Lake, and Lake Puckaway—are caused by the deposits of affluents which the main stream has not been able to wash away, indicating plainly that the present Upper Fox did not erode its course, for it has not even the power to keep itself free, and is filling up. Lake Buttes des Morts and Lake Winnebago are depressions which the present tendency is to fill up. The same is true of Lake Poygun, through which the Wolf River passes before joining with the Upper Fox.

1 x x

Lower Fox River.—This is simply an outlet of Lake Winnebago, whose surface is about 170 feet above Lake Michigan.

The waters descend with great rapidity over beds of limestone rock, forming numerous rapids. The valley is here narrow and gorge-like, and the sides are not to exceed 50 feet in elevation above the stream at the head of the Grand Chute.

Analogies between Lake Winnebago Basin and the Lake Winnipeg Basin in British America.—The Upper Fox River, like the Red River of the North, is separated by but low intervening grounds from a stream flowing in an opposite direction, with which there is an interchange of waters in floods. They both have a northerly course. The valleys of these two rivers are alike in being broad and undefined, and the banks but little elevated above the lakes into which they flow.

Both lakes have northeastern outlets, and these outlets are obstructed by rocks, and have rapids and falls. Both lakes have low shores and shallow water on their west sides, and high shores and deep water on their east sides.

Probable former extent of Lake Winnebago.—The low, level alluvial terrace bordering the west side of Lake Winnebago has a very considerable extent. I asked Capt. W. S. Edwards, chief engineer of the Green Bay and Mississippi Canal Company, to get for me the outline of the high ground bordering it, which he did. It is presented on the accompanying diagram, Plate IV, the outline shaded by horizontal ruling.

If this alluvial deposit was made in an ancient lake, this diagram gives an approximate outline of it.

Hypotheses consistent with above-noted conditions.—We have only to suppose that all the waters of Lake Winnebago Basin (including that of the Upper Fox) formerly drained to the Wisconsin River; that a slow change of level in this region elevated the southwestern part and depressed the northeastern part till a large lake was formed, which finally overflowed, forming the course of the Lower Fox. This explains the present doubling back in the course of the Upper Fox and tributaries, and it accounts for the close relation and yet opposite courses of the Fox and Wisconsin Rivers. As the level changed, the erosion at the outlet could not keep pace with it, and so prevent a lake forming, because a granite ridge lies near the surface, between the Wisconsin and Buffalo Lake. When the Lower Fox outlet formed, the loose material covering the rocks rapidly gave way, and lowered the lake-level down to the rock, which now keeps it at its present level. The period of this change I regard as post-glacial, because this alluvial terrace is free from glacial drift; which it could not have been if formed before in a region like this, surrounded with glacial-drift deposit.

A similar change in the course of the Red River of the North is treated of by me in my report on the Minnesota River. (See Annual Report of Chief of Engineers, United States Army, for 1875.) There the case of the Fox and Wisconsin Rivers, along with some others, is referred to; all regarded as indicating a relative elevation at the south and depression at the north, which has affected the continent.

Previous attempts at generalization in regard to the Fox River.—The only previous attempt at generalization of natural features along the Fox River, that I know of, was made by Mr. John B. Pettival, civil engineer, in report dated January, 1838, Doc. No. 102, H. of R., War Department, Twenty-fifth Congress, third session. He says, "That the succession of different valleys from Fort Winnebago (near Portage) to Grand Chute (Lower Fox River) was filled with water, making a chain of lakes. The barrier of the Grand Chute being thrown open by some

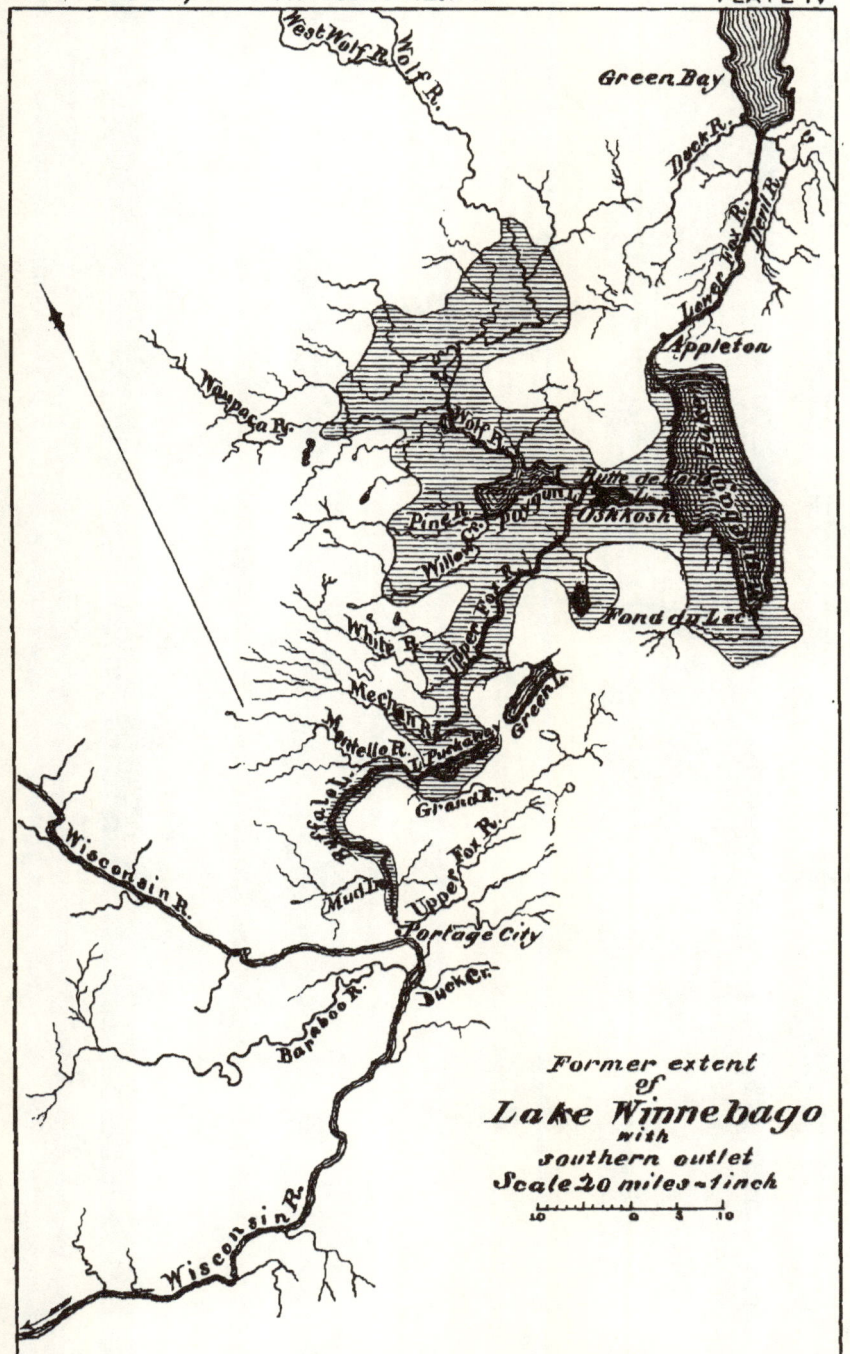

convulsion of nature, the more shallow lakes were drained, and the deeper remained sheets of water, and the river a meandering drain." He does not seem to have perceived the effect of such tributaries as the Montello River in causing some of these lakes, but his generalization, like mine, involves an idea of the recent formation of the outlet by the Lower Fox.

PROBABLE CHANGE IN THE DRAINAGE OF THE FOUR LAKES NEAR MADISON.

A like change of direction appears to have taken place in the drainage of the four lakes near Madison, Wis. These lakes now drain to Rock River, but formerly, I think, to the Wisconsin, along the valley of Black Earth Creek. The summit between this creek and the largest of the lakes, Mendota, is but little elevated above the lake, and is composed of the same pure white sand as is found along the margin of this lake, whence it was probably brought by the former southwestern outlet. So little is this upper portion of Black Earth Creek separated from the lake, that some years ago the building of a road and washings from cultivated land caused so much submergence of fields near the summit, by raising the level of a small lake about two feet, that the owners of this land cut a ditch to drain the waters the other way into Lake Mendota. This led to an injunction by a mill-owner lower down on Black Earth Creek, and after much litigation the final decision of the higher court was that the digging of this ditch must be stopped, and the obstruction which caused the overflow removed.

Explained by the same hypothesis, which is applicable to an extensive area.—The natural change in the direction of the drainage here can be explained by the same hypothesis made for the change of flow of the Upper Fox River, both of which are a part of a wide-spread exhibition of similar changes. It was first announced by me at the Chicago meeting of the American Association for the Advancement of Science, in 1868. It was also reported by me in outline in the Annual Report of the Chief of Engineers of that year.

CHAPTER V.

METHODS OF IMPROVING NAVIGATION.

PRELIMINARY REMARKS—Relations of the United States and corporate companies to the improvement—Difficulties heretofore not appreciated—Influences controlling former plans and operations—Future plans based on the new data—IMPROVEMENT BY CANALIZATION, REGULATION, OR RECTIFICATION—Hydraulic formulæ applicable—The Humphreys-Abbot formulæ adopted—Small practical bend effect—Width of rectified river at low water for different depths—Slopes for uniform depths and different widths—Requirements which must be met in works of construction for river rectification, so as to produce a desired navigable depth at low water—Conditions demanded at high water—How to begin the work discussed and illustrated by example—Section of regulated river for both high-water and low-water channels—Further protection against scour—ESTIMATE OF MONEY AND TIME REQUIRED FOR CANALIZING IMPRACTICABLE—Conclusions to be drawn from the success attending similar works on the Garonne—Example in the case of the Ohio River—Conclusion with regard to canalization of the Wisconsin River—IMPROVEMENT BY MEANS OF RESERVOIRS AT THE SOURCES—Doubtful possibility of success—Immense cost—Great danger attending such works—METHOD OF IMPROVEMENT BY DAMS AND LOCKS—Difficult and expensive, if not impracticable—Never recommended, and special data not obtained for depth to bed-rock—IMPROVEMENT OF NAVIGATION BY MEANS OF CANAL ALONG THE VALLEY—Data for making location—Provisional location—Objectionable features, and alternative to avoid them—CHARACTER OF CANAL AND LOCKS—Description of locks, with general directions as to construction—Bills of lock-material—Estimated cost of a lock—Summary of cost of all the lift-locks ; of all the guard-locks—Cost of feed-weirs connected with lock; of feed-pipes ; of culverts ; of waste-weirs; of bridges ; of walling ; of riprap; of grubbing; of clearing land ; of engineering ; the work to be done in two years—Grand total cost—Additional cost for five feet draught—Annual expense of superintendence and repairs.

PRELIMINARY REMARKS.

So far in this report I have been presenting the data and experience obtained from our surveys, and from the study of previous operations, to enable us to meet the question of further improvement. I have been uninfluenced by committal to any plan to which consistency might induce me to adhere beyond its intrinsic merits, and I have resisted the pressure for an immediate plan of operations until I could fully make up my mind as to what was practicable by elaborating our data, and thus be enabled to make a proper comparison of the Wisconsin with other rivers where improvements had been made, and be enabled to arrive at conclusions that should not be delusive.

Relations of the United States and corporate companies to the improvement.—At the time the work was under my charge as an officer of the Government, the route from Green Bay to the Wisconsin was under the control of a private corporation, and my investigations after 1866 were designed to furnish a plan for improving only the portion of the route along the Wisconsin. It is to that part I shall confine my attention in this chapter.

Difficulties heretofore not appreciated.—I have felt much concern in trying to find a suitable plan of improvement which should be acceptable to the public, for, from the first attempts at improvement till now, as shown in Chapter III, the difficulties have not been fully presented, if even understood. Year after year responsible persons charged with providing plans for making this improvement have regarded it as an easy matter, and in a few instances have applied with confidence such insufficient means as have been productive of no permanent benefit, and in fact so insignificant in themselves as to make it a matter of research to find out where they were employed.

Influences controlling former plans and operations.—The neglect to attempt more improvement of the Wisconsin arose mainly from the fact that in its natural condition the navigation was so much better than on the Fox Rivers, that its improvement was not so pressing a need as that of the other portions of the route. The United States law made the grant of lands proportional to the length of the route, excluding the distance along the Wisconsin; and although the legislature of the State required one-sixth of the proceeds of the sale of the lands to be applied to the Wisconsin, only a small proportion was actually thus used, as the whole was inadequate to the improvement of the route along the Upper and Lower Fox and the Portage Canal. To sustain the course adopted it is probable the managers represented the Wisconsin River in the best light they could, and their wisdom cannot be questioned in improving the Fox Rivers first. When the improvement passed to the control of a company it was not expected to improve the Wisconsin, and its financial necessities always inclined it to put the best face possible on this river's navigability. This influence was also brought to bear upon me early in these investigations, to induce me to attempt something at once; and while distrusting our ability to adequately improve the river itself, I suggested a method of operating by which it could be tested without great expense, and at the same time enable us to find out whether we could use the bed of the river for making crossings from a canal on one bank to one upon the other, should the canal plan be adopted.

Congress, in 1871, completed the legislation which enabled this trial to be made, but the control of the work had passed out of my hands. The engineer in charge consulted me on the subject, and proposed to follow my plan; but from the shoalness of the river he met with obstacles which compelled a modification of it, and the success which attended his work in 1871 led him to believe that any required depth could be produced by improvements in the river-bed, and my plan was abandoned. That these promises of success were illusory is apparent from subsequent experience, which has much reduced them, and I believe they must grow smaller until they are of no value.

Future plans based on the new data.—By means of the data obtained from our surveys and investigations, as exhibited by the descriptions and tables in the preceding chapter, and on the maps and diagrams there enumerated, we are enabled to take up the consideration of the improvement with facts at our command not possessed by any one before; and, if properly weighed and put together, they should give us more reliable conclusions. These we will now attempt to reach.

IMPROVEMENT BY CANALIZATION, REGULATION, OR RECTIFICATION OF RIVER.

The first method which has always suggested itself is that of contracting the water-way, thus increasing the depth, and, by confining the action of the water to a narrow channel, enable it to keep this free from sand or other deposit. This method, when most fully and successfully applied, consists in giving new banks to the river adapted to the end sought, and is known technically as the canalization, regulation, or rectification of the river.

Hydraulic formulæ applicable.—The flow of the water in such regulated rivers is subjected to uniformity of conditions that admit of the application of mathematical formulæ, and by these we may approximately proportion the dimensions of our proposed channel to meet the object in view, which, in our case, is to obtain a continuous proper navigable depth at low water. In the proposed problem of rectifying the Wisconsin, the survey has determined the volume and the slope which the present river has and which the improved river should have, and we may, therefore, give it the width which will maintain the desired depth. We have no way of determining this width except by mathematical formulæ or by expensive experiment, and we should, at least, do the best we can with the former as a preliminary step toward the latter.

There are two specially important requirements of a rectified river. It must be small enough to give the required depth at low water, and large enough to carry off the volumes of the floods, and arrangements must be made to secure the return of the stream to the low-water channel provided for the river on its reaching the low-water stage.

Here we have, in seeking for the required dimensions by the formula, to depend entirely upon the correctness of the factor in it representing the *slope*, the most subtle of all the quantities entering it. Disregarding for the present the effect which the new currents of the improved channel may have in destroying the permanency of the river-bed, we see that if the formula used should not properly express the effect of resistances—that is, for instance, that only part of the slope used according to the formula was found actually necessary to carry off the water in the regulated channel—then the unemployed portion of the slope would give increased velocity and diminish the depth. On the other hand, should it be found in practice that more slope than is called for by the formula at high water would be needed to move the floods, we would subject our new banks to inundations and dangerous injury. Large margins for safety in both directions must be allowed for, at best, in locating our new banks, but we are much less liable to error from the inapplicability of the formula than we are from the scour in the river-bed destroying that uniformity which it is our aim to give, and on which the applicability of all river formulæ is based. This question of maintaining the uniformity of the bed will be specially considered after we have determined by the formula the proportions the new bed should have.

The Humphreys and Abbot formulæ adopted.—As there are peculiarities under which all formulæ for rivers have been deduced, it is generally expected that the engineer in adopting one shall establish its applicability to his case. Feeling every confidence in the deductions of the "Physics and Hydraulics of the Mississippi," by Humphreys and Abbot, I yet endeavored to find confirmation of them on the Wisconsin, and especially on the Mississippi, near Saint Paul, where the conditions of the two rivers were similar, but under circumstances more favorable to the latter place for making nice observations. The natural difficulties at both places proved very great; so that while everything we could fairly conclude sustained the Humphreys and Abbot formulæ, these conclusions were not in themselves based upon observations that could add much weight to the evidence of their truth given by the authors of these formulæ, except as to the parabolic law of change of velocity from surface to bottom, which was fully sustained.

There was no part of the Wisconsin River, as we surveyed it, where uniform conditions existed through a distance that gave a possibility of measuring the corresponding slope, so no direct test of formulæ involving slope could be made. I have, therefore, taken several sections where the volume was known, and have applied the Humphreys and Abbot formulæ, to see what slope the river would have if it were straight and uniformly of that section. Irregular as these sections are, they furnish a much nearer approach to uniformity than the average of the iver. In a majority of cases the river is so divided and spread out

MISSISSIPPI RIVER AND LAKE MICHIGAN.

that, as far as the application of formulæ is proper, it is divided into several streams. The result is given in the following table:

Table of measurements on the Wisconsin, with column of calculated slope, deduced by application of the Humphreys-Abbot formulæ, showing the slope the river would have if uniformly of that volume and section; dimensions in feet.

Miles below Portage.	Discharge in cubic feet per second.	Area of section.	Mean velocity.	Width.	Wetted perimeter.	Hydraulic mean depth.	Slope.	Slope in feet per mile.	Height of surface above low water, 1867.	Remarks.
		a.	*v.*	*w.*	*p.*	*r.*	*s.*			
0.0	3360	1954	1.72	361	363	5.4	.00003586	0.189	0.25	
0.0	2765	1652	1.673	589	590	2.8	.00012020	0.63	0.12	Part of river.
2.0	3679	1762	2.088	353	356	4.96	.00008914	0.47	0.05	
7.0	3558	1280	2.780	270	287	4.46	.00031360	1.655	0.1	
8.0	3558	2030	1.743	759	761	2.66	.00016250	0.858	0.1	
15.5	3558	2730	1.303	300	316	9.1	.00000443	0.0234	0.1	
18.3	3275	2334	1.375	2040	2043	1.14	.00032470	1.714	0.0	
19.7	3275	2034	1.610	380	387	5.35	.00002898	0.153	0.0	
20.1	3275	2680	1.222	1900	1902	1.41	.00017040	0.900	0.0	
22	3275	1554	2.108	439	441	3.50	.00018770	0.981	0.0	
29	3210	1037	3.075	332	333	3.1	.00102500	5.41	0.0	Part of river.
29	3210	1554	2.065	390	392	3.964	.00013550	0.715	0.0	Mean of six sections.
57	6557	2059	3.184	364	367	5.75	.00033420	1.765	1.1	
61	5942	3241	1.833	912	915	3.5	.00003293	0.174	0.9	
75	5944	1896	3.135	480	485	3.95	.00068480	3.615	0.7	
79	5944	2701	2.201	642	645	4.0	.00015490	0.8178	0.7	
87	6568	2354	2.79	513	515	4.57	.00031970	1.687	0.65	
95	6568	3518	1.867	1700	1703	2.07	.00035680	1.884	0.75	
101	8111	2886	2.81	325	328	8.8	.00008476	0.4475	0.9	
110	2912	1493	1.944	501	504	2.96	.00019703	1.0403	0.7	River in two channels.
110	4065	2280	1.778	635	638	3.5	.00009327	0.4925	0.7	Do.

The sections of the river used in the preceding table were taken, except in two cases, where the water-way was not divided by islands, and in most of the cases the conditions were more than usually favorable to the flow of the water, thus requiring but little slope of surface. In one-third, however, the slope required, as deduced by the formula, exceeds the average slope of the river, and there is no doubt that if the sections taken represented a true average of the sections of the river, the above ratio of one-third would be increased. There can be no direct comparison of these deduced slopes with the measured slopes, because these latter are averages over considerable distances, while the calculated slopes are only for the immediate section. We can conclude, however, that the formula contains the proper factors for giving us the slope under all these fluctuating conditions, since it gives low slopes and high slopes, as nearly as we can ascertain, under the same conditions in which they exist in nature. Having, then, the volume at low water and the total descent of the river fixed, we may reasonably depend, to a very considerable extent, upon the formulæ of Humphreys and Abbot for determining the mean velocity and corresponding width and depth of the river when canalized or reduced to uniform conditions.

Small practical bend effect.—In regulating the stream it would, of course, be best to preserve the natural curves when not too sharp for navigation, and even increase them, when allowable, for the purpose of diminishing the slope by developing the low-water length of the stream, and also to consume a portion of the effect of this slope in overcoming the resistances of the bends. Unfortunately, we can do but little in this way, because the width required for the stream at high water, in some places, will occupy the whole available portion of the valley, and we could not allow the low-water channel to differ materially in direction from that at high water, without subjecting it to be filled up. The bend-effect, in consuming the slope in the rectified river, will be too small, as shown in the preceding chapter, to make it worth while to attempt to account for it before applying the deductions of the formula.

Width of rectified river at low water for different depths.—The original formula adopted to determine the width of the regulated river of required uniform depth is given on page 312 of the "Physics and Hydraulics of the Mississippi," No. 38, as follows:

$$p + W = \frac{195\, a\, s^{\frac{1}{2}}}{[0.93\, v + 0.167\, b^{\frac{1}{2}}\, v^{\frac{3}{2}}]^2}$$

In this W is the width; p the wetted perimeter; a the area of section; s the slope; v the mean velocity; $b = \dfrac{1.69}{(r + 1.5)^{\frac{1}{2}}}$. In this value of b, r is the mean radius.

The draught of water it is proposed to have at low water is in the neighborhood of four feet, with side slopes of 1 upon 2, thus:

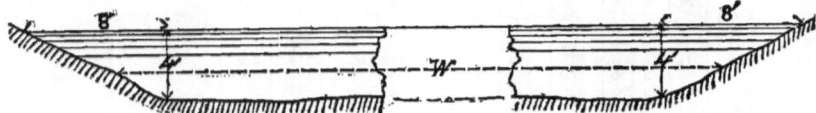

In this case $p = 1.01\, W$, nearly; W being the mean width, r will be the depth nearly; $r\, W$ will be equal to a; $v = \dfrac{Q}{r\, W}$, Q being the volume of water discharged in cubic feet per second.

Substituting these values in the equation for $p + W$, and solving with reference to $W^{\frac{1}{2}}$, we have—

$$W^{\frac{1}{2}} = \frac{0.1305\, b^{\frac{1}{2}}\, Q^{\frac{1}{2}}}{2\, r} \pm \sqrt{\frac{0.7267\, Q}{r^{3/2}} + \left(\frac{0.1305\, b^{\frac{1}{2}}\, Q^{\frac{1}{2}}}{2\, r}\right)^2}$$

In this value of $W^{\frac{1}{2}}$, where the river is as small even as the Wisconsin at low water, the second term under the radical sign may be omitted, and in large streams both terms containing b may be neglected. Letting $Q = 2,800$ cubic feet per second, as at low water at Portage, and with r varying from 2 to 10 feet, we obtain the following table:

Table of widths and velocities corresponding to different depths.

Depth in feet.	Width in feet.	Area of section in sq. feet.	Mean velocity, feet per second.	Probable maximum velocity.	Remarks.
2	790	1,580	1.772	2.215	Maximum velocity was obtained by increasing the mean one-fourth.
3	430	1,290	2.170	2.713	
4	275	1,100	2.545	3.183	
5	195	975	2.872	3.591	
6	149	894	3.131	3.914	
7	118	826	3.389	4.236	
8	96	768	3.646	4.557	
9	80	720	3.888	4.860	
10	68	680	4.117	5.146	

Slopes for uniform depths and different widths.—The mathematical condition under which the above table has been calculated requires uniformity of volume, slope, and cross-section, giving, with an unchanging bed, uniform widths and depths. But as uniformity of depth is the essential for navigation, and as uniformity of bed and slope cannot be always, if ever, attained, we may, where the river-bed is unyielding, narrow the width and increase the slope and velocity, and still secure the depth there, thus allowing us to somewhat widen the bed and diminish the slope at other places. How far this may be done is shown by the succeeding table giving slopes and velocities for a volume of 2,800 cubic feet per second, so as to secure a uniform depth of four feet, with width corresponding to the different mean velocities up to 5.81, and maximum velocity of 7.25 feet per second, or five miles an hour, which should not be exceeded. This value of s is deduced by means of the Humphreys and Abbot formula, (36,) page 312, "Physics and Hydraulics of the Mississippi," as follows:

$$s = \left[\frac{(p + W)\ (0.93\ v + 0.167\ b^{\frac{1}{2}}\ v^{\frac{1}{2}})^2}{195\ a} \right]^2$$

in which the quantities are the same as noted in this report when giving the formula for $p + W$.

Table of slopes and velocities for a uniform volume of 2,800 cubic feet and uniform depth of four feet, with corresponding widths.

Widths.	Area.	Velocity.		Slopes.		Remarks.
		Mean.	Max.	Sine of.	Feet per mile.	
275	1,100	2.545	3.181	.000298	1.57	
225	900	3.111	3.888	.000648	3.42	
175	700	4.000	5.000	.001735	9.16	
150	600	4.666	5.833	.003068	16.199	
135	540	5.185	6.471	.004641	24.50	
120	480	5.810	7.250	.007214	38.00	5 miles an hour.

If, now, our problem were to construct a channel which should carry all the low-water volume of the Wisconsin River by keeping near the natural slope of the valley, and give a channel navigable for vessels drawing four feet, and without locks, we know by consulting the last two tables the limiting hydraulic conditions which belong to it.

It must be noted by those investigating and considering this question of improving navigation, that the above tables exhibit the best results we have any reason to hope for, at low-water, near Portage, even with the greatest success in works of construction. Everything that can be measured is given as the result of actual measurements. The depths and corresponding widths, with this volume and this slope, are given in the first table; the variations the slope may have with uniform depths and different widths, in the second table—both from the best of formulæ for uniform motion of river-water. I have not extended the presentation to any but the low-water volume at Portage. For any other low-water volume at points lower down on the river, the widths for different depths and the same slope can be obtained near enough for our purposes by the simple proportion: as the volume used in the table (2,800 cubic feet per second) is to the other volume, so will the corresponding widths be for the same depth, &c.

The manner in which it should be practically executed will next be considered. It is a subject which may be further considered in a variety of ways, and I take the order which to my mind appears most natural. Others must make allowance for individual idiosyncrasies in endeavoring to follow me.

I will continue to confine myself at first to the conditions of low water, for this is so common in the Wisconsin, and exists during so much of the year when navigation is most needed, that any plan which is inadequate to ordinary low water must be given up.

Requirements which must be met in works of construction for river-rectification so as to produce a desired navigable depth at low water.

1st. The water-way must be so contracted as to give the required depth at low water.

2d. The works for improving the low-water navigation must not make navigation dangerous at higher stages, must provide for the proper discharge of the water in flood-stages, and must secure the return of the river, at the recurrence of low water, to the channel provided for it.

3d. The velocity of the water at all stages must be so small as not to injuriously scour or disturb the material forming the bed of the improved river.

By the data and calculations already given it is clear that a greater navigable depth than 4 feet is mechanically impossible, without reducing the average width to less than 275 feet, and this is as narrow as, if not narrower than, the interests of steamboat navigation will admit. To make this contraction we must prepare entirely new banks for the river. Experience on the Rhine, Garonne, and elsewhere in Europe has shown that straight lines for the banks should be avoided as much as possible, and that the banks should be composed of curves imperceptibly passing from one curve to another as the curvature increases or decreases, or reverses. One reason for this is that such disposition of the banks confines the action of the current to one side of the river—the hollow of the bend—and renders protection to the other side less needed. In rivers thus regulated the most difficult places for navigation occur at the points where the curve reverses, as the river passes from one side of the valley to the other. Sharp bends should be avoided, because they render reversals of curvature more frequent, are more difficult to navigate, and they produce more violent action of the current in scouring the banks and bed. No fixed rules can be laid down for determining the curvature, but it must depend upon the judgment at each place in meeting the conditions presented. In all the bends the low-water channel is naturally located on the concave side, so that on that side the high and low water bank can be the same; but in passing from a bend on one side of the valley to the other the low-water channel must cross the high-water one, and here great difficulty will be found in freeing the low-water channel after a flood-stage. (See diagram.)

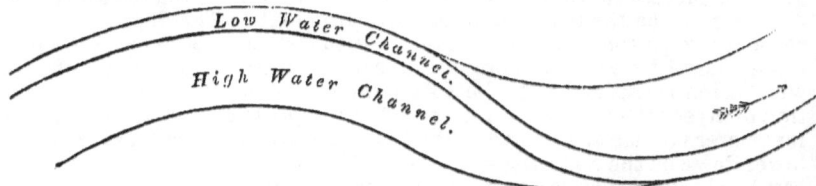

Conditions demanded at high water.—Suspending the further consideration of the low-water channel, we will take up that of the proper width for the high-water channel. It is evident that to secure a low-water channel we must control the course of the river at high water so that it shall not at that time cut out a new route for the water, and leave our low-water channel buried beneath the sand as the water falls. I have taken the high-water width for the first thirty miles to be that of the natural river at Skinner's Bluff, about 1,200 feet. It will have to be greater below that point, and if it should be necessary to have it wider at and above Skinner's Bluff, the natural river will in places require widening. The reason why it may require widening is that we cannot leave the present high-water bed unchanged, but must put in it such constructions as shall make it of a permanent form, sloping toward the low-water channel. The diminution of section which these works will cause it is expected will be compensated by the diminished resistances to the flow of water in the river of uniform width and sectional area, and by the increased depth by scour at shoal places. Such results have attended river rectification elsewhere. The high-water volume at Skinner's Bluff is 61,200 cubic feet per second; the mean radius, 11.5 feet; mean velocity, 4.46 feet per second; and maximum velocity about 6 feet per second, or four miles an hour. We may expect the occasional occurrence of higher velocities at places, especially in ice-gorges. The bend-effect of the improved channel for high water will be about the same as for the natural river.

How to begin the work discussed and illustrated by examples.—The natural course of procedure, I believe, is to lay out and build new high-water banks first. This is somewhat the way it was begun in very remote times by the riparians on the Garonne, for the simple purpose of securing an increase of cultivable area; and when, in the present century, it was taken up by the government of France and pursued systematically, the contraction of the natural river had in places gone far enough to enable the new low-water banks to be begun so as to improve the low-water navigation. The increase of cultivable-land area was still an object to be accomplished, the benefit to navigation being made subsidiary to it. Great care was taken not to raise the high-water banks so fast as to prevent the free admission of the silt-laden water to the low lands, sloughs, and marshes, farther from the river. The water was allowed to course slowly through these parts, and they were covered with cross-lines of stakes and wattlings, and willow-plantings to catch the suspended sediment, and by its deposit raise the level. So slow was this course of building up, that from 1833, at which time the work was begun under M. Baumgarten, down to 1848, as reported by him, only thirty-four miles of the river had been rectified.

This slow rate of progress would be fatal to any similar attempt to improve the Wisconsin. Moreover, it could not be applied because of the lack of silt in the waters of the Wisconsin, which could be used to build up the low lands, and, besides, the value of the land, even if gained, would not at all equal the expense. Furthermore, it may be noted here that the contraction to which the low-water channel of the Garonne was subjected is not half what will be needed to obtain the navigable depth at low water which the navigation of the Wisconsin demands.

Being then, from the conditions of our problem, unable to realize the benefits of the slow process on the Garonne, nor to stand the delays incident thereto even if we could, we are at liberty to construct the new high-water banks artificially at once, at such rate as is allowed by the means at our command and by the time required for the natural forces to adapt themselves and the included river-bed to the new banks given to the river. Experience has abundantly shown, in our western rivers of alluvial beds, that if by artificial works we deprive the natural bed of a portion of its area, the next high flood enlarges it again by removing an equivalent amount from some other place. My own investigations of the effect of the building of the high bridge-piers and embankment, by Mr. Sewall, at Saint Paul, and the building of the levees on the left bank by that city, show that an equivalent was taken from the opposite or right bank and the included island. This law of compensation is also noted by Mr. T. C. Clarke, in his valuable report on the construction of the Quincy bridge. It has also been noted as shown by the works at several other bridges, as at the bridge at Saint Joseph, on the Missouri River, and its auxiliary works, and at the Mississippi bridge at the town of Louisiana, Mo. Many other places might be named, but the most marked instance is that at Saint Louis, where the Mississippi, with its great volume, has been confined to a channel but little exceeding 1,500 feet in width by works on both sides and in the bed, and where the compensation is made by excavating the bed at high water.

It must be noted in all these examples that the contraction was over but a small space along the river, and that, therefore, it was but comparatively a small work for the river to free itself, and that the sand removed was soon so distributed as to find a resting-place where it would not produce noticeable effect.

From the foregoing facts and remarks we see that in building the new high-water banks for the Wisconsin, which we should do at low water, we shall compel it to enlarge the included space by deepening, and we must not build more between any two floods than the next one can safely clear, and from which it can remove the effects of the contraction. Suppose, for instance, we build five miles of new high-water bank during one spell of low-water, and that the succeeding flood be a full one. The enlargement by the moving of sand would begin all along our contracted position, but would not at first be felt in any but the upper portions, which would supply the lower with sand as fast as it was removed. The enlargement would, therefore, pass from the upper part downward, and in the mean time the water must be raised in the lower portion in proportion to the contraction, as long as it exists. It is obvious, then, that this will set a rate to our progress, for if we build too much we will have to raise, for each extension, the lower end of the new bank very high to prevent its being overflowed and destroyed before the enlargement by the flood will have been completed, and, if it stands, it will be much higher than the finally regulated river will need, and we shall have gained time only at great expenditure. It must not be left out of sight, in this connection, that the extreme floods in the Wisconsin are very rare. The ordinary flood only rises six feet above low water; the high ones ten feet. One has a volume of 29,390 cubic feet per second, the other of 61,200 cubic feet per second. Our river-work for high-water banks may, then, not be fully tested for several years, and it seems to me that it would be very hazardous to build more than ten miles at a time until that part should have been fully tested and adjusted. Analogous experience is frequently had in covered ways for streams in passing through cities, which, having capacity suited to ordinary rains, are burst up and destroyed with much attendant destruction during heavy rain-falls. Great as are the difficulties of constructing the new high-water banks for the Wisconsin, which must be continuous on one side, at least, all the way—often in the present river-bed and sometimes on both sides—let us suppose that by perseverance and ample means they are finally overcome, and that we have a section of high-water banks for ten miles along the river, at the upper end of the proposed improvement, done, and its capability to maintain itself established. Such bank might be built as an ordinary levee of proportions suited to its height, and thoroughly revetted on the river-side with riprap-stone or stone and brush. As soon as this ten miles was done the formation of the low-water channel might be begun along it, regard being had to the fact that the effect on this portion, regulated for high water, would be to lower the bed through it

Warren's Report on Wisconsin River — PLATE I

and a short distance above, and to raise it below, so that, as the extension downward was made, the lower part of the first division of ten miles would be lowered too.

Section of regulated river for both high-water and low-water channels.—We design the area of the section at high water, for the first thirty miles, to be nearly that of the natural high-water section at Skinner's Bluff; for the present canal should be brought down to at least below the mouth of the Baraboo River, and below that there is no considerable affluent for this distance. At this bluff the width is 1,180 feet, with average depth of 11.5 feet, giving an area of 13,570 square feet. Our proposed low-water banks should be 2 to 3 feet higher than low water, so that with the least accession of water we could get a depth of 6 feet for navigation. (The low-water banks prepared for the Garonne are 9 feet above low water, which is three times that proposed here—that river rises 30 feet above its low water, so that the ratio of the high and low water bed is the same.) Above that height the rising river should be allowed to spread rapidly, merely giving the bed such a gentle slope as will direct the water back to the low-water channel when the river falls. This influence of the high-water bed will be most needed at places where the low-water channel is crossing from the high-water bank on one side to that on the other. I would propose to give shape to the high-water bed at these places by driving rows of sheet-piles transversely to the stream between the high and low water banks, and cutting them off evenly, so as to give a slope rising about 2 feet between the low-water channel and the main bank. These piles would need to be bolted together by stringers, and protected by riprap down to a depth of from 3 to 10 feet from their tops on both sides, but particularly on the lower side. The distances of these rows apart and the depth to which the piles must be driven, will vary with circumstances. The low-water banks themselves, when not forming a part of the high-water banks, must be strongly built of suitable material, such as heavy piles and riprap. Special precaution must be taken on the Wisconsin on account of the ice, which alone would have greatly modified the work on the Garonne had it had the same climate. The same thing must be said about the aid to be secured from the growth of willows—for while they grow in both climates, it is at a much slower rate on the Wisconsin than on the Lower Mississippi, to which latter climate that of the Garonne may be compared.

The length of the new low-water-bank line would on one side equal the length of the river, and there would have to be two banks at all the places where the low-water channel crossed from one high-water bank to the other. The tie-lines between the low and high water banks would have to be at such distances apart as to keep the river in its place, and would be closer in proportion as there was greater force in the water to make a channel elsewhere. On the Garonne these distances apart varied from 130 feet to 325 feet.

The two diagrams, Plate V, represent sections of the river improved in the manner here considered. No. 1 is at a place where the low-water channel is in the middle of a crossing-place between the high-water banks with tie-banks between the low and high water banks, as already described. No. 2 is a section where the low-water channel is in a bend on one side of the high-water channel, the centrifugal force tending to keep the water in the concave bend. I have in this illustration given the tie-line the same rise from the low-water bank to the high-water bank opposite the bend, as in the previous case, thus making the slope of the high-water bed toward the low-water channel only half the amount allowed in the first case. Notwithstanding the effect of the centrifugal force to keep the deep water in the hollow of the bend, it is sometimes insufficient to prevent the low-water channel in rivers with sandy beds from cutting across the points so that tie-lines of piles would be needed there.

Both these sections have a high-water area slightly in excess of that we have considered in our calculation, but are thus taken to avoid fractional dimensions.

Further protection against scour.—With all these works thoroughly constructed and protected so as to withstand the floods, others must be used, if necessary, to prevent any local scour at high stages at points where the current from any temporary or local cause may become unusually strong, for the material thus scoured would be deposited at some other place, and probably in our low-water channel at the crossings. Whether such action could be prevented or not could only be proved by a long and expensive trial of some systematic plan like that I have presented. Experience on the Ganges Canal shows that inadmissible scour took place on sandy beds where the slope exceeded 15 inches per mile. This great canal has a volume of 6,750 cubic feet per second. It is 140 feet wide and 10 feet deep.*

ESTIMATE OF MONEY AND TIME REQUIRED FOR CANALIZING THE RIVER IMPRACTICABLE.

In preparing the method of canalizing the Wisconsin now presented, so as to endeavor to meet the requirements of the case, it was with a view to making an estimate of the cost and the amount of time required. What appeared as the most certain and direct in its results has been chosen. Notwithstanding this, the uncertainties as to length of time required, owing to the varying conditions of the river from year to year, prevent any reliable estimate of expense being made, even if the method itself was sure of success. The weight of experience elsewhere, however, (of which I shall next give some example,) is against the probable success of the method.

---

* Colonel Cantley, of the Royal Engineers, in his report upon the Ganges Canal works, vol. 1, page 199, quotes Major Baker, of the Royal Engineers, as follows : "The slope of 18 inches per mile was under any circumstances excessive, but its maintenance on a good soil aided by artificial expedients, was by no means considered to be an impossibility or likely to involve expenses of an extraordinary nature ; this could by no means be the case when the water was brought in direct connection with sand, or with lighter varieties of soil, that the admixture of sand leads to, nor could the design for the masonry works be considered appropriate to a channel where, although the surface of the bed might exhibit some trifling signs of durability, every foot in depth of excavation for laying in the foundations, plunged deeper and deeper into sandy soil. The necessities for modification not only in width of water-way, but in depth and solidity of foundations became under this evil apparent; and, although, from the advanced state of some of the works in the neighborhood of Mungloor and Liburheri, a redisposition of slope became somewhat inconvenient, as necessitating an alteration of work which had already been done, I determined at once to remodel the whole of the slope on a reduction of 3 inches to the mile from the Roorkee Bridge to Nanoon."

[To follow paragraph 2, p. 100, Warren's Report on Fox and Wisconsin Rivers.]

To give now, in brief, what must be done to secure a reliable and sufficient low-water navigable depth in the Wisconsin River by contraction, we will take the river to have an average width of 1,200 feet at high water, and reduce it to a width of 300 feet at low water. The low-water tie-banks must average a distance apart not greater than 300 feet, and, taking both sides of the low-water channel, an average length of 900 feet; that is, they will be equivalent in combined length to three times the length of the river. The lengths of the low-water banks must considerably exceed that of a single bank the whole length, and this excess, together with the protections to the high-water banks, will require fully as much work as another low-water bank the length of the river. The contracting and protecting works will then reach, in combined length, five times the length of the river, or 590 miles, or 3,115,200 linear feet. No matter how built, this would cost in the neighborhood of $3 per foot, or $9,345,600. In this estimate the cost of building the high-water banks, which I have proposed in order to limit the field of operations for maintaining a low-water channel, is not included. It is not a necessity, but if it is not built the extent of the low-water controlling works must be largely increased above what I have allowed. The progress of the work itself must be slow and tentative, waiting for the conforming changes of the river.

[To follow paragraph 3, p. 100, Warren's Report on Fox and Wisconsin Rivers.]

The danger that results from too much scour is, that deep holes form in some parts, with corresponding deposits in others, thus destroying the uniformity of the channel. At places of deposit the low-water channel will become engorged, the surface of the water will be raised and spread over our low-water controlling works, so that the navigable depth will be lost. The average slope is 18 inches per mile, and to get a depth of 4 feet we must have a velocity (calculated) at not less than 3 miles an hour. To get 10 feet of depth on this slope, we must have a maximum velocity (calculated) not less than 5 miles an hour, and this depth at least is what we know the Wisconsin has at high water, on an average slope of 18 inches per mile. Whatever the velocity may be, (whether more or less than 5 miles an hour,) we have the authority of Major Baker, of the Royal Engineers, as quoted below from Colonel Cautley's report on the Ganges Canal, that the maintenance of a sandy bed on this slope, with this depth, was impossible, without involving extraordinary expense, which, rather than undertake, he modified many miles of canal already constructed, so as to reduce the slope to 15 inches per mile. Even this reduced slope has since been found too great. On the Wisconsin, then, we shall have to succeed in maintaining a sandy bed where the volume reaches 60,000 cubic feet per second, when, with the same kind of bed and a volume not to exceed 7,000 cubic feet a second, the English engineers abandoned the attempt, although having at their command the cheap labor of the millions of people of the Indian Empire.

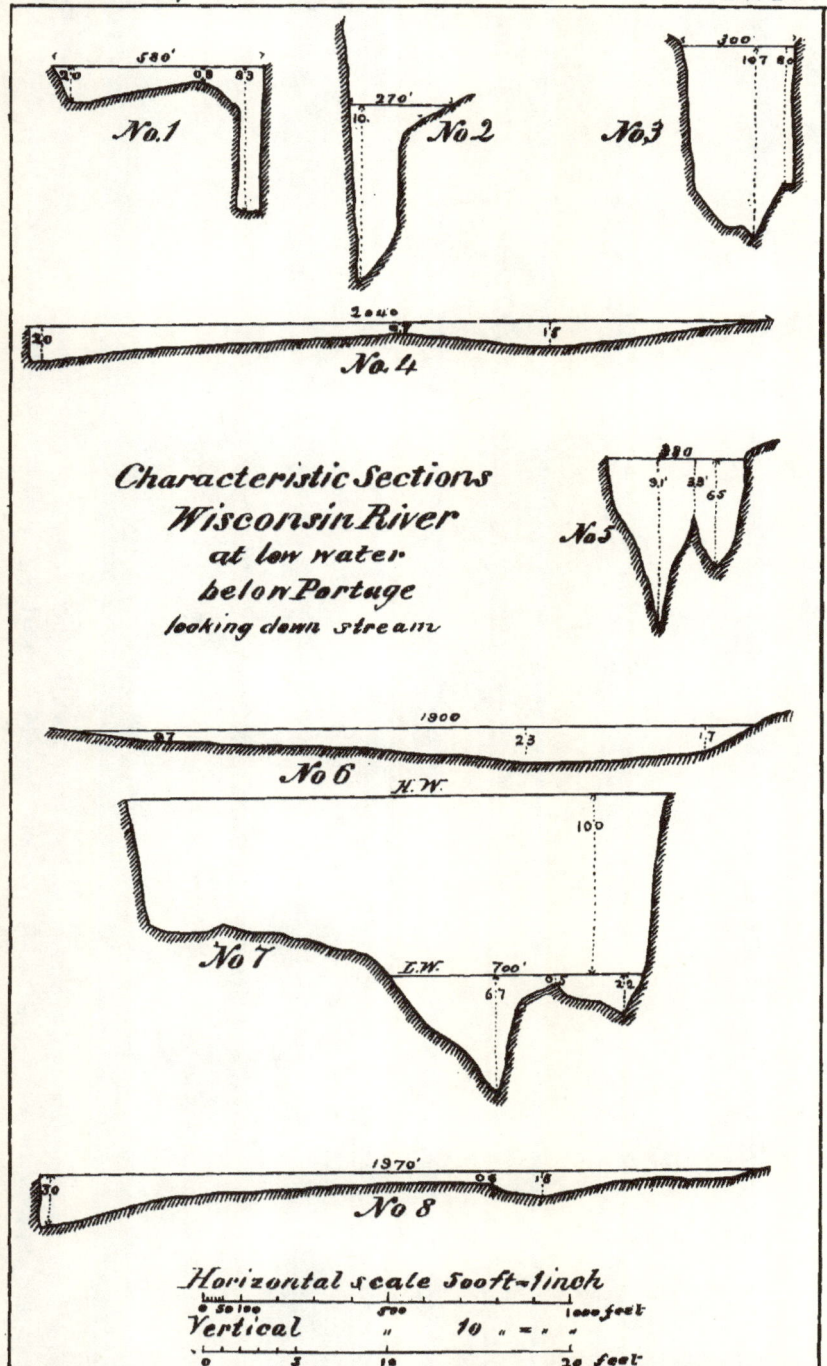

Warren's Report on Wisconsin River — PLATE VII

Wisconsin River
34 miles below Portage
Survey of 1867
Broken lines indicate crests of
under water bars
Course of deepest water for
navigation (20 inches)
shown by full line

Horey Cr.

Sand Terrace

remains of old dam

Magnesian Limestone

Scale of Miles
0   1/8   1/4   1/2   1

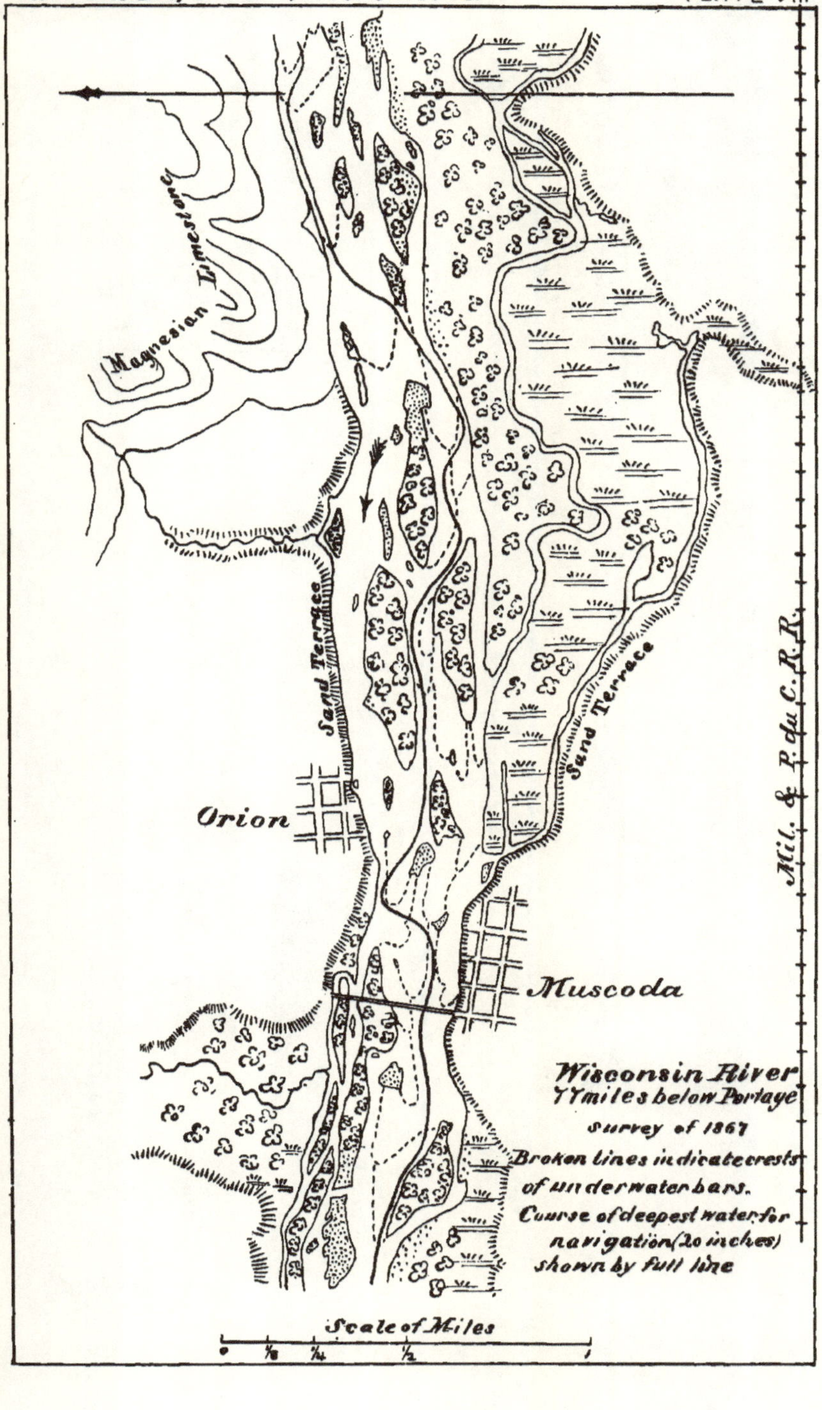
Magnesian Limestone
Sand Terrace
Sand Terrace
Orion
Muscoda
Mil. & P. du C. R.R.
Wisconsin River
77 miles below Portage
survey of 1867
Broken lines indicate crests of underwater bars.
Course of deepest water for navigation (20 inches) shown by full line
Scale of Miles
0
1/8
1/4
1/2
1

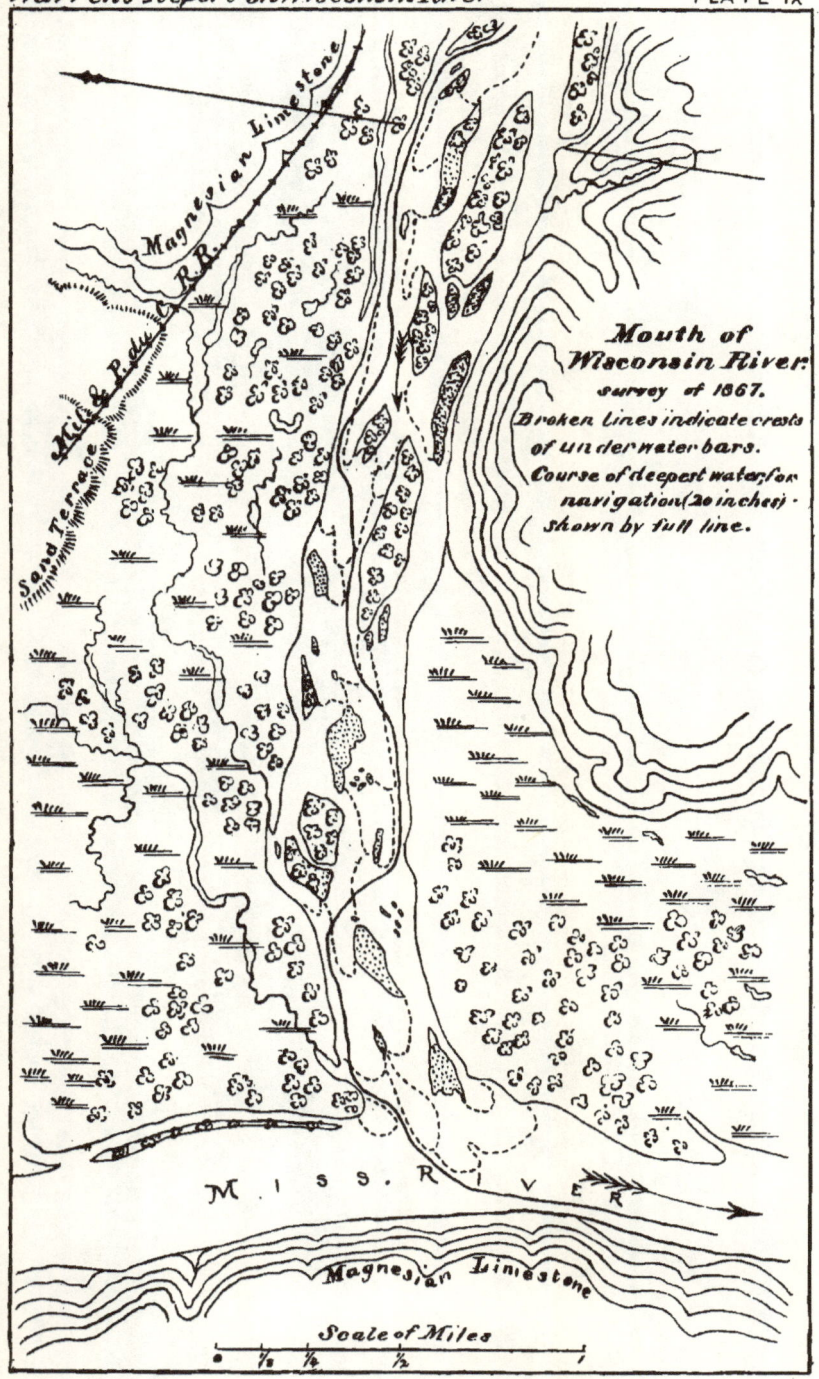

To enable the difficulties to be more easily comprehended, I have added to the text, Plate VI, showing a few characteristic low-water sections, enumerated below:

Section number.	Miles below Portage.	Area.	Hydraulic mean depth.	Remarks.
1	5	1460	2.51	At sand-bar just above Baraboo River.
2	7	1280	4.74	
3	14½	2730	9.1	
4	17¼	2334	1.14	Across a sand-bar.
5	18½	2034	5.35	
6	19¾	2680	1.41	Across a bar.
7	23	1722	2.43	
8	34	2207	1.12	Bar just above Honey Creek.

Also Plate VII, showing about 3 miles of river near Honey Creek.
Plate VIII, showing about 3 miles of river near Muscoda.
Plate IX, showing about 3 miles of river at the mouth.
The maps attached to this report show the whole river at the same scale.

Conclusions to be drawn from the success attending similar works on the Garonne.—I have cited heretofore the case of the rectification of the Garonne, because it is one of the most successful examples of this method of improvement. Col. W. E. Merrill, United States Engineers, in his report to the mayor of Saint Louis, in 1869, in regard to the rectification of the Mississippi River at that point, says of it, after such investigation of European examples as his opportunities enabled him to make:

From all that I have been able to gather from every source accessible to me, the river Garonne is the most complete specimen of a regulated river to be found anywhere, representing the most successful modern practice. The study of this river is particularly valuable, as the *Annales (des Ponts et Chaussées)* record its condition prior to the commencement of any work of improvement, and give a very complete history of the works and their effects from 1833, when they were begun, to 1848, when a large portion of the river (34 miles) had been successfully treated.*

The full account of this work on the Garonne up to 1848 is given in the memoir of M. Baumgarten, of which Colonel Merrill presents an abstract. This work I have consulted and had completely translated. The following comparison of the Wisconsin with the Garonne is presented, supposing the Wisconsin rectified to give a depth of four feet at low water.

* Mayor's message to the city council of the city of Saint Louis, April session, 1869 and other documents; also report of Col. W. E. Merrill, major engineers and brevet colonel United States Army, on the harbor of Saint Louis, which includes the report of Capt. T. J. Cram, United States topographical engineers, made in 1844, and the report of Robert E. Lee, lieutenant engineers, made in 1837-'38, on the harbor of Saint Louis. Printed for the city council, Saint Louis; George Knapp & Co., book and job printers and binders, 1869, p. 21.

Table of corresponding data for the Garonne River and for the Wisconsin, rectified to four feet depth at low water.

	Garonne.	Wisconsin.
Average slope per mile	1.4 feet	1.5 feet.
Volume at ordinary low water	5,800 cubic feet	2,800 cubic feet per second.
Volume at high water	272,700 cubic feet	61,200 cubic feet per second.
Rise from low to high water	*30 feet	10 feet.
Low-water width of rectified river	570 feet	275 feet.
High-water width of rectified river	1,950 feet	1,180 feet.
Draught at extreme low water	Depth not given, navigation suspended.	4 feet wanted.

* A flood of 33.6 feet is mentioned by M. Baumgarten, but the corresponding volume is not given.

To which may be added that the navigation of the natural river, in both cases, is suspended at low water; that the rate of progress of the rectification of the Garonne, after being regularly undertaken, was only three miles per annum; that the land reclaimed on the Garonne was of great value, while it would be of very little value on the Wisconsin; that there is little ice on the Garonne and a good deal on the Wisconsin.

From this comparison we see that with such rectification of the Wisconsin as the Garonne has received we should not get at low water more than 2½ feet. (See preceding table of calculated depths and widths.)

Example in the case of the Ohio River.—The works of improvement on this river, in the space between Pittsburgh and Cincinnati, 466 miles, are one of the best illustrations of improving low-water navigation, by contracting the flow of the water, which we have in this country. This part of the Ohio resembles the Garonne much more than the Wisconsin does. The range between high and low water is 35.6 feet at Pittsburgh, and 62.5 feet at Cincinnati. The coarse material forming the bed is due to the heavy scouring and transporting power of the large high-water volumes and depths. The works on the Ohio, however, have not been as systematic as in the case of the Garonne.

The public improvement of this river was considered by our Government as early, at least, as 1808; for on April 4 of that year, the Secretary of the Treasury, Albert Gallatin, referred to it in a report which was printed by the Senate. In 1822, a Board of Engineers, consisting of General S. Bernard and Maj. J. G. Totten, reported upon its improvement.* This report compares the river to the Loire, and recommends low dikes to contract the stream. They say:

> The expedient proposed above for obtaining a greater draught of water in the Ohio is the only one we can devise. The Board, however, are not sanguine in their belief in its efficacy in all cases requiring remedy. It is certain that by the dikes and narrow passages the water may be deepened at any required point, but it is to be feared that in some places, at least, the locality may be such that the very materials thus carried off by the rapid waters may be deposited when they become comparatively quiescent, in such a way as soon to form a new bar below. The very great importance of the object in view, and the want of any other resource will nevertheless justify an experiment.

The first experimental dam to overcome a sand-bar was begun by Maj. S. H. Long, at Henderson Island, two hundred miles below Louisville, and completed in 1825. It was 402 yards long, and cost $3,778.93. It was considered a success. The improvement of the river, by removing snags, was begun about the same time. The building of wing-dams at various places was begun and continued from this time annu-

---

* Transmitted by President Monroe to House of Representatives, January 22, 1823, and printed without plans by Gales & Seaton, 1823, as document No. 35.

ally up to 1839; the appropriations varied from $3,000 to $100,000, but a great deal of the money was expended in removing snags and rocks. The reports of the engineers in regard to the effect of the dams were generally hopeful as to what would ultimately be the result when the work should be thoroughly completed. But little benefit, however, was rendered, and the breaking and giving way of dams were continually reported. In 1839, Capt. John Sanders submitted an estimate of $312,000 for building dams in 1840.

In 1842, Capt. G. W. Hughes, United States Topographical Engineers, in an inspection report, (Doc. No. 50, H. R. War Department, Twenty-seventh Congress, 3d session,) gives a less hopeful account of the improvement. The usual appropriations were made for the years 1842, '43, '44. In 1843, Captain Sanders estimated that it would take $2,000,000 to complete the improvement so as to give a minimum draught of 2 feet between Pittsburgh and Louisville. No further appropriations were made till 1853, when $90,000 was appropriated for the Cumberland dam. This dam well illustrates the difficulty of making a dam across the sandy bed of a river.

Mr. Charles A. Fuller, agent for the Ohio, examined in 1853 the dams previously built and needing repairs, besides localities requiring several additional ones. Wherever they were built on sandy bed, as was the case with those below Louisville, they were in a very dilapidated condition. The Board of Topographical Engineers, Kearney, Long, and Turnbull, in the annual report for 1854, advised the abandonment of all the dams in the parts where the bed is sandy, except the Cumberland dam, and thought the only resource to be dredging at the shoals after every high water. The gap in the Cumberland dam was filled. In 1854, Agent Fuller partially repaired the dams in the Upper Ohio, using 800 tons of stone. I believe no further work was done till 1867, when appropriations were again made and have since been continued.

In 1866, Mr. W. Milnor Roberts commenced an examination and survey of the Ohio, and subsequently prepared a plan for a thorough improvement. We have his final report printed as H. Ex. Doc., No. 72, Forty-first Congress, third session, dated April 21, 1870—a book of 198 pages. Besides preparing the report, Mr. Roberts had charge of the improvement by dams in 1867, 1868, and 1869.

He says:

Former reports to the Department, made some years ago by different engineers and later by myself, concur in the opinion that the system heretofore adopted, to improve the navigation by means of riprap dams, although beneficent and useful, especially at low-water navigation, does not meet the requirements understood as belonging to the radical improvement of the whole river. * * All that has been promised or hoped for under this system, without the aid of artificial reservoirs, has been an increase of 12 to 18 inches in the natural river.

Mr. Roberts then gives a very thorough and exhaustive discussion of the other plans of improvement, and concludes that low dams requiring locks of about 6 feet lift furnish the best means of obtaining the desired navigation. He does not consider a continuous canal along the river, because it would not be an improvement of the Ohio; but it may be stated here that it would be a very expensive work on account of the difficulty of crossing the numerous large affluents.

Col. W. E. Merrill, United States Engineers, who has since had charge of the Ohio improvement, substantially agrees with Mr. Roberts as to the necessity for dams and locks, proposing, however, to adopt movable dams instead of fixed ones. This is a method which Colonel Merrill has thoroughly studied as practiced in recent years on some of the rivers of France, and he thinks it well adapted to the Upper Ohio. (See Annual Report of Chief of Engineers for 1874, pp. 406–410.)

Mr. Roberts, I believe, did no work at the Cumberland dam, in which a new break occurred after it was repaired by Agent C. A. Fuller. Colonel Merrill repaired this break only to have a new one occur at a succeeding high water. Such has been the experience in many dams on beds of movable material.

Conclusion with regard to canalization of the Wisconsin.—It seems to me, from what I have presented in this chapter, that no satisfactory improvement on the Wisconsin can be made by any system of contraction and rectification.

IMPROVEMENT BY MEANS OF RESERVOIRS AT THE SOURCES.

A project of this kind was suggested by Mr. C. D. Westbrook, jr., in his report to the Fox and Wisconsin Improvement Company, in December, 1854. He says:

> That remedy is the location of a dam upon the upper waters of the Wisconsin, where the public lands have not as yet been brought into market, that will create a reservoir in which a sufficient quantity may be stored from the high water in the spring of the year, to maintain an equable supply throughout the dry season sufficient for the uninterrupted navigation of the stream. Assuming this extra supply to average 100,000 cubic feet per minute, (1,666 cubic feet per second,) a dam 20 feet in height, flowing one hundred square miles, would be sufficient. The cost of such a structure, in comparison with its results, would be too insignificant to require an estimate of its probable amount, until it is determined by actual survey.

Mr. Westbrook assumes—

> That a sufficient supply of water for steamboat-navigation is had in this stream, except from the middle of August to the latter part of October, when, in common with all western rivers, so many interruptions exist, precisely at the period when their services are most needed, that they fail to meet the wants of the growing West, and are superseded to a considerable extend by railroad transportation.

Allowing the period Mr. Westbrook provides for to be 75 days, it would take 10,800,000,000 cubic feet.

Doubtful possibility of success.—The data obtained from our survey in 1867 enable us to deal with this question with more definiteness. If good navigation is to be made on this river, it must be by some plan which shall not fail in ordinary low water years at least, and so we may take the year 1867, which was observed, as a test case. The available depth at low water of that year was certainly not greater than 1½ feet. There were 93 days that year when the water was between low water and 1 foot above; 58 days when it was between 1 foot and 2 feet above low water; and 30 days when it was between 2 and 3 feet above low water. Allowing that each foot of rise would give us an additional foot of navigable depth, (too favorable a supposition,) and supposing that, during the periods just named, only half the quantity which we have determined to be necessary to raise the natural river each foot on the gauge would be required after a partial rectification, (also a favorable supposition,) we see that at Skinner's Bluff, according to the table in Chapter IV of volumes, at all stages at Skinner's Bluff, we would require—

 5,850 cubic feet per second, for 93 days;
 3,130 cubic feet per second, for 58 days;
 1,130 cubic feet per second, for 30 days;

or a total amount at Skinner's Bluff, to secure 4½ feet draught on the most favorable supposition, of 65,619,936,000 cubic feet. But if the natural river were improved in this manner, we should be compelled to supply double the above amount near the mouth.

[To follow paragraph 3, p. 104, Warren's Report on Fox and Wisconsin Rivers.]

It has been shown that it is a kind of improvement that, wherever applied and however successful, requires an amount of time that the present wants of transportation cannot wait for in this case; that it has never succeeded to any extent in this country nor in any other where the river's slope was as great as 18 inches per mile, the most favorable case being that of the Garonne River, in the south of France, having this slope, but whose navigation is suspended at low water; that works of contraction in the sandy bed of the Ohio River have been tried and given up by successive engineers; and, lastly, that the attempt to give requisite stability to such sandy beds, tried in India under the most favorable circumstances of engineering skill and abundant and cheap labor, has been pronounced impracticable.

Immense cost.—The reservoir capacity then would have to be about eight times greater than that estimated by Mr. Westbrook. If such reservoir is not absolutely impossible, it must be nearly so, and it is a sufficient estimate of what it would cost to state that it more than ninety-nine times exceeds the storage capacity of the water-works for supplying New York City.

Great danger attending such works.—It seems unnecessary to discuss further the project of keeping up navigation in the natural river by means of reservoirs, to retain the water in seasons of surplus, and distribute it to supply deficiencies in dry seasons. If the plan of making a thoroughly regulated or rectified river could be shown to be practicable, there would be much less volume required to raise it during low stages, and it might be well enough to consider the question of reservoirs in connection with that method. But if any other method can be designed, it will be advisable not to adopt the plan of reservoirs with their land-damages, their costly construction, maintenance, and use, and the ever-to-be-endured dread of destruction by the giving way of the dams and the deluging of the valley below.

METHOD OF IMPROVEMENT BY DAMS AND LOCKS.

Difficult and expensive, if not impracticable.—The difficulty of constructing dams in the bed of such a sandy river is very great. The scour on the lower side would probably remove the sand down to the bed-rock, and the construction of cribs filled with stone and well protected by riprap reaching down to the rock would then be necessary to give permanence. Such dams were built across the sandy bed of the Upper Wabash River in Indiana, and it was found that after giving way once or twice the third construction would generally stand, because the *débris* of the first two dams filling into the place scoured out below them made a foundation and an apron for the dam reaching down to the bed-rock.

Where experience has shown that dams could be built on sandy beds they have been constructed only at great expense. There is almost a certainty that the space above the dam will fill up with sand to the level of the top so that the pools in low water could not be navigated.

These dams on the Wisconsin would have to be frequent on account of the slope of the river being $1\frac{1}{2}$ feet to the mile, so that with locks lifting 7 feet they would probably be as near as every five miles, 23 of them being thus required. This number, with their very considerable lengths across the overflowed valley, would make them very expensive even if good foundations existed. Finally, we must take into the account that such works will be exposed to all the power of extraordinary floods.

Never recommended, and special data not obtained for depth to bed-rock.—I have never known any one to recommend locks and dams for the Wisconsin below Portage, and I have not thought it worth while to try to present an estimate of the cost of such improvement, or of the time required to build it. Special location of the dams and borings to the bed-rock must precede any reliable attempt at an estimate. My limited means would not allow of my making these even if I had thought that such a plan had any probable feasibility, and I think it has not.

IMPROVEMENT OF NAVIGATION BY MEANS OF CANAL ALONG THE VALLEY.

Data for making location.—When the survey was made in 1867, the object was to get a good hydrographical and topographical knowledge of the course of the stream, with a view to planning works of improvement in the bed of the river. The impossibility of doing anything with our dredge or scraper-boat was pretty well demonstrated in that year, and the results of the survey soon made plain the great difficulty of improving the river by canalization or any of the other methods treated of in the preceding parts of this chapter. Therefore, in 1868, I directed examinations to be continued so as to obtain a more definite idea of the margins of the flood-plain, of the heights of the terraces, &c., with a view to a survey for locating a canal and preparing estimates. In 1869 I made a reconnaissance of the valley, assisted by Mr. Jacob Blickensderfer, jr., a distinguished civil engineer and one well versed in canal construction. The funds at my command did not admit of making a thorough survey for canal line, so we made as good a location on our maps as the information we had allowed, and constructed an approximate profile of this line from which to estimate the amount of excavation and embankment. This profile was made by means of the level-notes of the survey of 1867, which gave the river-slope and bottom-lands, and the heights of the terraces generally. We also had the profile of the railroad along the bank. The uniform character of the valley enabled us to make this profile with some degree of reliability.

Provisional location.—The location proposed for the canal is shown on the small general map, scale six miles to one inch. This map also shows a profile of the route with the proposed positions of the locks, and in order to make it serve as a general map for considering the entire route from the Mississippi to Green Bay, it is made to embrace the whole extent.

The simple outline of the location estimated on is as follows: *First*, to continue the Portage Canal down to the mouth of the Baraboo River; *second*, to improve the river at this point so as to enable us to lock into it on the left bank, cross it, and lock out again on the right bank; *third*, the location to continue along the right bank, keeping up as high as practicable along the side of the valley so as to reach the Sauk Prairie; *fourth*, to continue the canal on the right side of the valley, locking down to low-water level after leaving Sauk Prairie, so as to get a new feed-supply as far as Pine River; *fifth*, in order to avoid an expensive aqueduct across Pine River, to improve the Wisconsin there, lock into it, cross to the other side, and lock out again; *sixth*, to continue down the left bank until the mouth of Green River be reached; *seventh*, to improve the Wisconsin between this and the mouth of the Kickapoo—distance of about three miles—and cross back to the right bank just below the mouth of the Kickapoo; *eighth*, the canal to continue on the right bank and lock into the Mississippi at Prairie du Chien. These crossings of the river are for the purpose of avoiding costly aqueducts over affluents, and to make the feed-supply for the canal ample and easily obtained.

Objectionable features and alternatives to avoid them.—The objectionable features of this location are the difficulties that may attend the satisfactory improvement of the river-crossing, and the trouble that river-sand at those points may give at the head and tail bays of the locks.

It may be necessary to keep out of the river entirely, and this may be done by continuing the Portage Canal on the left bank down to Merrimac, or Skinner's Bluff, or until a sufficient elevation is gained above the Wisconsin to build an aqueduct across it; after this, to continue all the way on the right bank, keeping high enough to pass all the affluents by aqueducts. With this arrangement the feed-supply becomes more difficult. The whole matter must be thoroughly gone over again.

location-surveys and comparative estimates being made before the best plan for a canal can be named.

Prairie du Chien is the natural terminus for a canal, on account of its large and deep harbor. This is the result of the influence of the sands brought into the Mississippi by the Wisconsin River, about four miles below. The Mississippi water is thus, as it were, held back by a dam, so that for many miles above the river has the features of a lake. The reverse conditions obtain below the mouth of the Wisconsin, where for many miles the Mississippi is made very shoal and rapid by the sands from this tributary.

CHARACTER OF CANAL AND LOCKS.

I submit the following approximate estimate on the first location named above. The canal is to be provided for steamboat-navigation, to be paved or otherwise protected, and to be fully 4 feet deep at low water and 100 feet wide at the narrowest places, with locks 165 feet long and 35 feet wide.

The location selected for this canal, and on which this estimate is based, is that which would make the cost of construction the least, and the proportions of the canal are only such as would make it certainly as good a line as that already constructed from Lake Winnebago to Green Bay, and better than there is any prospect of obtaining from improvements in the bed of the river.

It is well enough to say here that the improvement should eventually be much better than this, but as a preliminary estimate it is thought sufficient to only go thus far. A thorough improvement requires the reconstruction of the works on the Upper and Lower Fox rivers.

Description of locks, with general direction as to construction.—The lock designed is known as the "composite lock," and is constructed of stone, timber, plank, boards, and iron. The chamber is to be 165 feet long between the gates, and 35 feet wide at the bottom. The sides are to extend 27 feet, including the breast above the upper hollow quoins, and 20 feet, including the return-walls below the lower hollow quoins.

The head is to be an L of hydraulic masonry, carried back twelve feet, and to be further protected by a slope and protection wall. The foot of the lock is to have an apron, and the bottom and sides of the canal are to be paved for one hundred feet below.

The foundation, except at the miter-sill, is to be of pine, 10 inches in depth by 12 inches wide, of sufficient length to extend at least one foot beyond the walls of the lock; to be laid so as to cover two-thirds of the surface, and the space between the timbers to be puddled. The timbers under the lower miter-sill are to be of white oak, and to cover the whole surface for a space of 8 feet. The foundation-timbers are to extend at least one foot above the breast-wall and 25 feet below the return-walls, for an apron.

There should in all be four rows of sheet-piling extending across the foundation, one at each end and one under each miter-sill; to be of 2-inch pine plank, and to extend from four to six feet below the surface of the foundation, and to be lined with inch pine boards—the whole to be properly secured to the foundation-timbers. Ditches are to be excavated to receive the piling, and, when placed and fastened, the space on both sides is to be carefully puddled so as to render the work impervious to water.

The whole foundation is to be covered with pine plank two and a half inches thick; that part of the foundation between the side walls of the lock, extending from the breast down to the return-walls, except under the miter-sills, is to lined with 2 inch pine plank in such a manner as to make a water-tight floor.

Cross-sills of sufficient length to extend into the walls at least 3 inches are to be laid across the floor, and fastened to the foundation-timbers with screw-bolts, V-thread. Of these, fourteen in the chamber and two immediately below the lower gates are to be of white oak, 9 inches deep and 10 inches wide. On. the apron are to be two sills of pine, 9 inches deep and 12 inches wide.

The side walls are to be rubble masonry, laid up dry, except 4 feet square about each hollow-quoin post, which is to be laid in hydraulic cement; the side walls are to be 11 feet wide at the bottom, including the front sill, and are to be carried up on the inside with a batter of one-fourth of an inch to the foot, and on the back or outside with such a batter in offsets as will give 6 feet width at the top. The breast-wall and head-wings are to be laid in hydraulic cement, the height, width, &c., to be determined by the lift of the lock and location.

The necessary sills, girts, and posts are to be placed in front of the chamber and recess walls, to receive the plank and boards requisite to make the lock water-tight; the sills to be bolted to the foundation, and the posts anchored into the wall.

The quoin-posts are to be inserted in the wall, and securely anchored to the same.

The chamber is to be lined with two courses of pine plank, the first to be 2-inch, placed longitudinally, and properly fastened to the posts. The second course, of $1\frac{1}{2}$-inch plank, is to be placed vertically in front of the first course of planking, and secured to coping, girts, and sills.

The coping is to be of white oak, not less than 9 inches thick and 15 inches wide. It is to receive the head of the chamber and quoin-posts, and to be connected by anchor-timbers to a longitudinal timber on the outside of the lock-wall.

The frames of the gates are to be of white-oak timber; the bars and posts to be bound together by wrought-iron straps and balance-rods, the lower ends of the heel-posts to be banded with wrought-iron bands, and the posts to rest and turn upon pivots and sockets of the best cast iron.

Fender-cribs 16 feet long and 8 feet wide are to be placed at the head of each lock, in such a position as to form an entrance to and a protection for the lock.

Estimate has been made for building thirteen weirs, in connection with the locks, for passing feed-water from one level to the next below. In locks with weir-connections the lower return-wall is to be continued 14 feet beyond the usual length. From this point it will slope up and down the canal, making a retaining-wall for the bank of the weir. A sluice-way is to be made in the lower return-wall, the bottom to be 3 feet below the surface of the water in the upper level, and 12 feet in width. In addition to the increased length of the return-wall, there will be timber for foundation, sheet-piling, hydraulic masonry, embankment, &c. The cost of these feed-weirs is not included in the cost of the lock, but is given separately in the detailed estimates.

A puddle-wall of suitable material, 10 feet wide and 55 feet long, transversely of the canal, shall be carried up from the foundation to the surface immediately in front of the breast, in addition to the puddling around the sheet-piling and between the foundation-timbers.

An estimate for the excavation of the lock-pit has been made in the case of each lock, at the rate of 30 cents per cubic yard when above water, and $1.25 when under water. The embankment is included in the total for canal-embankment.

MISSISSIPPI RIVER AND LAKE MICHIGAN.

Bill of lock materials.

Bill of lumber for a composite lock 160 feet long, 35 feet wide, and of 8 feet lift.

No. of pieces.	Where used.	Length, feet.	Width, inches.	Depth, inches.	Cubic feet. Pine.	Cubic feet. Oak.	Board measure. Pine.	Board measure. Oak.
	Foundation.							
39	Upper and lower recesses, breast and below gates	64	10	12	2,080			
18	Under miter-sills	64	10	12		960		
112	In chamber	60	10	12	5,600			
2	Miter-sills	40	16	12		106⅔		
4	....do	20	16	12		106⅔		
2	....do	7½	18	12		22½		
18	Under lower return-walls	12	10	12	180			
21	Cross-floor timbers	36	10	8	420			
	Floor—First course of foundation		2½				32,350	
	Second course of foundation		2				14,164	
	Sheet-piling, 4 courses		2				3,072	
	....do		1				1,536	
					8,280	1,196	51,122	
	Chambers, recesses, &c.							
12	Oak sills and girts in recesses	24	14	10		230		
30	Oak sills and girts in chamber	30	14	10		875		
4	Oak coping in recesses	29	18	9		131		
10	Oak coping in chamber	30	15	9		281		
2	Oak coping below lower recess	20	20	9		50		
2	Oak coping return-walls	24	20	9		60		
6	Oak anchor-timbers	24	10	8		80		
10	....do	29	10	8		161		
21	....do	18	10	8		210		
98	Oak posts in chamber and recesses	5	10	8		272		
196	....do	5½	10	8		599		
2	Oak posts in corner of upper recess	17	12	12		34		
2	Oak posts in corner of lower recess	17	20	10		47		
4	Oak posts for hollow quoins	17	6	9		26		
4	....do	17	13	13		80		
4	....do	17	13	15		92		
4	Oak blocks on top of gates	4½	18	24		54		
						3,332		
	Gates.							
4	Oak miter-posts	19	14	14		103		
4	Oak quoins	19	14	16		119		
8	Oak arms at top and over paddles	20	10	14		156		
4	Oak arms at bottom	20	12	14		93		
28	Oak arms	20	8	12		373		
16	Oak paddle-studs	4	15	14		93		
4	Oak spars to shut gates	28	8	8		50		
						987		
	Planking.							
	Chamber—First course	181	2				12,308	
	Second course		1½				9,231	
	On gates		2				2,000	
	Oak fender-planks, upper gates	12	2					288
	Oak tongues		¾					150
6	Oak ties	8	5	8				160
60	....do	6	5	8				1,200
							23,539	1,798

RECAPITULATION.

Foundation	8,280	1,196	51,122	
Chambers, recesses, &c.		3,332		
Gates		987		
Planking			23,539	1,798
	8,280	5,515	74,661	1,798

Bill of iron for a composite lock 160 feet long, 35 feet wide, and of 8 feet lift.

No. of pieces.		Length, inches.	Width, inches.	Thickness, inches.	Pounds.
	Wrought iron.				
40	Round sill-bolts	20	1¼	....	222
24	Round miter-sill screw-bolts, V-thread	20	1⅜	....	237
8	Round hollow-quoin bolts	84	1¼	....	231
8	Flat anchors to same	20	2	½	44
72	Round chamber and recess bolts	72	1¼	....	1,780
72	Flat anchors to same	20	2	½	403
4	Flat heel-post bands	50	2	½	56
40	Flat heel-post straps	98	2½	½	1,372
40	Flat miter-post straps	74	2½	½	1,036
160	Round bolts to same	15	¾	....	296
8	Flat diagonal braces	288	3	⅝	1,210
8	Round tops of same	28	1¼	....	78
20	Round swivel-screws	60	1¼	....	410
12	Round braces to blocks	144	1¼	....	593
12	Flat anchors to same	72	3	½	365
4	Round journals in top of quoin-posts	12	3	....	94
16	Round pins on top of blocks	6	1¼	....	33
4	Flat collars in blocks	16	3	¾	40
4	.....do	14	3	¾	35
8	Round bolts to same	20	¾	....	20
12	Square bars to paddles	168	1	1	564
168	Nuts, ¾-inch bore	2½	2½	¾	163
8	Square plates in blocks	1¾	1¾	¼	260
168	Washers	2	2½	1⅛	15
72	.....do	....	....	....	11
					9,568
	Cast iron.				
	Paddle-gates, &c	....	....	....	9,012
	Spikes and nails	....	....	....	2,000
					11,012

Estimated cost of a lock.

Estimated cost of a lock 160 feet long, 35 feet wide, with 8 feet lift.

Pine, 74,661 feet, board-measure, at $22	$1,642 54
Oak, 1,798 feet, board-measure, at $32	57 54
Pine, 8,280 cubic feet, at 20 cents	1,656 00
Oak, 5,515 cubic feet, at 30 cents	1,654 50
Dry wall, 2,192 cubic yards, at $8	17,536 00
Hydraulic wall, 313 cubic yards, at $15	4,695 00
Puddling, 400 cubic yards, at 50 cents	200 00
Wrought iron, 9,568 pounds, at 15 cents	1,435 20
Cast iron, 9,012 pounds, at 8 cents	720 96
Spikes and nails, 2,000 pounds, at 6 cents	120 00
Snubbing-posts, 6, at $5	30 00
Capstans and spars, 4, at $20	80 00
Painting gates	30 00
Timber fender-cribs	564 00
Total	30,421 74

This should be increased for locks located where the foundation is insecure, as follows:

Piles for foundation and protection, 474, at $5	2,370 00
Bolts for fastening foundation to piles, 471 pounds, at 15 cents	70 65
Total cost of lock	32,862 39

The details of the estimate for each proposed lock are given in the appendix to this report.

Summary of the cost of all the lift-locks.

Number of lock.	Lift.	Cost.	Number of lock.	Lift.	Cost.
	Feet.			Feet.	
Lock No. 1	9	$39,836 38	Lock No. 13	8 3-10	$32,565 61
Lock No. 2	8	31,431 79	Lock No. 14	9	32,689 48
Lock No. 3	8	31,087 99	Lock No. 15	9	32,526 93
Lock No. 4	8	32,520 49	Lock No. 16	8	33,096 79
Lock No. 5	7	31,746 43	Lock No. 17	8	33,096 79
Lock No. 6	8	32,143 59	Lock No. 18	7	31,745 18
Lock No. 7	7	32,546 43	Lock No. 19	7	30,980 18
Lock No. 8	8	31,929 54	Lock No. 20	9	34,744 48
Lock No. 9	8	31,929 54	Lock No. 21	9½	40,183 70
Lock No. 10	8½	32,765 61			
Lock No. 11	9	33,531 03	Total		701 219 19
Lock No. 12	9	38,121 23			

Summary of cost of all the guard-locks.

Guard-lock No. 1	$37,132 04
Guard-lock No. 2	36,882 04
Guard-lock No. 3	36,882 04
	110,896 12

Cost of feed-weir connected with lock.

For continuation of lower return-wall of lock, 153 cubic yards of hydraulic masonry, at $10 per yard	$1,530 00
128 cubic yards of dry masonry, to be made hydraulic at an increased cost of $5 per yard	640 00
Timber, 5,500 feet, board-measure, at $25	137 50
Puddling, 38 cubic yards, at 50 cents	19 00
Spikes	3 00
Planking, 1,385 feet, board-measure, at $20	27 70
Sheet-piling, 320 feet, board-measure, at $20	6 40
Embankment, 1,910 cubic yards, at 30 cents	573 00
	2,936 60

Cost of feed-pipes about one mile below Honey Creek.

Two cast-iron pipes 60 feet long, 36 inches inside diameter, and 3 inches thick, with two stand-pipes 6 inches in diameter, and 15 feet long; in all, 49,797 pounds, at 8 cents	$3,983 76
Gate-stems, wrenches, &c., 450 pounds, at 15 cents	67 50
,688 pounds cast-iron in gates, at 8 cents	215 04
00 feet, board-measure, sheet-piling, at $20	10 00
Bedding timber and watch-house	100 00
	4,376 30

Cost of culverts.—Estimates have been made to pass Honey Creek. Blue River, and Grand Gris Creek under the canal with culverts. In determining the amount of water-way requisite to pass these streams we have used the following rules :

1. For every mile in length give 2 feet span.
2. For every square mile drained give 1 foot area in opening.

At Honey Creek we have allowed more space than either rule calls for, because when the Wisconsin River is high the culvert will be submerged and the flow of the water in the creek obstructed. We have estimated for two semicircular arches of 28 feet span each; these arches are to rest on two rows of piling. The wing-walls are to be 24 feet long, making an angle of one hundred and twenty degrees with the face of the culvert, and to be built on piling also. Over the arches a parapet, or retaining-wall, 3 feet high, is to be constructed. The material between the crown of the arches and the bottom of the canal is to be well packed and puddled.

Bill of timber, masonry, &c., for Honey Creek culvert:

Piles under arches and wings, 836, at $5	$4,180 00
Pine timber under arches, 1,312 cubic feet, } 1,792 feet, at 20 cents	358 40
Pine timber under wings, 480 cubic feet, }	
Plank under arches, 1,804 feet, } 5,048 feet, B. M., at $20	100 96
Plank under wings, 720 feet, }	
Iron bolts, 3′ × 1″ with nuts, 68, 750 pounds, at 15 cents	112 50

Hydraulic masonry:

In arches, 1,151.4 cubic yards, }	
In wings, 298.5 cubic yards, } 1,633 cubic yards, at $15	24,495 00
In parapet, 183.0 cubic yards, }	
Puddling, 1,932 cubic yards, at 50 cents	966 00
Riprap, 163 cubic yards, at $1.50	244 50
Pit excavation under water, 9,081 cubic yards, at $1.25	11,351 25
	41,808 61

For the Blue River we have estimated for two semicircular arches of 20 feet span, the arches to rest on a timber foundation covered with plank. To prevent scour a row of sheet-piling is to be placed at each end of the foundation, and the bed of the creek is to be riprapped.

Bill of timber, masonry, &c., for Blue River culvert:

Timber in foundation, 3,816 cubic feet, at 30 cents	$1,144 80
Plank, 11,550 feet, B. M., at $20	231 00
Sheet-piling, 1,200 feet, B. M., at $20	24 00
Riprap, 50 cubic yards, at $1.50	75 00
Spikes, 550 pounds, at 5 cents	27 50
Excavation, 2,935 cubic yards, at $1	2,935 00
Puddling, 1,044 cubic yards, at 50 cents	522 00
Masonry, 5,983 cubic yards, at $15	8,974 50
	13,933 80

For Grand Gris Creek a semicircular arch of 10 feet span is estimated for.

Bill of timber, masonry, &c., for Grand Gris Creek culvert:

Timber in foundation, 2,059 cubic feet, at 30 cents	$617 70
Plank, 6,176 feet, B. M., at $20	123 52
Sheet-piling, 1,040 feet, B. M., at $20	20 80
Spikes, 390 pounds, at 5 cents	19 50
Excavation, 1,875 cubic yards, at $1	1,875 00
Puddling, 630 cubic yards, at 50 cents	315 00
Riprap, 30 cubic yards, at $1.50	45 00
Masonry, 227.3 cubic yards, at $15	3,409 50
	6,426 02

Cost of waste-weirs.—Estimate for eighteen waste-weirs has been made; this allows one to every level of any considerable length. This appears to be a liberal estimate for a canal of this length, but the fact of the greater part of the canal being located at the foot of bluffs makes it necessary to provide for a large amount of surface drainage. The cost of these weirs depends so much upon location that we have allowed for an equal number of each of two kinds, an estimate for one of each being given.

Bill of materials for a waste-weir to consist of a center-crib 100 feet long and 7 feet high, with two wings 10 feet long and 10 feet high:

Pine timber (10″×10″) in foundation, 1,010 cubic feet, at 20 cents	$202 0
Sheet piling, 1,200 feet, B. M., at $22	26 4
Pine timber in center crib, (12″ × 12″,) 1,120 cubic feet, at 20 cents	224 0

Pine timber in end cribs, (12″ × 12″,) 1,200 cubic feet, at 20 cents	$240	00
Plank to cover center and apron, 3,200 feet, B. M., at $22	70	40
Spikes, 5-inch, 135 pounds, at 6 cents	8	10
Stone to fill cribs, 215 cubic yards, at $1.50	322	50
Riprap to protect bank at end of apron and about ends of weir, 100 cubic yards, at $1.50	150	00
	1,243	40

Bill of materials for a waste-weir to consist of a single timber 100 feet long, with two wings 10 feet long:

Pine timber, (12″ × 12″,) 100 cubic feet, at 20 cents	$20	00
Pine timber, (12″ × 12″,) for wings, 20 cubic feet, at 20 cents	4	00
Sheet-piling, 1,000 feet, B. M., at $22	22	00
Spikes, 50 pounds, at 6 cents	3	00
Riprap, 94 cubic yards, at $1.50	141	00
	190	00

Total cost for eighteen weirs, nine of each kind $12,900 60

Cost of bridges.—We have estimated for twenty highway-crossings—though it is probable that a less number will accommodate the public when the canal is built—and one railway-crossing.

Estimated cost:

20 highway-bridges, at $1,400	$28,000	00
Embankment for approaches	1,921	25
1 railway swing-bridge	2,500	00
	32,421	25

Cost of walling.—We have provided for walling or paving the inner slope (if artificial) of the canal in all cases where the width is less than 80 feet, from 4 feet below to 2 feet above the water's surface.

Estimated cost $192,210 00

Cost of riprap.—The outer slope, the slope next to the river, is to be wrapped from the bottom to above high water in all cases where the canal is located along the bank of the river.

Estimated cost $291,264 00

Cost of grubbing.—We have allowed for 383½ acres to be grubbed, at $75 per acre.

Estimated cost $28,762 50

Cost of clearing.—There would be about 1,446 acres of clearing, estimated to cost $25 per acre.

Estimated cost $36,150 00

Cost of engineering, the work to be done in two years.—The entire improvement can be made in two years, and the engineering expenses will be as follows:

1 chief engineer, at $600 per month	$14,400	00
2 assistants to chief engineer, at $200 per month each	9,600	00
1 engineer, 1 rodman, and 1 axman, on each of ten divisions into which the line will be divided, $250 per month for each division	60,000	00
1 engineer and 1 rodman, one year, on each of the 24 locks, at $200 per month	57,600	00
1 clerk and 2 draughtsmen at $150 per month each, for office	10,800	00
rent of office, fuel, and attendance, 2 years	4,000	00
paper, drawing-material, &c	2,000	00
24 leveling and 10 transit instruments, with target-rods and chains, at $60 each	5,440	00
traveling and incidental expenses	10,000	00
	173,840	00

There will be constant employment in the canal for one dredge-boat, scows, and tug.

Estimated cost $25,000 00

Grand total cost.

Summary of estimate for canal, 86 feet least width at bottom, and 4 feet draught, with locks 165 feet by 35 feet, clear, for boats:

Embankment	$1,200,564 9?
Excavation	737,279 7(
21 lift-locks	701,219 1!
3 guard-locks	110,896 1!
Feed-weirs	38,175 8!
Feed-pipes	4,376 3!
Culverts	62,168 4
Waste-weirs	12,900 6
Bridges	32,421 2
Walling	192,210 0
Riprap	291,264 C
Grubbing	28,762 5
Clearing	36,150 (
	3,448,388 !
Engineering	173,840 (
Dredge-boat, and scows and tug	25,000 (
Contingencies	352,771 !
	4,000,000

Additional cost for 5 feet draught.—The miter-sills have been so place in the foregoing plan and estimate as to have 5 feet draught over them, s that the canal might be made to allow of 5 feet draught instead of four l additional excavation amounting to 550,000 cubic yards, at 30 cents p yard..$165,000

Annual expense of superintendence and repairs.—The annual expen of superintendence and care of the work after it was completed wou be as follows:

One superintendent	$3,000
Twenty-six lock and feed tenders	17,000
Operating dredge and tug, fuel, laborers, engineers, &c	30,000
	$50,000

www.ingramcontent.com/pod-product-compliance
Lightning Source LLC
Chambersburg PA
CBHW022132160426
43197CB00009B/1246